Remaking the Modern

Space, Relocation, and the Politics of Identity in a Global Cairo

Farha Ghannam

UNIVERSITY OF CALIFORNIA PRESS

Berkeley / Los Angeles / London

Parts of Chapters 3 and 5 originally appeared in a chapter by the author in Ayse Oncu and Petra Weylands, eds., *Space, Culture, and Power: New Identities in Globalizing Cities,* London: Zed Books, 1997.

Parts of Chapters 3 and 6 originally appeared in "The Visual Re-Making of Urban Space: Relocation and the Use of Public Housing in 'Modern' Cairo," *Visual Anthropology* 10 (1998) © OPA (Overseas Publishers Association) N.V., with permission from Taylor & Francis, Ltd.

Parts of Chapter 6 originally appeared in "Keeping Him Connected," *City & Society,* 1998.

University of California Press
Berkeley and Los Angeles, California

University of California Press, Ltd.
London, England

© 2002 by the Regents of the University of California

Library of Congress Cataloging-in-Publication Data

Ghannam, Farha, 1963–.
  Remaking the modern : space, relocation, and the politics of identity in a global Cairo / Farha Ghannam.
    p.   cm.
  Includes bibliographical references and index.
    ISBN 0–520-23045-0 (cloth : alk. paper). — ISBN 0–520-23046-9 (pbk. : alk. paper)
    1. Urbanization — Egypt — Cairo.   2. Cairo (Egypt) — Social conditions. 3. Cairo (Egypt) — Economic conditions.   4. City and town life — Egypt — Cairo.   I. Title.
HT384.E32 C3444   2002
307.76'0962'16 — dc21   2001006438

Manufactured in the United States of America
11   10   09   08   07   06   05
10   9   8   7   6   5   4   3   2

To Hans and Lena

Contents

List of Illustrations ix

Acknowledgments xi

Introduction: Researching "Modern" Cairo 1

1. Relocation and the Creation of a Global City 25

2. Relocation and the Daily Use of "Modern" Spaces 43

3. Old Places, New Identities 67

4. Gender and the Struggle over Public Spaces 88

5. Religion in a Global Era 116

6. Roads to Prosperity 141

Conclusion: Homes, Mosques, and the Making
of a Global Cairo 167

Notes 183

Bibliography 195

Index 207

Figures

1. Map of Cairo   3
2. View of "modern" areas of Cairo   31
3. View of Bulaq   32
4. Some of the project buildings are arranged in *murabba'at* (squares)   47
5. Interior of an apartment of a better-off family   56
6. Exterior of apartment building   58
7. A sheep in the kitchen before the Sacrifice Feast   65
8. Example of interior remodeling done by better-off family   97
9. A stand adjacent to an apartment block selling basic groceries and household supplies   107
10. Diagram of various mosques in *el-masaakin* and *el-ahali* that Um Ahmed frequents during the week   128
11. Magdy's original apartment   154
12. Magdy's brother's apartment   155
13. Magdy's apartment after the latest additions   156

Acknowledgments

This project was made possible by the cooperation, hospitality, and friendship of the people of al-Zawiya al-Hamra. To protect their privacy, I regret not being able to name each one of the men, women, and children whose words and practices are at the center of this book. I can only express my deep gratitude and appreciation for their kindness and warm friendship.

I am also grateful to my teachers and mentors at the University of Texas at Austin: James Brow, Bob Fernea, Clement Henry, Ian Manners, and Katie Stewart. My supervisor, Bob Fernea, has been a great source of inspiration during and after my graduate studies. His provocative questions and stimulating ideas have promoted my critical thinking and analysis of social life. I very much appreciate his deep knowledge of the Middle East and his dedication to his students. During my graduate studies at the University of Texas, I was fortunate to have the chance to study with two great teachers: James Brow and Katie Stewart. They both have been very influential in shaping my thoughts and have provided me with methodological and analytical tools that will continue to shape my work in years to come. I will always be indebted to them. Elizabeth Fernea has been extremely supportive since I first arrived in Austin. I very much appreciate her thoughtfulness and generosity.

I am grateful for the help and support of my friends and colleagues Jessica Chapin, Ben Feinberg, Petra Kuppinger, Barbara Ibrahim, Emily Lee, Sharon Nagy, Abou-Zeid Rageh, Lucine Taminian, Seteney Shami, and Huda Zurayk. Many thanks also to my friends at Swarthmore

College, especially Bruce Grant, Miguel Diaz-Barriga, and Rose Maio. Some of my students at Swarthmore read parts of the manuscript and gave valuable feedback. A major part of this book was revised while I was a fellow at the International Center for Advanced Studies at New York University. The fellows (especially Smriti Srinivas) and the director of the center, Tom Bender, were of great help, and their feedback enriched my work in many ways. I am also thankful to Michael Gilsenan, who read and commented on an earlier draft of this manuscript. Special thanks to Marcelle Thomas for help with the drawings and Susan M. Lee for help with the formatting of the text. I would also like to thank Lynne Withey, Kate Warne, and Elisabeth Magnus at the University of California Press for their help and support. The financial support provided by the Middle East Awards, the Wenner-Gren Foundation, the Ford Foundation, and the International Office at the University of Texas at Austin is very much appreciated.

My parents, although illiterate, have been strong believers in education, and their love has motivated my work throughout the years. Hans Löfgren, my husband, has been generous with his time and support since I started my fieldwork in Cairo. His love and unfailing support are present on every page of this book. I dedicate this book to him and to our wonderful daughter, Lena, who was born during the last stages of this project.

Thank you all very much.

Researching "Modern" Cairo

If you manage to find a taxi driver who will agree to drive you from the center of Cairo to al-Zawiya al-Hamra,[1] the trip may take only thirty minutes. Most taxi drivers, however, are not willing to go to this neighborhood, located in the northern part of the city. One driver explains that the road is "very bad" and that his car will be damaged if he drives there. Another insists on determining the fare before you get into the cab and then charges more than for similar rides to other parts of city. Other drivers simply do not "feel comfortable" going to al-Zawiya. It is cheaper to take the state-operated city bus (*otobis*). But to do that you have to be skillful and know how to use it. You need to know how to jump when it slows down as it nears your station. You also have to know how to jump into the bus before it speeds up and joins the flow of traffic. But above all, you need to learn how to fit your body among the masses on board while paying close attention to your belongings. In addition, you need to acquire the skill not only of quickly grabbing any vacant seat but also of sharing it with young children and older people. A good way to avoid the hassle of either the relatively expensive taxi or the overcrowded cheap city bus is to take the metro to Hadayiq al-Qubba and then get into one of the small privately owned buses. These seat around fifteen passengers, and you can usually manage to find a spot. But many people in al-Zawiya put up with the annoying city bus because it is cheaper. While the trip in the city bus (*otobis*) costs ten piasters (around three cents), the trip by the metro and the "micro-bus" (as people call it) costs around fifty-five piasters. To ride the micro-buses, you need to learn at least two skills.

I

First, you need to learn how to find the doorknob. Most often the inner knob is broken and you have to stick your hand out the window to the outer handle to open the door quickly. Second, you need to know how and when to ask the driver to stop: "next to the mosque *ya usta*," "at the corner of the street," or "in front of Ragab" (a local restaurant). You have to call upon the driver in a voice that is higher than the loud music and at the right time — that is, before you reach your stop but not too early so that you do not irritate him or end up walking to your destination.

My daily trips from al-Tahrir Square to al-Zawiya al-Hamra (see Figure 1) over more than two years usually combined these different means of transportation. I often took the metro in the morning, when I knew that it was impossible for me to get inside the city bus. I preferred to take the latter at night, however, because it was less crowded and took me directly to al-Tahrir Square. During the first nineteen months that I spent studying al-Zawiya, learning how to use these different vehicles was an important achievement. I became confident not only about finding the doorknob and talking back to the screaming driver but also about collecting the fare from the rest of the passengers and passing the money to the *usta*. Interestingly, it was learning such skills that gave me a sense of familiarity and knowledge of life in al-Zawiya al-Hamra and the daily struggles of its inhabitants.

Al-Zawiya al-Hamra attracted my attention when I planned to study how modern discourses are articulated in the production of urban space. This neighborhood seemed the right choice because it housed part of the five thousand Egyptian working-class families who, during 1979–1981, were moved from Bulaq (in the center of Cairo) to public housing in al-Zawiya al-Hamra and 'Ain Shams. The relocation project was one of President Sadat's attempts to rehabilitate the city center and "modernize" the housing conditions of Cairo's poor as well as to build a global metropolis that would meet the demands of tourists and foreign investors. My review of the state public discourse circulated in national newspapers revealed an intriguing utilization of modern images and discourses in justifying the relocation project. Notions such as *hadith* (new or modern), *'asri* (contemporary or modern), and *madani* (civilized or refined) were widely used to justify the project. Moving the urban poor to "modern" housing, the state discourse promised, would transform them into more productive agents who would be active in the making of their country. To further legitimize this project of "modernity," state officials depicted members of the group as drug dealers, criminals, and troublemakers and viewed relocation as crucial for disciplining, normalizing, and integrating

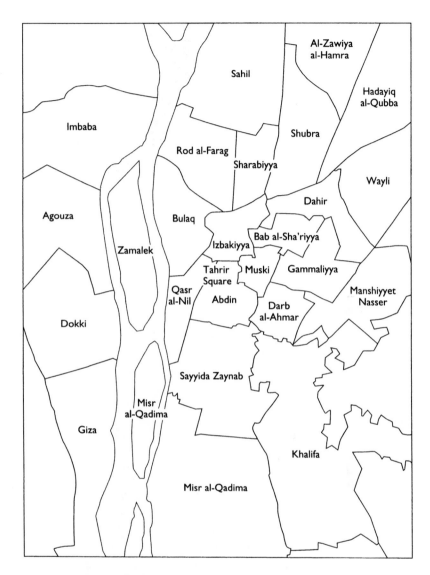

FIGURE 1. A map of Cairo showing the location of the main sites referred to in this book. Bulaq is in the center of Cairo on the east bank of the Nile. Facing it on the other side is upper-class Zamalek. Al-Zawiya is located in the far north. Adapted from map by Eric Denis, Centre d'Études et de Documentation Économiques, Juridiques et Sociales, Cairo, Egypt.

them into the nation. Theoretically and methodologically, al-Zawiya seemed the right place to examine how state planners have translated notions of modernity into physical forms and how ordinary men and women appropriate and physically transform these forms.

I focus on this relocation project as one concrete example of how global forces (such as investments and tourism) are articulated in national policies and people's daily practices in the making of urban spaces. Studies on resettlement in different parts of the world have documented the socio-economic consequences of relocation (see, for example, Perlman 1982; Hansen and Oliver-Smith 1982; Cernea and Guggenheim 1993; Shami 1994). As suggested by such studies, the project reordered relationships among the relocated population and rearranged their links with the city. Their economic insecurity was exacerbated by the disappearance of old neighborhood relations and the assurances provided by direct and long-lasting personal bonds. Those who depended on close personal relationships in their business were hit hard by relocation. For example, women who used to buy cheap fabric and clothes from local markets and sell them to their neighbors for a small profit lost this source of income when some of their customers were moved to 'Ain Shams, some were dispersed in the new housing project, and the rest remained in Bulaq.[2] This book, however, is not about the economic consequences of relocation. Rather, it examines the spatial practices of the relocated population and the cultural identities that they are constructing for themselves and that are being attached to them by other residents in al-Zawiya.

A View of al-Zawiya

> [Al-Zawiya al-Hamra] is one of the bleakest landscapes in Cairo
> as few roads, amenities, or services interrupt tract after tract
> of apartment buildings. Public housing suffers from all the
> unfortunate aspects of contemporary, inexpensive "modern"
> architecture where identical cubicle-like buildings rise out of the
> dusty roads and lack any influence from indigenous architecture.
>
> Diane Singerman, Avenues of Participation

Although the trip from the city center to al-Zawiya is relatively short, the social distance that separates it from upper- and middle-class areas is huge. Not only for taxi drivers, but also for many other Egyptians, Al-Zawiya al-Hamra is constructed as "the Other." It is often perceived as remotely located, and its people are viewed as drug dealers, criminals, troublemakers, and, most recently, fundamentalists and terrorists. For many, it is a reminder of the 1981 sectarian clashes between Muslims and Christians (discussed in chapter 5), which, as indicated by one young man, placed the neighborhood "on the map."[3] Middle- and upper-class people perceived my work there with mixed feelings, usually of surprise and uneasiness, expressed by describing me teasingly as "*ra'na*" (headstrong, but also with a touch of foolishness), as a well-known Egyptian sociologist once did.

Al-Zawiya is not attractive to tourists, and you rarely see it on Cairo's maps,[4] for it lacks the "authenticity" of Old Cairo and the luxury of upperclass quarters. It is not attractive to researchers either. While *baladi*[5] neighborhoods such as Bulaq, Bab al-Sha'riyah, al-Gamaliyya, and al-Musky have attracted the attention of researchers (El-Messiri 1978; Rugh 1984; Campo 1991; Early 1993; Singerman 1995), newer neighborhoods like al-Zawiya are often considered by researchers to be "less authentic" and thus outside the scope of academic interest. The concepts and perceptions of *baladi* people are depicted as the "most representative of the post-colonial Egyptian Muslim Identity" (Campo 1991: 96).[6] In the words of an Egyptian writer, "the old alleys" are "the real Cairo" where one finds the "authentic Egyptian life . . . the Egyptian whose attributes did not change over thousands of years" (Muharram 1989: 5). These groups are considered the holders of the "present and the future of Egyptian society, as well as its definition of what Islam is and will be" (Campo 1991: 97). In contrast, neighborhoods such as al-Zawiya, which are located on the outskirts of Cairo, are considered to be outside the urban landscape and are viewed as part of the "rifi subculture," which is based on "attachment to local custom, family honor and solidarity, and the land" (Campo 1991: 90).

This construction of al-Zawiya and similar neighborhoods on the outskirts of the city is largely based on their recent history. Al-Zawiya, currently a densely populated area, was mainly agricultural land until the early 1960s. The oldest inhabitants were agricultural workers. They cultivated corn, rice, and vegetables and lived in clusters of mud-brick houses. The situation changed drastically after the 1952 revolution. Land was redistributed to many of the families who used to work as agricultural laborers. At the same time, the state began constructing roads, and the area was soon connected with the rest of Cairo via a tramway. Many new immigrants (Muslims and Christians) who came from Upper and Lower Egypt found cheap housing in al-Zawiya. They constructed or rented rooms in red-brick houses that are called *biyuut ahali* (private houses). In the early 1960s, the neighborhood expanded rapidly with the establishment of the first public housing project (*el-masaakin el-qadima*). This project was part of Nasser's policy that aimed to provide housing for low-income groups. It is located to the west of the main street. Many of those who moved to this project could not afford housing in the center of the city, had lost their housing units through urban clearance, or were immigrants from other cities and villages. In the late 1970s and early 1980s, the second or the new housing project (*el-masaakin el-gidida*) was established on the east side of the main street at some distance from the old project. *El-masaakin el-gidida* houses part of the population moved from Bulaq, the main focus of this book. The project also houses families who moved from the city center seeking cheaper housing or who were moved by the state from other parts of Cairo.

The social and physical distinctions between public and private housing are significant in this neighborhood. Private and public housing differ in many aspects, such as size, color, architectural design, division of the unit, and use of space. Although their residents have similar socioeconomic backgrounds, differences between private and public housing are highlighted and invested with many social meanings. These differences are signaled, for instance, in the labels used to refer to these two areas. *Masaakin shaʿbiyya*, usually translated as "public housing" or "housing for the people," is the full expression that formally refers to the housing project. Currently, the word *shaʿbiyya*, with its positive connotations (as discussed further in chapter 3), has been dropped from the name. Only the word *masaakin*, which simply refers to the housing structures, is used to refer to public housing. In contrast, *biyuut ahali* is the full expression used to refer to privately constructed houses. The word *biyuut*, or "houses," is dropped, and *ahali*, or "people," which has positive connotations related to life there, is used to refer to the private housing. Following the people's usage, I use the word *masaakin* to refer to the public housing project and *ahali* to refer to private housing.

Life in both *el-masaakin* and *el-ahali* is diverse. This diversity is manifested first in the activities that people are engaged in. There are petty traders, vendors, plumbers, metal and construction workers, shoemakers, factory laborers, craftsmen, mechanics, drivers, waiters, low-level government employees, teachers, and owners of small businesses (such as a barbershop or an iron shop). There are families with relatively high income, especially those with members who are skilled workers or who work in oil-producing countries, and there are unskilled workers with little income who can hardly sustain their families. Many men work more than one job to meet the needs of their families. A man may, for example, work during the day as a teacher in a professional school where he earns around one hundred Egyptian pounds per month and work in the evening as a house painter, which earns him more than two hundred pounds.[7] Young women are usually factory workers, sales people in local shops (especially clothing), or secretaries (inside or outside al-Zawiya). But they tend to quit after securing enough money for their trousseau. Most stop working outside the home after marriage, but many become engaged in various economic activities around the housing unit.

The population in al-Zawiya al-Hamra consists of groups who migrated from various areas at different time periods. There are migrants from villages in Lower and Upper Egypt, from other cities, and from various neighborhoods in Cairo. While most of its residents are Muslims, it is estimated that 12 percent of the population is Christian (Central Agency for Public Mobilization and Statistics 1986: 343).[8] The diversity of the residents not only has implications for the generalizations that can be made about al-Zawiya. More importantly, as discussed in chapters 3 and 4, it contextualizes and shapes how the relocated population views al-Zawiya compared to other areas in general and Bulaq in particular.

I Was There

In my experience, fieldwork is, above all else, surprising.
Candace Slater, "Four Moments"

This book is based on more than two years of fieldwork. Most of the research was conducted during 1993–1994 and 1997. I also visited the area during 1995, 1996, 1998, 1999, and 2000. Letters, cards, and occasional phone calls still connect me with my close informants. My data are derived from diverse sources: participant observation, interviews with people in and out of al-Zawiya, novels, newspapers, and television serials. Participant observation, in particular, was very valuable in acquiring intimate knowledge of people's feelings and reactions to the project, their current dreams, and future aspirations. It was during activities such as stuffing cabbage or sorting rice in the living room or frying fish in the kitchen that women shared with me their memories of relocation, life in Bulaq, the first days in al-Zawiya, and their feelings about other residents in the area. It was, however, unexpected encounters such as a ride in the city bus, a letter or tape from a relative in Kuwait, a song in a wedding or engagement party, or a weekly lesson in a local mosque that often enriched, in ways that I had not anticipated beforehand, my understanding of daily practices and struggles. For example, transnational connections became central to my research when women asked me to write to sons and husbands who worked in the Gulf. This task directed my attention to the significance of flows of money, information, and goods from Kuwait, Saudi Arabia, and Libya in shaping life in the neighborhood. As illustrated in chapter 6, through an exchange of letters, audiotapes, and phone calls, male labor migrants in oil-producing countries are kept connected with their families. Despite their physical absence, migrant workers maintain an active role in making important decisions such as arranging the marriage of a sibling or adding a new room or balcony to the housing unit in al-Zawiya.

STUDYING THE CITY

> *Fieldwork cannot appear primarily as a cumulative process of gathering "experience" or of cultural "learning" by an autonomous subject. It must rather be seen as a historically contingent, unruly dialogical encounter involving to some degree both conflict and collaboration in the production of texts.*
>
> James Clifford, *The Predicament of Culture*

I arrived in Cairo in early 1993 with promises from Egyptian friends to introduce me to some families in al-Zawiya al-Hamra. The first families that I met were not part of the relocated population and did not live in *el-masaakin*. Over a short time, I found myself part of a wide network of relationships with people living in *el-ahali*. Although I toured the housing project (where the group was relocated), I did not want to just walk into one of the apartments and introduce myself as a Palestinian-Jordanian graduate student at an American university who was doing research, especially after the recent Gulf War and the increasing suspicion of outsider involvement in armed attacks in different parts of Egypt. What struck me early on was the resistance and hesitation of my new acquaintances to introduce me to "such people." This resistance was based on a genuine concern for my safety. Informants residing in *el-ahali* strongly believed that the resettled group consisted of drug dealers, criminals, and troublemakers. One informant suggested that I only go with her son, a policeman, something that I, of course, rejected. It was not until I went to a wedding with a friend in *el-ahali* that I met two sisters from the relocated group. I realized how lucky I was, since weddings attended by residents of both *el-ahali* and *el-masaakin* are rare. In this particular case, the two young women had worked with the bride in the same sewing workshop for more than two years, first outside and later inside al-Zawiya. Through these two sisters, I managed to establish a separate network with the relocated group. This was facilitated by the physical separation between *el-ahali* and *el-masaakin,* which allowed me to visit one part of the area without being monitored by members from the other. This invisibility was important so that I could maintain relationships with both parties and avoid pressures, mainly by informants from *el-ahali,* to control my mobility. Although my relationship with the two groups was based on a continuous negotiation of various selves rather than a fixed identity, I believe that my interaction with people in al-Zawiya al-Hamra was shaped primarily by my gender and marital status on the one hand and by my religious identity on the other.

''AROUSA' IN THE FIELD

Like several other female anthropologists in the Middle East (see, for example, Shami 1988; Joseph 1988), I found that being a woman facilitated my work in that it allowed me access to private and public spaces and provided direct contact with males and females. I joined women when they attended mosques, clinics, and local markets, as well as when they visited their relatives and friends in different neighborhoods. They invited me to participate in social functions such as weddings and birthday celebrations. I also helped in cooking, taking care of children, and helping some students with their homework.

My marital status shaped to a large extent my interaction with men and women and access to information. Because I was newly married ('*arousa*) when I started my fieldwork, women felt a certain kind of responsibility for introducing me to married life. They shared with me information about sexuality, procreation, and childbirth. Pregnancy became especially important in our discussions. Women were expecting me to get pregnant during the first few months and expressed their sorrow each time I said no. For all my informants, children are central to married life. As reported by other female anthropologists (Joseph 1988; Inhorn 1994), women repeatedly pressured me about having a baby and often emphasized its priority over education and professional objectives. They discouraged me from using contraception, especially the pill, which all women believe causes infertility. Then they tried to convince me to see a doctor to make sure that I was capable of conceiving children and continuously prayed to God to grant me a baby. Many told me stories about themselves or relatives who did not have children for a while but then through medical treatment or "traditional" methods had several.

The many questions that were asked (both by men and women) about my husband and his background made me quickly realize the central role of the husband in a woman's life. I learned that, as a good wife, I should present my husband as a source of authority in my life. I discovered how strange it sounded when I agreed to participate in various activities without first consulting with him. I also learned the advantage of having the husband as an authority in the life of a woman and how that can be actively used to achieve certain purposes and avoid undesirable social obligations. Men and women rarely argued when the decision was presented as being made by the husband. Occasionally, I used my husband's authority in the same way. So it was sufficient to tell my friends that *he* did not allow me to do this or that when I did not want to take responsibility for rejecting a proposal to participate in some activities.

In al-Zawiya, unlike some other communities in the Middle East (see, for example, Altorki 1988; Abu-Lughod 1986, 1988), there was, except in a few cases of extreme religiosity, very little sex segregation in daily life. Men and women interacted with each other at home and outside it. My being married meant that I did not threaten women; many felt very comfortable having me around and tried to promote conversations with their husbands and male relatives. Men were eager to "advise" me about how to conduct fieldwork, what I should ask and whom. However, many of them were working most of the week. Thus, my interviews with men, except for those with unemployed or part-time workers, were limited to evening sessions, holidays, group trips, and social occasions. I played cards, chess, and dominoes and watched television and videotapes with them. We discussed various topics that ranged from politics, terrorism, and soccer games to resettlement and intergroup relationships. Still, my gender limited my participation in other men's activities such as drinking beer, smoking hashish, and socializing in coffee shops. My information on such activities is based mainly on limited observations and men's accounts.

When I arrived in Cairo, I was totally convinced that I should live in al-Zawiya. My attempts, however, were quickly frustrated. Housing options were limited, and the apartments of my close informants were often too small for their own family members. Another important reason for not living there was that, while it was easy for people to understand my interest in researching life in al-Zawiya and participating in their daily activities, it was hard for them to understand why I was ready to live there and leave my husband alone in Garden City (where he was close to his workplace at the American University). Being a good wife demanded that I stay with my husband, but being a good student demanded that I spend a lot of time in al-Zawiya. So I visited almost every day, and at times, when my husband was out of town or when there was a special occasion, I stayed up to two weeks with my close informants.

At first, I felt very uneasy about this arrangement because a good anthropologist, the rules say, stays twenty-four hours a day in the field to observe and participate in "every activity." However, I soon discovered the advantages of such an arrangement. Over a short period, I managed to form relationships that allowed me to spend several nights when I wanted with families, both in *el-ahali* and in *el-masaakin*. When my husband was outside Cairo, my close informants insisted on having me with them, sometimes for up to two weeks. Due to the limited interaction between residents of *el-ahali* and *el-masaakin*, I would have been more restricted had I chosen to live in a specific part of the area. Coming from outside allowed me more freedom to visit various families in different parts of the neighborhood. My regular trips to the area also continuously reminded me that al-Zawiya is connected with the rest of Cairo and that the practices of its residents shape the city in various ways. Many men and women make similar daily trips to go to workplaces and shopping centers or to visit relatives and friends. Stories in the city bus, encounters with taxi drivers, and events on the metro became important in analyzing life in the area and its connections with other parts of the city. At the same time, they disrupted the sense of familiarity that was emerging over time. Trips to upper-class areas, for example, continued to defamiliarize life in al-Zawiya. Not only were the visual signs and organization of streets very different in Madinat Nasr and Zamalek, but each time I visited the large apartments in Zamalek and Garden City, I was reminded of the shock that I had felt the first time I sat in a tiny living room in the old *masaakin*. In contrast to upper-class neighborhoods, space in al-Zawiya is always limited. In some cases, the kitchen in a fancy apartment in Zamalek was as big as a one-bedroom apartment that housed five to seven family members. I also came to learn different things about al-Zawiya by being outside it. Moving between al-Zawiya and upper- and middle-class areas felt like "tacking between cultural spaces" (Scott, quoted in Clifford 1997:

214). Reactions of upper- and middle-class Egyptians to my work became part of my analysis, especially the location of al-Zawiya in the social space and in the imagination of other groups in Cairo.

"PRAYING LIKE A FROG":
RELIGION AND THE ANTHROPOLOGICAL ENCOUNTER

In addition to my gender and marital status, being Arab but not Egyptian shaped my interaction with people. First, I was not associated in any way with the Egyptian government. People were not hesitant to express antigovernment feelings and discuss various "illegal" issues such as drugs, gangs, and prostitution. Second, I was really surprised to see people who had spent between twenty and thirty years in Cairo identifying with me because "we are all strangers in this city." Third, questions asked by informants about Jordan and how life there compared with certain aspects of life in Egypt taught me a lot about what informants regarded as important and unique to life in Cairo. They repeatedly brought up marriage, the housing shortage, and the transportation system in discussions with me and my relatives when asking about life in Jordan.[9] Still, being non-Egyptian left me vulnerable to political changes. With the increasing number of armed attacks and the attempts to blame outsiders for these attacks, I often felt insecure about how people would react to my presence. Religion, however, was of greater importance than nationalism in shaping my relationships with many people in al-Zawiya.

When I planned my fieldwork, religion was not one of the topics that interested me. But I realized its significance as soon as I arrived in al-Zawiya. The emphasis on praying and performing religious duties, wall and car decorations, the importance of the mosque in bringing people together, the role of Muslim activists in providing various services, and the tension between Muslims and Christians were all signs that signaled the significance of religion in daily life. One of the first questions people always asked was about my religion and if my husband and I performed our religious duties. Each time I answered that I was a Muslim, Muslims expressed relief and repeated *"al-hamdu lillah"* (thanks be to God). I was politely asked by my first informants to wear a scarf to be able to "blend" into the community, especially when going with women to local markets and mosques. This was particularly important because I was married and the scarf was needed to distinguish me from Christian women. The fact that I was strongly identified as a Muslim allowed me to go to the mosque and facilitated my interaction with Muslims. However, it restricted my relationship with Christians. Although I did interact with some Christian families, my relationship with them continued to be superficial and was structured by the limited daily interaction between Muslims and Christians.

Even though people tolerated not praying, it was totally unacceptable not to fast. Like the others, I fasted during Ramadan and prayed throughout the month. I also occasionally attended the Friday prayer as well as weekly lessons in local mosques. Being a "Muslim" in al-Zawiya, however, was not an easy task. I soon discovered that there were many subtle differences between what I had learned as a child in Jordan and what people practiced in al-Zawiya. Although I used to pray on a regular basis while growing up, it was in al-Zawiya that I attended the mosque for the first time in my life. I was not sure what I was supposed to do. At first, I thought that it was sufficient, as the informant who invited me to go with her to perform the Friday prayer suggested, to imitate other people who were praying, but soon I realized that there were other things that I needed to take into consideration. On a couple of occasions, I felt very embarrassed because other women praying corrected the way I bent my knees and stretched my hands. That embarrassed me because it happened in front of other people and because I thought that "I knew the right way" to pray. One of the sources of my pride when I was ten years old was the fact that my teacher used me as a "model" to teach other students how to pray. Because I was one of the few students who had learned to pray at an early age, the religion teacher used to call me to her various classes to pray on the table in front of the whole class. To my astonishment, in al-Zawiya, my way of praying was not "correct." One woman even said that I "prayed like a frog" because my hands where separated when I was bowing down (*sujoud*). On another occasion, a woman scolded me because I did not move quickly to secure a space for another worshiper who was trying to fit in the line with us. For me, there was no space, and the line behind us was totally empty. In the mosque, I learned later, we should stand as close to each other as possible to prevent the devil from entering among us and dividing our unity. These incidents brought to my attention the important role of religion in disciplining bodies and souls and in constructing collective identities and reinforcing gender inequalities. Discourses circulating in the mosque also informed people's attempts to appropriate modern discourses and objects and their discussions of mundane issues such as wearing wedding bands, watching TV, and obeying one's husband. Religion thus became central to my research and understanding of people's daily struggles.

"Being Here": Returning to Academia

> *It is Being Here, a scholar among scholars, that gets your*
> *anthropology read . . . , published, reviewed, cited, taught.*
> Clifford Geertz, *Works and Lives*

In August of 1994, one day before going back to the States to start writing my Ph.D. dissertation, I visited one of my first and key informants. Over the two years that I spent doing my fieldwork, Abu Hosni, a man in his mid-fifties, took the role of directing my research and providing me with tips about various issues that ranged from interacting with others and using the city bus to my personal life and how I should treat my husband. During my last visit, he interrogated me about the chapters that I intended to write. I tried to avoid the discussion because I could not provide answers to his questions at that time. In fact, I did not want even to think about how I was going to organize the dissertation and what I was going to include in each chapter. As usual, Abu Hosni insisted on giving me some tips, in this case about how to write a "good dissertation." His work as a driver and his relationships with Americans and middle-class Egyptians provided him with access to information not available to others, which he referred to when discussing various topics with his wife, children, and neighbors. He recounted his most recent experience when he had attended the defense of a master's thesis of the wife of one of his supervisors. He described how tough the committee had been on the "poor" woman and analyzed the situation, linking it to previous conflicts between the committee members. Then he shifted to discuss my committee and how tough I expected them to be. The key, he suggested, was my supervisor, whom I used several times as an authority figure to justify the need to work hard in the field or to leave my husband in Cairo while going back to the United States to write my dissertation.

He asked about my advisor's religion. I was puzzled and surprised by the question and did not really know the answer. After a few seconds of silence I picked my thoughts and decided to say with hesitation: "I think he is Christian." I was sure that saying that he was Christian would be much better than trying to explain the complexity of the situation and what role religion might play in the life of Bob Fernea. Abu Hosni did not like the answer. "You think? What do you mean by 'I think?'" Knowing my supervisor's religion, he proceeded to explain, was central to my success. "You should know his sect also." He advised me to learn about these issues as soon as I returned to Austin, but in a subtle way. He said, "Look around in his office for clues and indirectly ask the secretary about his religion." Then, Abu Hosni suggested, I should choose some parts from the Bible, especially those that my supervisor might like, and quote them in the introduction. This, he emphasized, would be sufficient to "soften" his heart and make him read the dissertation with sympathy. For Abu Hosni, the key to success was not only my "good work," accurate description of life in al-Zawiya, or the professional training of Bob Fernea and the rest of the committee. It was also my ability to write what would appeal to them. Abu Hosni reminded me that we always write for a specific audience. Not only do we need to provide details of "Being There," but we also need to impress and please the reader. Above all, we strategically use other texts to construct our authority as writers and to support or legitimize what we write.

Given that Abu Hosni is a good Muslim, one might be surprised by his willingness to deal with the situation through what could be considered a "compromising" of my religious identity. But through his advice, Abu Hosni was pointing to a central feature of the daily life and the importance of the "tactics" (de Certeau 1988) that enable the weak to gain victory over the powerful. A tactic is "a clever trick" that depends on time and involves waiting to manipulate emerging opportunities and "cracks that particular conjunctions open in the surveillance of the proprietary power" (37). By quoting the Bible, I was not compromising my religion as much as I was "tricking" my supervisor into being more sympathetic while reading my dissertation. Working on the feelings of the other and making him or her supportive of your causes and demands is one of the main tactics that people employ in al-Zawiya al-Hamra when dealing with the powerful, especially state officials.

"Tricking" the powerful is done in various ways. People always tell stories that show their ability to trick parents, husbands, older siblings, merchants, teachers, employers, drivers, and policemen. Showing respect, "sweet talking," pleading, making fun of others, and conning those in power are all skills celebrated by people in al-Zawiya al-Hamra. These skills signal courage and resourcefulness in responding to emerging challenges and crises. For instance, Huda had to find a way to locate her fiancé, Ahmed, who had disappeared after one of their frequent quarrels. Since they had become engaged two years earlier, Huda and Ahmed had been facing many problems. After one of their big fights, Ahmed threatened to leave Huda and allegedly stole *el-qayma,* the list that documents all the articles and household equipment that would belong to Huda in case of divorce.[10] Huda tried to find him and visited his family in Bulaq, but they claimed that they did not know where he was. With the support of her neighbors, some of whom posed as witnesses, Huda went to the police station and claimed that along with *el-qayma,* Ahmed had stolen £E 500. She had to claim that, as she explained, because there was a need to motivate the police to take more interest in her case. When the police located Ahmed, she dropped the charges and they wrote a new list. Not one of her neighbors saw Huda's claim as "a lie"; instead, they viewed it as a legitimate way to motivate the police to search for Ahmed and to force him to listen to her demands. Huda simply employed one of the many clever tricks that people use in their daily life to encourage the police to find Ahmed because she could not do that by herself.

This book traces similar tactics and examines their impact on the housing project and Cairo at large. It also examines some more formalized strategies that people use to transform social and physical realities. The study focuses on these strategies and tactics to illustrate how the city is made and remade through social actors who articulate the discourses and policies of the state and various global forces with their daily needs and cultural dispositions. I aim to go beyond the usual tendency to link the construction of Middle Eastern cities in general and Cairo in particular to planners and political figures. The focus is usually on the "series of grand political designs" (S. E. Ibrahim 1987: 87) that produce "the City" (with a capital C). We read about the strategies of the powerful and the role of 'Umar Ibn al-'Aas, Ahmed Ibn Tulun, Nasser, Sadat, and other rulers in the construction of Cairo (Abu-Lughod 1971; S. E. Ibrahim 1987). We continue to see the palaces, castles, opera houses, and grand mosques that preserve and remind others of the efforts of these leaders. We also hear about grand plans, economic systems, the international division of labor, global corporations, political processes, and colonial powers that have produced certain cities (Gottdiener 1985; Mitchell 1988; Rabinow 1989; Abu-Lughod 1990). In contrast, little attention is devoted to "the ordinary practitioners of the city" (de Certeau 1988: 93). While we often hear about the great achievements of the dominant group, the role of Cairo's dwellers is usually brought up only when discussing disorder and urban problems such as crowding, squatting, housing shortage, and informality (Nadim et al. 1980; Rageh 1984; Al-Safty 1983; Oldham et al. 1987; Shorter 1989). In such studies, the city is often viewed as a mere container for the practices of its residents, and such studies continue to be *in* the city rather than *of* the city. For example, women's practices are often viewed in the city. We read about the networks that women form (Singerman 1995) and about women's daily activities (Early 1993). But we rarely read about how these practices shape the city and the specificity of urban life in producing and shaping the activities and relationships forged by women.

In this book, I draw attention to people's spatial practices and analyze how they transform the state's efforts to construct a modern capital. I provide "thick contextualization" (see Ortner 1995) to explore the shifting meanings and multiple consequences of these practices. This contextualization entails examining how social agents articulate local values, national policies, and global forces in their daily struggles. To this end, I use a mixture of tactics and strategies that I learned in al-Zawiya to try to convey some of the mechanisms that structure daily practices and construct cultural identities. I provide stories, quotes from Abu Hosni and his neighbors, pictures, clips from local newspapers, plans of apartments, and analysis of different practices and processes. My purpose is to understand the logic of these practices (Bourdieu 1990) and to examine their transformative power in various contexts.

This is therefore a study of Cairo but from a very particular angle. It takes us, I hope, beyond the classical reductionist obsession with the role of religion in the production of urban space and the constitution of the "Islamic city" (Grunebaum 1955; Hourani and Stern 1970; Serjeant 1980; Hakim 1986).[11] It does not, however, try to present a "holistic" view of the city (Basham 1978: 27). Nor does it try to convey the city as a pregiven bounded entity. It aims to draw attention to the role of social actors (such as Abu Hosni, Huda, a five-year-old girl, a young factory worker, and a labor migrant in Kuwait) in the creation of modern Cairo and the attachment of meanings to urban space. What are the structures that constrain and enable their participation in the production of their neighborhood and Cairo at large? How do they transform Cairo's private and public spaces? How do they invest these spaces with memories, dreams, and aspirations? How do they create and recreate homes and localities in a constantly changing world?

Globalization beyond Westernization

> *The city becomes the dominant theme in political legends, but it is no longer a field of programmed and regulated operations.*
> Michel de Certeau, *The Practice of Everyday Life*

Of course, Egypt was never isolated from the rest of the world. Trade, travel, diplomacy, and pilgrimage connected Cairo with other cities. The Geniza documents revealed a cosmopolitan Cairo that, since the tenth century, had been connected (especially through trade) with different parts of the globe, from Tunisia and Morocco to Aden, Samarkand, Andalusia, and India. (For more on this topic, see Rodenbeck 1998; Ghosh 1992.) There has been, however, a remarkable increase in Cairo's connectedness with the rest of the world over the past fifty years. Modern means of communication and transportation in particular have had a profound impact on expanding and intensifying connections between the Egyptian capital and other Arab, African, and Western cities. In particular, Sadat's policies, starting from 1974, as will be discussed in the next chapter, marked the beginning of a strong orientation toward the outside (especially the United States), an emphasis on economic liberalization, and a boom in construction and consumption. The relocation project examined in this book was one of his attempts to enhance these policies and create a modern city that would satisfy the demands of tourists and investors.

In addition to the spatial transition from Bulaq to al-Zawiya, the study traces a temporal transition from the late 1970s into the 1990s. It shows how these two transitions contextualize memories of the past, uses of space, desires of consumption, dreams of travel, and constructions of identity. Abu Hosni and his neighbors are not fax users, e-mail receivers, jumbo jet travelers, or satellite owners. They are part of Cairo's low-income groups whose experience of globalization is structured by their economic resources and position in social space. They, especially men, experience global discourses and images through their movement in the city, their interaction with foreigners (as employers and tourists), and their work in oil-producing countries such as Saudi Arabia, Kuwait, and Libya. Working in one of these countries is often seen as the only hope for young men to secure an apartment, a necessary requirement for marriage, and various consumer goods, which are rapidly becoming signs of distinction. Many of them come back from abroad with color televisions, VCRs, tape recorders, carpets, and Moulinex blenders. Families without relatives working abroad participate in saving associations (*gam'iyyat*) to secure money to buy such goods. Above all, many of Abu Hosni's neighbors experienced the forces of globalization in their displacement from their neighborhood in the center of the city. Their houses were demolished to be replaced by buildings and facilities that catered to upper-class Egyptians, international tourists, and the transnational community. Relocation, therefore, is one concrete example of the structured globalization of Cairo that I discuss in this book. It is important to emphasize here that relocation is only one force, albeit a very important one, that shapes people's current identities, practices, and memories of the past.

Recent theoretical developments in anthropology and cultural studies have demonstrated that the growing flow of information, capital, and labor between different parts of the globe is not producing one unified culture (Lash and Urry 1994; Featherstone 1995; Appadurai 1996). Rather, global processes and practices are being juxtaposed in complex ways in "local" contexts (Hall 1991a, 1993). Thus, contrary to the old conceptualization of the world as becoming a "global village," local differences and identities are not eradicated but are being supported in many cases by global forces and processes (Hall 1991b, 1993; Ray 1993; Massey 1994). My ethnography aims to highlight the significance of grounding our theorization of globalization and locality in concrete experiences and precise enactments. This grounding is essential to account for the multiple flows that shape social imagination and cultural practices in different contexts. If we are to recognize that social agents in different parts of the globe are doing more than simply rejecting or passively absorbing global discourses, images, and goods, we need ethnographies and rich contextualization that capture how global trajectories operate, the contradictory desires they stimulate, the competing identifications they generate, and the structures of feeling that they facilitate. It is important, I aim to show, to go beyond the current explicit or implicit division of the globe into the West and the Rest. There is much talk about "compression of the world" (Robertson 1995), "time-space compression" (Harvey 1990; Massey 1994), transnational connections (Hannerz 1996), and global flows (Appadurai 1996). In spite of this, however, globalization is still viewed as essentially flows between the West (or the rich North) and the Rest (or the poor South). This view has been taken for granted in previous attempts that have aimed to show that the globe is being "homogenized" or "Westernized," and it is still largely present in recent studies that aim to show the complexity of the articulation between global forces and local contexts (see, for example, Hall 1991a; Hannerz 1996; Featherstone 1995; Sassen 1996). Such a view excludes a major part of the complex flows that are central to the growing connectedness between different parts of the world and weakens the analytical potentials of the concept of globalization. The problems with such a view are clearly seen in how globalization is frequently reduced to notions such as "neocolonialism," "McDonaldization," "cultural imperialism," "Americanization," "clash of civilizations," or even "Jihad versus McWorld" (Barber 1995; Ritzer 1996; Huntington 1993; Waters 1995).

While the "American conception of the world" (Hall 1991a: 28) may be hegemonic in various contexts, people experience the influence of a multiplicity of other discourses and images. People in al-Zawiya al-Hamra not only experience the American culture that is transmitted to them in movies starring Arnold Schwarzenegger (known, especially among young people, as "Arnold") but also experience global images and discourses through oil-producing countries where their children and male relatives work as well as through the mixture of people who visit and work in Cairo from different Arab countries. For example, women use oil for their hair that comes from India via their sons who work in Saudi Arabia, and they collect their wedding trousseau from clothes, sheets, and blankets brought by brothers from Kuwait. Although many of the consumer goods are produced in the West, their meanings are given to them by their active users in al-Zawiya al-Hamra. For many, consumer goods, especially VCRs, are investments that can be exchanged for cash when needed. Several families use their refrigerators to cool water during the summer but turn them into closets during the winter to store household appliances.

Globalization, especially through the media, is introducing new forms of identification among the subjects of its processes. People in al-Zawiya al-Hamra, for instance, enjoy watching television, especially global sports events such as the World Cup in soccer. Young men and women follow these games very closely; they know the names of the Brazilian, German, and Italian players. While they are watching these games, different identities compete for priority: the audience shifts from supporting African and Arab teams to cheering for any team from the third world when they play against Europeans (Brazil against Germany, for example). The 1998 championship, which took place while I was visiting al-Zawiya, was of special significance because it revealed another dimension of the growing complexity of identification in the context of increasing movement of people and images between different parts of the globe. On the basis of my observation of the 1994 championship, I expected that most people would support the Brazilian team in the final match. In 1998, however, there was strong support for the French team. Many felt that the Brazilian team was arrogant and careless, especially after they lost to Norway, which caused an early end to the participation of the Moroccan team. Most, however, supported the French team because it had several African players, including, most important, the Algerian Zineddine Zidane. The joy of victory was tremendous when Zidane scored two goals and secured the championship for France. Many supported Zidane because he was "Arab"[12] and Muslim. This exemplifies how people do not experience globalization as a coherent set of discourses and processes that is trans-

mitted from the West to the rest of the world but rather experience fragments and contradictory pieces filtered through multiple centers that do
not present a unified "conception of the world."

Central to the globalization of Cairo is the circulation, largely facilitated by the development in media and communication systems, of discourses and images of "modernity." Men and women in al-Zawiya al-
Hamra are not outside the discourses and processes of modernity. They
struggle daily with various aspects of what they perceive to be "modern."
Notions of "modernity" are embedded in various aspects of the daily life
of the people, even though they rarely reduce it to a single bounded
definition. Only when I started asking them about how they understand
modernity did they try to present a definition. Most often, however, they
ended up providing concrete examples of what it means to be modern,
which are referred to in the following chapters. For now, it is sufficient
to emphasize that rather than assuming that except in the cases of Europe
and Japan, "modernization occurred under dependent conditions, which
led to distorted, inauthentic modernity" (Sharabi 1988: 22), this book
examines modernity as a set of discourses and processes that emerged in
Europe (Giddens 1990; Berman 1988) but have been widely circulated
and selectively appropriated by various social groups in different parts of
the world. Rather than searching for an essence that defines "modernity"
or assuming that there are multiple alternative modernities (Miller 1995;
Watts 1996), this book examines concrete struggles that illustrate how
notions of the "modern" are contested, made, and remade in Cairo. In
short, I want to focus on "the politics of selection." What makes modernity unique in a country like Egypt is the people's view that it is not a master narrative that should be taken or rejected as a whole. Instead, there is
a general feeling that one should be selective about what to appropriate
and what to discard. Thus, the next chapters address questions such as:
Who appeals to "modernity," and what defines a discourse, an object, an
image, a space, or a practice as modern? How are various discourses and
images that are viewed as "modern" appropriated and reworked to
empower and/or to control certain groups as well as to construct and
transform specific identities?

Multiple Spaces

Space is central to this book.[13] A growing number of studies focus on the
production of space and how it shapes and is being shaped by power rela-

tionships, practices, identities, and subjectivities (Bourdieu 1977; Foucault 1979; Lefebvre 1991). Foucault (1984), for example, emphasized that space is central not only to communal life but also to any exercise of power. He showed in his study of the history of the penal system that discipline of bodies and souls "proceeds from the distribution of individuals in space" (Foucault 1979: 141).[14]

Most of the studies that have been trying to present a complex theorization of the relationship between space and time tend to focus more on the production of space (mainly by dominant groups) and pay less attention to how spaces are actively used and reconstructed by social actors who are not the original makers of these spaces. Thus, the focus has been on colonial attempts to redefine local spaces (Mitchell 1988; Rabinow 1989), governmental endeavors to restructure urban space (Massey 1994), and efforts to discipline bodies and souls through spatial orders (Foucault 1979). The following chapters aim to direct attention to the fact that spatial forms and arrangements are never totalized and that urban space is always a contested domain. I focus on the "spatial practices of the ordinary practitioners of the city" (de Certeau 1988: 93) to show that the dominant image of the city is contested and struggled over. As active users, men and women reshape the city through their daily practices. The analysis shows how power relationships are embedded and manifested in the struggle over space and how various groups strategically use and manipulate space to evade attempts to discipline them and regulate their relationships and activities. As will be discussed in the following chapters, the relocation project examined here is but one form of this contestation. Each chapter discusses space as the locus of a struggle that is central to the construction of collectivities and the representation of the self in everyday life. Family members, genders, and religious groups struggle over space and negotiate how it should be used and represented.

The relocation project examined here was part of Sadat's attempts to modernize Cairo and its residents. Chapter 1 provides a brief historical background of modern Cairo and situates the project within the broader context of Sadat's open-door policy (infitah). It presents a textual analysis of the state public discourse used to justify the project and examines how this discourse used modern images and appealed to global demands and models to legitimize the relocation project. Modernity was to be objectified in visible forms that could be gazed at by visitors and upperclass Egyptians. I pay particular attention to how the relocated group was represented in the state public discourse and how government officials defined "modern" housing. The new apartments, local newspapers emphasized, promised to transform people's daily life and to create modern subjects who would be able to contribute to the construction of the nation. These new apartments are examined in chapter 2 as structured spaces that manifest the state's understanding of modernity. Drawing on the writings of Bourdieu and de Certeau, I explore the "tactics" and "strategies" employed by the relocated population to articulate this understanding and the state's hegemonic construction of space with their cultural dispositions, religious beliefs, and daily needs. People not only have utilized the new spaces in ways that were not intended by state planners but also have physically transformed these spaces. I examine the logic of these changes and analyze how they are shaped by the continuous flow of images circulated through different channels, especially state-controlled media.

Chapter 3 investigates how relocation, together with other global forces and discourses, is shaping identities in al-Zawiya al-Hamra. It pays particular attention to how the state discourse, which stigmatized the group before and during relocation, has informed the views of other residents and shaped how the newcomers have been situated in al-Zawiya. The housing project brought different groups from Cairo to live in the same location, attend the same coffeehouses, and shop at the same markets. This mixing of people and the growing globalization of culture are introducing new identifications and uncertainties that have to be negotiated in people's daily life. In chapter 4, I examine how these uncertainties have been shaping social views of public spaces such as the vegetable market and the coffee shop. Such spaces, which bring members of the different groups together, are often viewed in negative terms. After exploring the shifting meanings of privacy and publicness and how these meanings are linked to gender inequalities, I focus on the coffee shop and the workplace to examine how the access of young men and women to these spaces is restricted by their families and government officials. Rather than limiting the restrictions on women's access to public spaces to the need to control their sexuality, I aim to broaden the discussion to examine how these restrictions aim to control the knowledge acquired by young men and women.

Chapter 5 shows how the mosque, unlike the negatively constructed coffee shop and the vegetable market, is perceived as a "safe" place that brings people together as a collectivity. Residents of *el-masaakin* and *el-ahali*, old inhabitants and newcomers, the better off and the needy are all being brought together by Islam and the mosque. This chapter examines the relationships between Muslims and Christians, especially in light of the 1981 clashes, to show how religion has been used to mobilize the two groups. It also maps notions of modernity in al-Zawiya and argues that the growing hegemony of religious identity is closely linked to people's daily struggles to appropriate what they view as positive aspects of modernity and avoid what they see as negative. I show that this struggle is situated between the efforts of the Egyptian government to duplicate Western modernity and the attempts of some Muslim extremists to restrict access to and utilization of modern objects and discourses.

In addition to religious identity, men and women situate themselves in al-Zawiya through their active role in its making. Chapter 6 focuses on how locality is produced and reproduced. As a structure of feeling, a material reality, and an attachment to a situated community (Appadurai 1996), locality has to be created and recreated over time. This becomes a challenging process with the increasing flow of people, capital, and goods between Cairo and other Arab and Western cities. Focusing on male migrants in oil-producing countries, this chapter examines how young men are kept connected with their families through the flow of information, ideas, and money and through the construction of homes in Cairo. I first analyze these flows and the apartments constructed in al-Zawiya as techniques for the production of locality. Then I place them within a wider spatial and historical context to show that even when these spatial practices primarily intend to satisfy some immediate need of the family, their unintended consequences transform the project and the neighborhood at large. They play a significant role in situating the group in the new location and in objectifying to themselves and to others their active role in the making of the neighborhood. The transformative power of these practices, I argue in the conclusion, goes beyond individual units and the project itself and extends to reshape the image of Cairo that the state tries to control and beautify. Looking at newly constructed homes and mosques, I argue that the city is not merely a ready-made container for the practices of its residents but a flexible entity that is made and remade through these practices. Religion along with the new apartments inscribes the presence of the group and displays the active role of its members in the making of Cairo at large. I also examine recent global and national transformations that have been shaping the neighborhood and how these transformations privilege and challenge the role of religion in shaping identities and practices in al-Zawiya al-Hamra.

CHAPTER I

Relocation and the Creation of a Global City

Nationalism, as a model of imagining community, articulates with, rewrites, and often displaces other narratives of community.
Akhil Gupta, "The Song of the Nonaligned World"

The phrase *Umm al-Dunya* (Mother of the World) is used by Egyptians and Arabs to refer to Cairo. The mixture of actions, buildings, people, and activities gives the impression that the entire world is represented in Cairo and that it represents the world. The diversity of its neighborhoods, old quarters and new Western-style areas, high-rise buildings around the Nile, satellite dishes, foreign fast-food chains (such as McDonald's, Pizza Hut, Kentucky Fried Chicken, and I Can't Believe It's Yogurt), the World Trade Center, the crowded streets, the walls that are covered with advertisements for many international companies (such as Sony and Citizen), and the life that never stops — all of these phenomena blend together to give Cairo its magic and recreate the feeling that this city is "the Mother of the World" and that it has something to offer everyone. It attracts poor immigrants from rural Egypt who come seeking work and a better life and foreigners who work for international organizations, educational institutions, and embassies, as well as Arab and international tourists who are attracted by the pyramids, the Nile, and the nightlife.

Touring Cairo's streets and alleys, one cannot but feel both the presence and absence of the government. The large number of policemen, who are guarding buildings, searching bags, regulating traffic, watching the people, and socializing with each other, give the impression that Cairo is under control. On the other hand, the traffic is in chaos, people occupy streets and sidewalks to sell various products or to park their cars, and drivers are madly honking to attract the attention of numerous pedestrians and other drivers. This makes it hard to think that Cairo is under control, and one is left with the impression that the city is beyond any attempts to discipline it. Yet efforts to regulate the city and organize its space have been intensified since the nineteenth century.

Contemporary Cairo, which in 1900 had a population of six hundred thousand (S. E. Ibrahim 1987: 93), currently houses almost eight million inhabitants in the city proper (*al-Ahram Weekly*, December 2–8, 1999: 7) and sixteen million in Greater Cairo (*Al-Ahram Weekly*, August 31–September 6, 2000: 2). Containing around one-quarter of Egypt's population, Cairo is by far the largest city in the country. It is the economic, political, and cultural center of Egypt. Its supremacy is reflected in the tendency of Egyptians to use the Arabic word *Misr* to refer to both Egypt, the country, and Cairo, the capital. This gigantic city is the product of a rich and complex history that goes back more than five thousand years. The date of the foundation of Cairo proper goes back to A.D. 969, when the Fatimids (the Shi'ite dynasty that controlled Egypt at the time) gave her its current name, *al-Qahira* (the Victorious), after "the planet Mars the Triumphant" (Rodenbeck 1998: 67). Over the years, Cairo has been shaped by the Pharaohs, the Arabs, the Ottomans, the Mamluks, the French, the British, and more recently by Italian, German, Canadian, and American architects and planners. Volumes have been written about this rich history, and I would have to write another one to cover even a fraction of Cairo's past.[1] Hence, I provide only a brief background on the most recent attempts to modernize the Egyptian capital.[2]

Histories and Spaces

Cairo's modern spaces are largely shaped by the strategies of the successive political powers that have ruled Egypt since the early nineteenth century. A few years after the unsuccessful French attempt to colonize Egypt (1798–1802), Muhammad Ali, an Albanian Ottoman officer, took over Egypt. With the help of French consultants, Muhammad Ali aimed to modernize Egypt's economy, military, administration, and educational system. Although Cairo became the capital of Muhammad Ali's dynasty, it remained marginal in his grand plans to modernize Egypt's economy and army (Raymond 1993). Aside from building new royal palaces in the peripheries of Cairo, he did little to change the structure of the city (Habitat 1993). His French-educated grandson, Ismail (1863–1879), however, invested heavily in modernizing and Europeanizing Cairo and its landscapes. New districts were created, parts of Medieval Cairo were renovated, two avenues were opened in the old city, and a road that connected the pyramids with the city center was constructed (Habitat 1993). The Europeanization of Cairo became urgent before the arrival of representatives of European royal families to celebrate the opening of the Suez Canal. Khedive Ismail wanted to turn his capital into "another Paris" and "a showcase" to impress his guests (Rodenbeck 1998: 168). His plans, which mainly focused on the Western part of the city, included the construction of parks, open squares, roads, bridges, villas, an opera house, a theater, a library, and residential palaces for his European guests (S. E. Ibrahim 1987; Rodenbeck 1998). Ismail's policies, however, left the country bankrupt. He had to give up the throne for his son Tawfiq, and the British soon after colonized the country. A master plan was created for Cairo and other Egyptian cities, and specialized authorities were created to provide services and manage different urban problems (Habitat 1993). From 1881 to 1922, the British managed Egypt as an investment with the aim of generating revenues to pay back the European creditors, maintain control over the Suez Canal, and open Egypt as a market for British products. For these purposes, the British mainly invested in "the maintenance of order and the expansion of infrastructure" such as roads, tramways, and dams (Rodenbeck 1998: 179). They also constructed new modern areas for foreigners (especially Europeans) and a small segment of Egypt's population, who enjoyed special benefits under the British. Meanwhile, the old part of Cairo was rapidly deteriorating, and the needs of its inhabitants were ignored. In effect, the British created a dual city: the old part, which represented the Orient and its "backwardness," and the new part, which represented the West and its modernity (Mitchell 1988).

By the time of the 1952 revolution, Cairo was a rapidly urbanizing capital that suffered from unemployment, housing shortage, and a lack of adequate services (Habitat 1993). The Egyptian president Gamal Abdel Nasser promoted the idea that "Egypt could be modern without selling out to the West," and he adopted a socialist policy that aimed to provide land, education, and housing for peasants, the working class, and the lower segment of the middle class (Rodenbeck 1998: 225). Cairo's new factories and workshops (constructed with the help of the Soviet Union) attracted many immigrants from the countryside. Massive public housing projects, factories, and bridges were constructed in different parts of the city. It was during this period (the early 1960s) that the first housing project was erected in al-Zawiya al-Hamra. This project, which is currently very crowded, attracted thousands of low-ranking officials and working-class families. The state also built areas for the middle class, such as Madinet Nasr and Madinet al-Mohandessin (or "The City of Engineers").

Under Nasser, Cairo became the center of the Egyptian bureaucracy, a flourishing capital of the Arab world, and a center that inspired Asian and African national movements (Rodenbeck 1998; S. E. Ibrahim 1987). However, it suffered from regional political instability during the 1950s and 1960s. After the nationalization of the Suez Canal in 1956, the French, British, and Israelis attacked Egypt and caused major destruction to the country's landscape. Due to this confrontation and continuous conflict with Israel (especially the 1967 war), attention was directed towards the army and the reconstruction of towns and cities in the Suez Canal area. Meanwhile, Cairo's infrastructure deteriorated in the 1960s. In 1965, the sewage system broke down, and it took the government three months to repair it. The city suffered from traffic congestion and high density, and its old part was decaying (Habitat 1993). It was under these conditions that Sadat took over the presidency of Egypt. Not unlike Khedive Ismail, Sadat hoped to Westernize Cairo. But whereas Ismail had tried to recreate Paris in Cairo (Rodenbeck 1998), Sadat's ideals were American cities like Los Angeles and Houston (S. E. Ibrahim 1987).

Heading West

> With her vast capabilities, the United States is bound in duty, even naturally expected, to assist all those striving for a better future alike for themselves and for the whole world.
>
> Anwar el-Sadat, *In Search of Identity*

In *In Search of Identity* (1978), Anwar el-Sadat strongly criticizes Nasser's policies, arguing that they destroyed Egypt's economy and kept the country isolated from the rest of the world. To remedy the country's chronic economic and financial problems, Sadat reversed Nasser's policies by cutting most of the ties with the Soviet Union and reorienting Egypt toward the West. He turned to the United States in particular for assistance in resolving Egypt's conflict with Israel as well as for supporting the economic and technological development of the country. With the tremendous popularity he won after the 1973 war, Sadat crystallized his new visions and ideas when declaring "the open-door policy" or *infitah* in 1974. This policy aimed to "open the universe . . . open the door for fresh air and remove all the barriers and walls that we built around us to suffocate ourselves by our own hands" (Sadat 1981: 12). As Sadat explained to a group of young Egyptian men, his *infitah* was motivated by his belief that each one of them would like to "get married, own a villa, drive a car, possess a television set and a stove, and eat three meals a day" (12).

Sadat's policy strove to modernize the country by accelerating planned economic growth, promoting private investment, attracting foreign and Arab capital, and enhancing social development (Ikram 1980; Waterbury 1983). Laws were enacted to secure the protection needed to attract foreign investors and to facilitate the operation of private capital (Waterbury 1983). Private domestic and foreign investments were expected to secure the capital needed to construct modern Egypt. Investments in tourism were especially important because they were expected to "yield high economic returns and provide substantial foreign exchange and well-paid employment" (Ikram 1980: 309). Sadat's economic openness and orientation to the outside required several spatial transformations. As the capital, Cairo became central to Sadat's policies. Cairo was to be "renewed to become a city that fits its international position through providing it with the necessary infrastructure, modern [*haditha*] communication systems, and the facilities needed for work as well as economic and touristic activities" (Sadat 1974: 47). Many changes were needed to facilitate the operation of capital and to meet the new emerging demands. Sadat encouraged private developers and land speculators to build new hotels and buildings, and Egyptians were encouraged to work in oil-producing countries and invest their remittances in the building of their home country. Construction boomed in and around Cairo, hotel chains dotted the Nile Corniche, bridges and new roads were constructed to facilitate the circulation of goods and people, and conspicuous consumption soared. For example, the growing demand for luxury and middle-class housing by the transnational community and Egyptians who worked in oil-producing countries inflated the price of land, especially in the city center, and increased the cost of construction materials (Rageh 1984). At the same time, high-rises proliferated around Cairo to meet the demands of private and foreign investors for work-oriented spaces.

Two tendencies were expressed in the discourses and policies of urban planning that aimed to promote the *infitah* policies and to rebuild a modern capital. The first tried to integrate within Cairo areas of significance to Egypt's glorious past, especially those that were attractive to tourists, such as the pyramids and Islamic monuments. The second tendency, the subject of this book, attempted to remove the "less desirable" parts, especially the old quarters, which did not represent the "modern" image of Egypt.

The State, the "Modern" City, and the Old Quarters

The identity of the modern city is created by what it keeps out. Its modernity is something contingent upon the exclusion of its opposite.
Timothy Mitchell, *Colonising Egypt*

As part of Sadat's larger plan to restructure the local landscape and build "modern" Cairo, around five thousand Egyptian families were moved during the period 1979–1981 from Bulaq in Central Cairo to public housing projects (*masaakin sha'biyya*) built by the state in two different neighborhoods: 'Ain Shams and al-Zawiya al-Hamra (*al-Akhbar*, May 19, 1979: 1).[3] Bulaq, once the site of the winter residences of the rich, then a major commercial port, and later an industrial center (Rugh 1979; Abu-Lughod 1971), had become unfit for the modern image that Sadat was trying to construct. This large area, which over the years had housed thousands of Egyptian low-income families, overlooks the Nile. It is adjacent to the Ramsis Hilton, next to the television station, around the corner from the World Trade Center, across the river from Zamalek (an upper-class neighborhood), and very close to many of the facilities oriented to foreign tourists (see Figure 2). Its old houses and crowded streets were not things that tourists[4] and upper-class Egyptians should see. At the same time, the location became very valuable because Sadat's policies, as he proudly announced, increased the price of the land. The old crowded houses were to be replaced by modern buildings, luxury housing, five-star hotels, offices, multistory parking lots, movie theaters, conference halls, and "centers of culture" (*al-Ahram*, December 27, 1979: 3).[5] Officials emphasized the urgent need to remove the residents of this old quarter because many international companies were ready to initiate economic and tourist investment in the area. Expected profits from these investments would contribute to national income and assist the state in financing new houses for the displaced population (9). The plan to build

FIGURE 2. Behind these modern buildings overlooking the Nile, including the grand building of the Ministry of Foreign Affairs, the heavily guarded television station (in the middle), and the Ramses Hilton Hotel (in the far back), Bulaq still houses hundreds of thousands of Egyptian families. Photograph by Farha Ghannam.

modern Cairo placed great emphasis on the visual image of urban space. Aiming to imitate Western modernity, Sadat's policies privileged the gaze of tourists and upper-class Egyptians.[6] The privilege of vision over the other senses is manifested clearly in presenting Cairo as "the face" of the Egyptian "body" that should be maintained, cleaned, and beautified (*al-Ahram*, December 27, 1979). The removal of the old quarters, inhabited mainly by low-income groups, with their "depressing shacks," from the land overlooking the Nile was seen as "central to the creation and beautification of this face" (3). Beauty was defined in objectified forms (i.e., modern buildings) that should replace the old housing of Bulaq (see Figure 3). The removal of the old quarters was also seen as necessary to "beautify the face of the Cairene society" by "extricating" (*intishal*) thousands of Egyptian families from "inhuman" housing conditions that did not "fit the image of Cairo as the capital of Egypt" and providing them with more suitable housing that fit the Egyptian people and "modern" life (*al-Ahram*, April 23, 1979: 8).[7]

FIGURE 3. A view of Bulaq from the Ramsis Hilton Hotel. Sadat hoped to remove the whole neighborhood, but his death in 1981 put an end to this idea. Photograph by Farha Ghannam.

These ideas were also shared by Egyptian architects and intellectuals (see Hanna 1978; Hamdan 1993). Milad Hanna (1978), a construction engineer and a member of a leftist party at that time, for example, described how the few big buildings in the old quarters that overlooked main streets functioned like "the golden peel that covers the surface," hiding "the miserable conditions" of the popular areas (65). He described the pain and "terror that hits Egyptian intellectuals when passing with a foreigner through one of these streets where one sees the most amazing things and where housing is turned into a distorted image that makes the hearts of those who still have feelings bleed" (65). He emphasized that the population of Bulaq should be "relocated to the periphery so that the large space that they occupy can be replanned to become the second lung of Cairo's center in the next century" (67).

Similarly, relocation was seen in the state public discourse as "the scientific solution" practiced in many other modern countries (*al-Ahram,* December 29, 1979: 3). It was viewed as essential to solve the capital's housing crisis as well as to create a "new heart for Cairo" (*al-Akhbar,* December 27, 1979: 3; *al-Akhbar,* May 19, 1979: 1).[8] Pictures and numbers derived from a "social scientific study" were used to show the "inhuman" housing conditions that had prevented the group's "effective contribution in the development of the country" (al-Ahram, July 19, 1979: 9). The Minister of Construction and New Communities announced that 45.6 percent of the families to be relocated lived in one room, 31.5 percent shared a single room with another family, and only 8 percent lived in separate apartments (Al-Ahram, December 29, 1979: 3). He added that 75 percent of the relocated families did not have their own separate kitchen and that 77 percent shared a bathroom with neighbors. These figures were used to emphasize the idea that there is a "time and a place for everything," an idea central to the project of modernity (Harvey 1990: 217). This was especially manifested in the importance of privacy, which was seen as essential to create a "healthy" family and a "modern" society. Newspapers strongly criticized the fact that family members of both sexes slept and bathed in the same room because these practices were believed to be "unethical" and "antisocial" occurrences that lead to "transgression" (al-Ahram, December 29, 1979: 3). The absence of separate bathrooms and kitchens was also strongly attacked because it was considered physically harmful and socially unsafe (sharing these with neighbors caused conflicts). The area itself was described as dirty, unhealthy, and built according to an old style (for example, roofs were mainly made from wood). For all these reasons, the area was seen as backward, isolated, and "uncivilized" (hadariyyan mughlaqa), highly inappropriate given that it was located in the "heart of the capital of the Middle East and Africa" (al-Ahram, December 27, 1979: 3). The solution was the replanning of this area.

It is important here to note that this project and the state public discourse were based on what Foucault (1984: 8) calls "dividing practices." They started by separating and stigmatizing the targeted population as an expedient rationalization for policies that aimed to modernize, discipline, normalize, and reintegrate them within the larger community. Not only were the housing conditions attacked by state officials, but the people themselves were stigmatized and criticized.[9] Playing on the popular ambiguity toward Bulaq and its inhabitants (as discussed in chapter 3), the state discourse presented only negative images of the residents who were to be moved. The social scientific study mentioned earlier revealed, as stated by the Minister of Construction and New Communities, that the area of Bulaq had been a shelter for qiradatiyya (street entertainers who perform with a baboon or monkey), female dancers,[10] peddlers, and drug dealers (al-Ahram, December 27, 1979: 3). Thus, the removal of these groups from the center of the city was seen as "the most dangerous plastic surgery, crucial to beautify Cairo's face," and relocation was seen as "the scientific method" that was going to move the people from "the dark to the light" (3).

Compared to the old conditions, the new settlement, official statements assured, was planned according to the "most modern lifestyle" (*al-Ahram*, November, 1979: 10). As in other modernist projects (Holston 1989), housing, work, transportation, and recreation were seen as central components of rational planning. In the words of the head of the section that designed and planned the project, the new housing promised to secure "healthy units" and "integrated social life" (*al-Sha'b*, September 11, 1979: 12). The promised "modern" lifestyle was characterized by the construction of "good and beautiful houses" that would consist of separate apartments with separate kitchens and bathrooms.[11] The new units would fit the demands of both "the Egyptian family" (assumed to be a nuclear family that would occupy its own separate apartment) and "modern life" (*al-Ahram*, November 27, 1979: 10). Modern facilities such as piped water, electricity, and sewage were to be installed before people moved into their new housing units. According to the plans, fifteen- to twenty-meter-wide streets were to connect the area with the rest of the capital (10). Officials promised to establish "green areas," not available in the most "advanced" (*arqa*) areas in Cairo, that would "secure a healthy environment." The new location was to include schools, playgrounds, markets, shops, clinics, religious buildings, and, perhaps more importantly, a police station.

All these modern facilities were going to produce more productive social agents who would be integrated into the nation and who would contribute positively to the construction of the mother country. "Thanks to President Sadat's backing of the project, those people will now enjoy a new and decent life" (*Egyptian Gazette*, December 27, 1979: 1). The move in space promised a leap in time that would bring prosperity, progress, and modernity to people's lives. In short, relocation was perceived as a necessary step to create "modern" subjects.[12] They were to become productive, disciplined, and healthy citizens. Through relocation, Sadat's policies aimed at the construction of the Egyptian identity through "negation" (Stallybrass and White 1986: 89): they aimed at destroying an "image" that did not represent the "modern" Egyptian and at constructing "modern" houses as a basic part of the creation of the "modern" Egyptian identity and the constitution of new productive subjects.

Sadat, the Hero of Construction

*[T]he only kind of agency modernism considers in the making of
history is the intervention of the prince (the state head) and the
genius (architect, planner) with the structural constraints of existing
technology.*

James Holston, *The Modernist City*

Sadat, the developer, presented himself as the leader who could bring
both material resources (as the Hero of Construction, or *Batal al-Bina'*)
and spiritual resources (as the Believing Leader, or *al-Rais al-Mumin*) to
transform people's lives and create modern realities. In an interview, he
said that he had heard of 'Ishash al-Turguman, the part of Bulaq that was
removed first, and its problems before the 1952 revolution. One day, after
waiting for more than thirty years, Sadat called the Minister of
Construction and told him that he would not allow "the problem of
'Ishash al-Turguman" to continue and ordered him to secure apartments
for the people before removing their housing (*Mayo*, June 22, 1981: 3).
The minister executed the command immediately. Sadat's visions and
plans were turned into concrete structures that promised to positively
transform people's lives. It is worth noting that Sadat was both present
and absent throughout the project. Although state officials emphasized
that they were following the guidance and commands of Sadat in planning and carrying out the project, he remained absent in the media until
the people were moved to the new area. Only in the last part of the project, when giving the green light to demolish the old houses and when presenting new apartments to the relocated group,[13] did Sadat appear in public, with Egyptian newspapers referring to him as "the Hero of
Construction."[14] On more than one occasion, Sadat described his feelings
after touring the project, visiting some apartments, and talking to their
residents (*Egyptian Gazette*, December 30, 1979: 2). In one interview, he
said: "I was really glad to see joy on the faces of the new inhabitants. They
had left their shacks [*'ishash*] and moved to healthy houses in an area that
was planned in accordance with modern systems" (*Mayo*, June 22, 1981: 3).

Neither Sadat nor the government-controlled press referred to the fact
that the police were sent to the area to force people to move and to crush
any attempt to resist. Instead, daily newspapers described in detail Sadat's
visit to the housing projects in al-Zawiya al-Hamra and 'Ain Shams and
how he was received with love. The *Egyptian Gazette* described how,
while visiting a school, Sadat "cheerfully acknowledged the standing ova-

tion accorded to him with a wave of his stick" (December 30, 1979: 2). Other newspapers reported the conversations that he had with members of the relocated population, all of whom expressed their deep happiness with the project and declared their appreciation to the president who was the only one to "make their dreams come true." Pictures of Sadat kissing small children, playing one of his favorite roles as the "head of the Egyptian family," and talking to women were included to document and prove how delighted the people were with the move (al-Ahram, December 30, 1979: 3). Women were especially happy and expressed that by ululating and singing. One happy young woman said that the new apartment "would bring her the suitable bride-groom." She added, "We were ashamed of our dilapidated houses . . . where we could never receive a suitor. Long live Sadat. . . . In the new house, . . . I will get married and I will give birth to only two children, one of them will be a soldier to defend peace and the other will be an engineer to build the country" (Egyptian Gazette, December 27, 1979: 1). The move, therefore, was expected to bring positive changes to every aspect of people's personal lives and to ease the accomplishment of some important national goals such as family planning and the material development of the country.

Voices that protested the relocation were quickly silenced, and objections raised by the displaced population were considered "selfish." Officials emphasized that the benefit of the "entire nation" should prevail over everything else (al-Ahram, July 9, 1979: 9). The project thus was centered on "progress and nationalism," which were "two central constructions of space and time in the constitution of modernity" (Friedland and Boden 1994: 11). Reports on people's resistance and negative reactions to the project were restricted to a few newspapers with limited circulation, such as the Islamist-oriented al-Sha'b (in Arabic) and the Egyptian Gazette (in English).[15] A representative of Bulaq in the People's Assembly wrote: "The people in Bulaq live in a boiler [mirjal] . . . that is capable neither of cooling down nor of exploding" (al-Sha'b, September 11, 1979: 2). The Egyptian Gazette reported that a group filed a suit against the governor of Cairo to stop his attempts to relocate them and expressed their resentment because he "reached an agreement with an investment company to exploit" their old area and called on the government to help them in reconstructing their neighborhood (Egyptian Gazette, November 4, 1979: 3). The newspaper explained that "the people expressed deep concern over the decision of Cairo's authorities to demolish Eshash al-Turguman slums in order to build modern communities" (3). They complained because the expected price of the land was going to be one thousand

Egyptian pounds per square meter while the government was paying them only thirty pounds per square meter as compensation.[16] A widow expressed her anger because the compensation was too small relative to her foregone rental income, which had been sufficient to cover her daily expenses. A man who had lived in the area since 1913 was quoted: "We strongly oppose the demolition decision and call upon the authorities to help us rebuild our district" (3). The interviewed residents emphasized that those among them who had money were ready to contribute the capital needed, while the poor were willing to provide labor to improve and reconstruct the neighborhood. These efforts, however, did not succeed, and their calls upon the government to include them in the reconstruction of their area were denied.

Relocation and the Disciplining of Cairo

> *Faust has been pretending not only to others but to himself that he could create a new world with clean hands, he is still not ready to accept responsibility for the human suffering and death that clear the way.*
>
> Marshall Berman, *All That Is Solid Melts into Air*

There was another reason behind Sadat's sudden change of heart and his prompt orders to the Minister of Construction and New Communities to "improve the housing conditions" of Bulaq's inhabitants. President Sadat referred to the area when he was talking about the "communists" who tried to destabilize Egypt during the 1977 riots. These riots, widely known as "the Food Riots" but labeled by Sadat as "the Uprising of Thieves," protested the increase in the prices of basic daily goods, especially bread. They started as peaceful demonstrations by workers and students in Cairo and Alexandria but soon turned into widespread riots. Rioters attacked and burned buses, stores, nightclubs, and bars. The demonstrators also chanted publicly against Sadat's policies and targeted *infitah*-related facilities such as five-star hotels and nightclubs (Abdel Razaq 1979).[17] These riots shocked Sadat. Ahmed Baha' al-Din (1987: 127) reported that Sadat felt betrayed and threatened and strongly resented the demonstrators, who almost reached his house in Giza. Sadat described the language used by the *al-ghawgha* (mob or rabble) as "obscene." After these riots, Sadat, according to Baha' al-Din, hated Cairo and its residents, whom he described as "*arzal*" (rude or insolent).

Reflecting on these riots, Sadat described how three communists tried to set fire to the paper storage place of two daily newspapers, *Al-Akhbar* and *al-Ahram*. When the security forces chased them, they disappeared in 'Ishash al-Turguman, where it was impossible to reach them, since narrow streets prevented the use of police cars.[18] The relocated group was seen by Sadat as having participated in "a conspiracy organized by communists" that aimed to distort the achievements of *infitah*. Hence, this area became an obstacle to his policies. It symbolized the sort of community that the bourgeoisie feared in different parts of the world. It represented the community that "the police could not penetrate, which the government could not regulate, where the popular classes, with all their unruly passions and political resentments, held the upper hand" (Harvey, quoted in Scott 1998: 63). So the city center was to be replanned to allow more effective control and policing of Cairo, and the group was divided into two parts, each relocated in a different neighborhood.

It is within this context that the state public discourse and planning policies must be understood. They strategically appealed to hegemonic images of modernity and discourses of social engineering to legitimize relocation and to restructure the local urban scene. Pictures were shown to compare the old dilapidated houses with the new "modern" units constructed in al-Zawiya al-Hamra and 'Ain Shams. Words such as *hadith* (modern or new), *'asri* (contemporary or modern), *madani* (civilized or refined), *hadari* (civilized), and *tatawwur* (evolution or development) were widely utilized in the state public discourse. The appeal to modernity was also manifested in the emphasis on progress, scientific solutions, statistical facts, and rational planning, the importance of international investment and the tourist's gaze in representing Cairo, and the separation of the home from the workplace, as well as on the importance of personal and public hygiene, child rearing, family structure, clean environment (through, for example, emphasizing health, hygiene, and green areas), and consumer goods in creating productive agents who would contribute to the construction of a modern national identity. This appeal to modernity was used to offer the people a "Faustian bargain" (see Berman 1988) that forced the relocated group to pay a high price for Egypt's opportunity to be "modernized." Using force (the police) and seduction (by appealing to images of modernity and offering alternative housing), the project removed them from the center of the city and deprived the group of the benefits associated with modern facilities and new changes that *infitah* promised would bring prosperity for everyone. The group lost a major part of its economic, social, and symbolic "capital," to use Bourdieu's (1984) term, all of which were linked to their central geographical location. Resettlement restructured most of the group's informal economy, altered their access to many cheap goods and services, destroyed a major part of their social relationships, and reordered their personal lives.

In many ways, Sadat seems to be a "pseudo-Faustian" developer who, like many leaders in the third world, managed to manipulate "images and symbols of progress . . . but [was] notoriously inept at generating real progress to compensate for the real misery and devastation they bring" (Berman 1988: 77). After fifteen years of relocation, there are no hotels, no restaurants, no high-rise buildings, and no international investments in the area evicted. This area is currently used as a parking lot. A well-known Egyptian engineer who was working in the public sector and who participated in formulating housing policies during Nasser and Sadat's eras explained to me that "no one in his right mind would take the risk of investing in a small area adjacent to Bulaq, with its bad reputation and miserable conditions." The original idea, he stated, "was to remove all Bulaq and turn it into a promising area. We wanted to turn the area into a neighborhood for embassies." Since the project stopped after the removal of only one section of Bulaq, no investors were willing to invest any money in the area. Some argue that the pressure placed by Egyptian intellectuals on the government against its emphasis on foreign investments terminated the project. There are also indications that Bulaq's residents became more vigorous and organized in resisting the attempts to remove other parts of Bulaq (see al-Sha'b, July 21, 1981: 8).[19]

For many of the relocated population, the empty land signifies the typical failure of the Egyptian bureaucracy to deliver what it promises. Others feel that the government just tried to kick them out of the city center and was never serious about investing in the area. Some think that the land turned out not to be suitable for hotels and big buildings. Many say the project died with Sadat, who was killed a few months after the relocation of the residents of a small part of Bulaq. But did the project really die with Sadat? It is true that the removal of the rest of Bulaq was halted with his death.[20] But the fact that Sadat's policies were translated into physical forms allows us to go beyond this question to examine how a project like this (still common in different parts of Egypt and the rest of the world) has reshaped the urban space and continues to influence the lives of thousands of Egyptian families. Displacement is examined in this book not merely as part of state policies that are motivated by the public good, as the official discourse tries to present them, or that can be subsumed under "resettlement due to development projects" or "planned change" (see, for example, Guggenheim and Cernea 1993; Hansen and Oliver-Smith 1982). Rather, relocation is produced by certain economic and political inequalities and is part of the state's attempts to control the production of urban space and objectify its hegemony in physical forms. As the project under study reveals, resettlement is central to the rearrangement of power relationships and a manifestation of many of the economic and political changes that Egypt has experienced. Studying relocation as part of the continuous struggle over urban space, I argue, reveals many of the political mechanisms that restructure urban space and avoids reducing such factors to attempts to solve some basic problems related to housing, hygiene, or poverty alleviation. As will be shown in the next chapters, not only the state hegemonic construction of space but also its public discourse, which one may be tempted to dismiss as empty talk, is powerful and continues to shape people's aspirations, identities, and use of space after years of relocation.

Discourses, Desires, and Hegemony

I still remember my strong shock, which I managed to hide successfully, when I saw Anwar el-Sadat's picture decorating the living room of the first family I visited in the housing project. The husband pointed to the picture and said, "Do you know how much we pay for this apartment? You will never guess! We only pay three pounds every month. Can you believe that? It was Sadat who moved us to these units that we will own soon." Except for most ex-owners, who lost their material and symbolic capitals by relocation, most people tend to appreciate Sadat's attempts to improve their housing conditions, and one woman compared his policy with Nasser's redistribution of land that benefited farmers. This was one of the main things that I did not anticipate before starting my fieldwork. Informed by studies of this and other projects (Al-Safty 1983; Hassan 1985, 1991; Perlman 1982), I was sure that people would be resentful of the state and would criticize Sadat and his policies. For instance, Nawal Hassan (1985), who studied a relocation project from the old part of Cairo, argued that although such resettlement projects were designed to create "modern Egyptians," they have led the displaced communities toward a "slow but certain economic death" and the "destruction of indigenous cultural identity" (61).

While acknowledging the negative aspects of relocation and the social destruction it caused, people in al-Zawiya also emphasized the positive aspects of this project and often highlighted the advantages of the new units. Many argued that they had acquired better and more "modern" housing, which they expected to formally own after fifteen years of resettlement. I was also struck by how pervasive the state discourse was in shaping people's views. For example, people internalized the associations that the state-controlled media had made between, on the one hand, the location and the size of the dwellings in "unplanned" areas ('ashwa'iyyat) and, on the other hand, many social problems and transgressions. Similarly, several men and women emphasized that the increasing moral corruption (fasad) and female transgression (inhiraf) were a direct result of the fact that many parents sleep in the same room as their children. Drawing on the media, they suggested a relationship between old quarters (hawari) and unplanned areas and the increasing number of armed attacks in Egypt. A woman expressed her astonishment when she heard that a man had started shooting at people in the subway in New York: "We have terrorism because we have unplanned areas ['ashwa'iyyat] and old narrow neighborhoods [hawari], which produce ignorance and backwardness, but why do they have crime in advanced America [amrika al-raqiya]?"

Therefore, the state public discourse should not be dismissed as mere rhetoric or empty talk. Rather, it is powerful and continues to shape people's identities and their use of space after relocation. As Foucault (1979, 1980a) emphasized, power does not only repress, exclude, and censor. In addition, it "produces effects at the level of desire and also at the level of knowledge" (Foucault 1980b: 59). This is not to say that people embraced everything they heard in the state-controlled media. In fact, they were usually very critical of what they heard, often dismissing it in favor of what they heard from other sources, such as the mosque. They frequently questioned how the country was run, discussed the many problems they faced daily, and linked their problems with the corruption of state officials. These contradictory reactions present another theoretical and methodological issue related to how to conceptualize the relationship between the shifting feelings and views of people in al-Zawiya al-Hamra and the state public discourse. How is it possible for people to both accept and oppose the dominant representations of modernity when these are encoded in physical forms around them? In the coming pages, I aim to account for the desires and effects that the state discourse stimulates without reducing the spatial practices of the "ordinary practitioners of the city" (de Certeau 1988: 93) to a mere reflection or rejection of the state policies. I examine the multiple meanings of these practices and analyze their intended and unintended consequences. While men and women welcomed the new apartments and considered them superior to their old units, their narratives and the ways they utilized the new apartments provide a critique of the state project of modernity. As active users, I show in the next chapter, the project dwellers utilized various strategies and tactics to transform the new apartments physically and socially.

CHAPTER 2

Relocation and the Daily Use of "Modern" Spaces

Short of a certain threshold of likelihood, only magical solutions remain. Magical hope is the outlook on the future characteristic of those who have no real future before them.

Pierre Bourdieu, *Algeria 1960*

One day in 1994, Amal, a five-year-old girl, sat on my lap to tell me a story. "Praise the Prophet. Once upon a time, there was an old woman who used to live in an apartment that was as small as that tiny table [Amal was pointing to a small table in their living room]. Each time the old woman swept the floor, she found either one pound or fifty piasters that she kept hidden in a place in her window.[1] The old woman was saving to buy a larger apartment. But one day, a thief stole all the money she had saved. She was very sad. An *'afriit* [demon or ghost] appeared and asked the old woman what she would like to have. She asked for a larger apartment. The *'afriit* asked her, 'Would you like the apartment with a balcony?' She answered, 'yes'. He asked her, 'Would you like a television set, a fan and a bottle of water?' [Amal was describing some of the things that were in front of us in the living room]. The old woman said yes. Then he asked her, 'And would you like some pictures of Samira Sa'id and Latifa?' [These are two popular female Moroccan and Tunisian singers whose posters were decorating the wall of the living room]. The woman again answered yes. The *'afriit* brought all these things to the old woman. She was very happy and cried out with joy. That same day, however, she smelled the *birshaam* that was hidden behind the television set [this *bir-*

shaam is a type of drug that is often believed to be produced and circulated by the United States and Israel; it is a pill that is taken orally and not sniffed as Amal implies]. This caused her heart to collapse [*gham ala albaha*], and the old woman died."

Amal's narrative was contextualized by her family's attempts to find a larger housing unit to move into from the one-bedroom apartment to which her parents had been relocated in 1980. Amal's parents had been trying without success to save enough money to move to a larger housing unit. Before the story, Amal informed me that she had asked her father, who was going to receive his pay "in the morning," to buy them an apartment that was as big as my apartment, which she had visited a few days before narrating the above story. Her father, a worker in a government-owned factory and a part-time barber, promised to buy the new apartment "tomorrow." She realized that "tomorrow" was too distant, so she asked the father to repaint at least the walls of their apartment because the current color was, as described by her eldest sister, very "depressing." Her mother and sisters had been trying to persuade him to replace the current dark green color, which he thought would be more durable and would not get dirty easily, with an off-white color that the mother's sister, who lived in another neighborhood, had chosen when she repainted her apartment.

As is the case with many other children, Amal's images of the desired home are constructed from global images transmitted through television programs, school textbooks, and visits to different parts of the city. Her dreams, as well as those of her sisters, of the future apartment are informed by the movies and soap operas they like to watch: a big apartment with a balcony, a spacious kitchen, modern furniture, and organized spatial arrangements inside and outside the housing unit. These images contradict the material realities of Amal's life and create desires that cannot be satisfied even through some magical means. Like the dreams of many other low-income people, Amal's discourse "proceeds in a jagged line, the leaps into daydream being followed by relapses into a present that withers all fantasies" (Bourdieu 1979: 69). As signified in the end of the story, disappointment and frustration continually disrupt the dreams of Amal and many of her neighbors.

The story of Amal not only expresses the frustration of young children with the shrinking amount of space allocated to them but also communicates the unsatisfied expectations of the many young men and women who try to find housing in Cairo. Amal's oldest sister, Zahra, has been engaged for two years. She is becoming more and more frustrated with her fiancé's inability to save enough money to rent an apartment. Karim, her fiancé, has been working as a waiter in a restaurant outside the neighborhood and cannot save enough to secure the key money (an advance that is paid to the owner before moving into the apartment) that is required by owners. Like many low-income couples, Karim and Zahra cannot afford housing in the capital, and they are pushed to new communities such as Madinat al-Saalam and the 6th of October outside Cairo.

Amal's family is lucky compared with other low-income families who are pushed outside the city. They still have an apartment that is relatively close to the capital center, they pay low monthly rent, and they expect (according to the promises of the government) to become its legal owners within two years. The limited housing options available for low-income groups and the continuous increase in rents reinforce the role of the dwelling in providing the family with security and social prestige. When "all that is solid melts into air" (Berman 1988), being rooted in a particular place gains more significance and becomes central to the representation of the self and the formation of identities.

El-Masaakin: A Dream and a Reality

> *The techniques of enframing, of fixing an interior and exterior, and of positioning the observing subject, are what create an appearance of order, an order that works by appearance.*
>
> Timothy Mitchell, *Colonising Egypt*

Amal and her family live in the new housing project that was constructed in the late 1970s and early 1980s. This project is divided into identical blocks (or *bilokat,* as they are called in al-Zawiya) that consist of five-story apartment buildings with separate entrances. Each building is divided into individual apartments with separate doors.[2] The smallest unit is called *qatou'* ("chopped off"). This is usually a single bedroom with a hall-way (*turqa*) and is disliked due to its small size and the absence of a separate room to receive guests.[3] The most common-sized units are those with one bedroom and a *saala* (a living room) and those with two bedrooms and a *saala.* The largest, which is the least common, has two bedrooms with a larger living space that can be divided into a *saala* and a third bedroom. These apartments usually have one small bathroom with a shower. The kitchen is either a tiny separate space, which is the dominant form, or a corner in the hallway where a gas stove and a sink are placed.

Some of the blocks are organized in parallel rows and others are organized in square shapes or *murabba'at*. A square usually consists of 12 blocks with a piece of land that is called *wist al-murabba'* or the middle of the square (see Figure 4). This land was cultivated with flowers when the group was moved to the area. Currently most of it is used by residents for activities such as socializing, raising animals, and gardening, as well as for weddings and receiving condolences after funerals. While the *hara* or the narrow street was a main social unit in Bulaq, the *murabba'* has become the point of reference in collective activities and interaction in al-Zawiya. These two units resemble each other (and the *shari'* or street in *el-ahali*) in terms of the social obligations that bind people who live in the same *hara* and *murabba'*, especially in major rites of passage. Weddings that are conducted in the same social unit (*murabba'*, *shari'*, or *hara*) are usually opened to all the people who live there, who are also expected to pay condolences when someone in that unit dies. The obligations between the residents of these social units are manifested in various ways. For example, a family that is celebrating a wedding is expected to ask for permission from the family of a deceased person who lives in the same unit if the celebration is taking place within forty days of the date of the death.[4] However, similar to a housing development that Eickelman (1989) described in Morocco, the project in al-Zawiya shows only limited solidarity compared with relationships in Bulaq, a topic closely examined in the next chapter.

Many members of the relocated group, especially women, welcome the new apartments and see in them a big improvement compared to their previous housing. The monthly rent is small, and the residents have been promised ownership of their apartments fifteen years after the relocation date. Ownership is considered a big advantage from the people's point of view, especially given the lack of affordable housing in Cairo. However, soon after the resettlement, the new arrivals started to face problems. In addition to shabby construction (sewage, for example, always leaks, and thus several apartments are stained; in at least one case, water was dripping over people's heads while I was visiting with them), the size of most of the new "modern" apartments does not fit the changing size and structure of the family.

Most families got the same number of rooms that they had in the original settlement. Only when there was more than one nuclear family living in the same housing unit was each family given a separate apartment.[5]

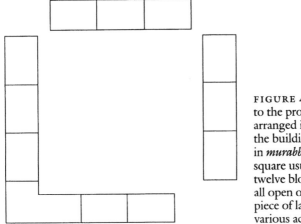

FIGURE 4: In addition to the project buildings arranged in rows, some of the buildings are arranged in *murabba'at* (squares). A square usually consists of twelve blocks. The blocks all open on the same shared piece of land that is used for various activities.

Many refer to how the rooms that they used to occupy in the old location were large enough to carry out all their daily activities and that the new apartments did not add substantially to the private space that they had in Bulaq. What the project did, however, was to try to separate spaces and assign certain activities to specific locations. Thus, a space for preparing food was labeled "kitchen," another space for personal hygiene was called "bathroom," a third space, the *saala* was designated for socializing, and the family was expected to sleep in one or more "bedrooms."

The new division of the apartment, seen in the state public discourse as the main feature of modern housing, did not solve the privacy problem, emphasized by the Minister of Housing as a motivation for the resettlement. Most families received one bedroom with a small living space. Despite the concern expressed by officials over males and females sleeping in the same area, there were no extra rooms for children or guests. Because many parents, just like Amal's parents, believe that children should not sleep with them in the same room and that it is better to conduct different activities in designated areas, they soon had to convert the *saala* to a bedroom for the children. Amal's parents had two daughters when they were first moved to their one-bedroom apartment. Over the last fourteen years, three more daughters have been added to the family. A bed and a couch in the living room are now shared by Amal and her four elder sisters, whose ages range from ten to twenty years. The parents occupy the bedroom. Sometimes the mother is forced to take Amal to sleep with them in the bedroom, something that she considers inappropriate. Other daughters are also moved to sleep on the floor in the parents' bedroom when visitors stay for the night. Recently, Amal's father has been pressuring his wife to get pregnant again in hopes that they might have a son. Amal's mother resists the pressure, using their small apartment as a "weapon." She argues that their living conditions will get worsen with the birth of another child. Other families in the project have also grown and have found it impossible to live in the apartments allotted to them by the state without adding a small room (if they are fortunate enough to live on the first floor) or a balcony (if they live on other floors). Unfortunately, Amal's parents live on the fifth floor, which makes it very hard to add an extra room or a balcony without the full cooperation of their neighbors. In addition, their apartment overlooks a main street near the police station. This immediately exposes any alterations to the apartment to the gaze of officials, who could terminate the construction and penalize the family.

As a structured space, the modern apartment objectifies the state's understanding of modernity. The official discourse, as discussed in the first chapter, assumed that people, after having entered the "modern" apartments, would be transformed into productive subjects who would contribute positively to the progress of the country. In other words, the state promoted the modern apartment as a way to create healthy families and remove social conflicts and "immoral" behaviors. But can the modern apartment determine how it should be used? Can it regulate how people organize their relationships and practices? How do people use the new units? What changes do they introduce to their apartments, and what are the sociocultural meanings of these changes?

Negotiating Modern Space and Daily Life in *el-Masaakin*

> *The modern apartment is an element in a system and, as such, it requires its occupants to adopt a certain life-style; it presupposes and calls for the adoption of a whole complex of practices and representations.*
>
> Pierre Bourdieu, *Algeria 1960*

In his analysis of public housing in Algeria, Pierre Bourdieu (1979) showed that the move to modern housing is not sufficient to produce "modern" practices and dispositions but that there are objective conditions that structure people's appropriation of the modern apartment. In this analysis, Bourdieu maintained a clear distinction between the more and less privileged fractions of the working class. The "adaptation"[6] to modern housing is bounded by a cultural transformation that segments of the working class with low incomes are not capable of achieving because they lack the economic means and the dispositions, which cannot be "formed in the absence of those means" (85). Because the less privileged fractions are unable to acquire "the higher level of adaptation required by the modern estate," they "seek to create a form of adaptation at a lower level, at the cost of a 'shanty townization' of the estate" (87). Only members of the most privileged fraction of the working class, with their economic resources, education, and aspirations, are capable of transforming their practices and cultural dispositions to meet the demands of modern housing. They find in the modern apartment a perfect match to their "desires which hitherto were formulated only in imagination and were concretely thwarted to find the material conditions for their realization" (90).

Bourdieu's distinction between the different fractions of the working class and how they differently appropriate space should be taken into consideration in the study of urban space. This differentiation, however, is excessively deterministic in the Algerian study, since it assumes that the objective conditions (i.e., economic resources) of the social agent totally regulate how the modern space is used and appropriated. Even when people linked their dissatisfaction with the housing project to the fact that their units were different from the "European" apartments, Bourdieu saw in such statements mere attempts to escape their objective situation or to deny their cultural and economic shortcomings.

Although various issues could be examined in Bourdieu's interesting study of the Algerian rehousing project, here I limit the discussion to two points that are relevant to my study of *el-masaakin* in Cairo. First, Bourdieu's model works only if we accept a monolithic definition of modernity inscribed in cultural forms that dictate how they are to be used. In this framework, any deviation from the dictated pattern of usage reveals the inability of the actor to "adapt" to modern life. The inability to provide the necessary furniture and utilities for the "modern" apartment "appears as a sort of scandalous absurdity; it objectively testifies to the occupant's incapacity to take real possession of the space available, an inability to adopt the modern life-style which such housing offers" (Bourdieu 1979: 83).[7] In contrast, I examine modernity as a contested set of discourses and images and argue that, as with any other cultural form, the meaning of a "modern" apartment is not stable but is continuously negotiated by different agents with different powers, capacities, and conceptions.

The second point draws on de Certeau's (1988) critique of Bourdieu's concept of "strategy," a key concept that Bourdieu utilized to challenge the mechanical assumptions that were rooted in structuralism and to avoid the dichotomy between objectivism and subjectivism (Honneth et al. 1986). A strategy, Bourdieu (1990) argued, "is the product, not of obedience to a norm explicitly posited and obeyed or of regulation exerted by an unconscious 'model'" (15), but of a "practical sense of things" (Lamaison 1986: 111) that enables "agents to cope with unforeseen and ever changing situations" (Bourdieu 1977: 3). His usage of this concept aimed to show that "actions can be goal-oriented without being consciously directed towards them or guided by them" (Honneth et al. 1986: 41). A strategy thus is not a conscious or calculated action but the "intuitive product of knowing the rules of the game" (Mahar et al. 1990: 17).

Bourdieu's use of the term *strategy* has been criticized by several authors (see, for example, Jenkins 1992; de Certeau 1988) because, among other things, it limits the options available to social actors and ignores other forms of action. De Certeau (1988) presented a useful distinction between *strategies* and *tactics*, which Bourdieu's work did not address. A strategy assumes a proper place and serves as the basis for generating relations with an "exteriority composed of targets or threats" (de Certeau 1988: 36). A tactic, in contrast, is "a calculus which cannot count on a 'proper' (a spatial or institutional localization) locus" (xix). It is "a clever trick" that depends on time and waits to manipulate any emerging opportunities in a system of domination. Tactics and strategies are distinguished by the kinds of "operations and the role of spaces" (30). Thus, while strategies can create, arrange, and control spaces, tactics can only use, maneuver, and invert these spaces.[8]

The distinction that Bourdieu made between the privileged and less privileged segments of the working class corresponds with a distinction that can be made within the relocated group in Cairo. Although the latter is heterogenous in terms of occupation and income, the majority of its members are low-income earners who work in local factories, small crafts, low-level government services, and petty trading. Some members of this group work as skilled or semiskilled laborers in Cairo or in oil-producing countries. This segment enjoys more income and stability in the job market than the rest of the group. Neither the petty trader nor the skilled worker, however, has accepted the "modern" apartment as allocated to them by the state. They both have introduced various changes to the housing unit. I analyze the practices of both of these fractions in al-Zawiya al-Hamra as "strategies" and "tactics," employed to articulate their cultural dispositions with the modern construction of space imposed on them by the state.

Later in this chapter, I will also discuss gender, an important dimension that was not addressed by Bourdieu's analysis of housing in Algeria, as vital to the understanding of the appropriation of modern housing. Women are key agents in dealing with the Egyptian bureaucracy; they followed the paper work through government offices, answered questions posed by researchers and officials who visited them before the relocation, and bargained for a larger unit or a better location. Women also resist the limitations imposed on them by their economic conditions. They manage the budget, negotiate the family's needs, save money to introduce physical changes to the unit, and cooperate with neighbors to form savings associations (*gami'yyat*) to secure enough money to buy many of the consumer goods (such as color TVs) that are becoming signs of distinction. In short, women take care of their family's apartments, alter how they are used, and organize their spaces. Women's views of modern life, therefore, are vital in shaping the housing project in al-Zawiya.

Struggles over the Modern

> *If we think of modernism as a struggle to make ourselves at home in a constantly changing world, we will realize that no mode of modernism can ever be definitive.*
>
> Marshall Berman, *All That Is Solid Melts into Air*

The new apartments have brought many changes to people's lives, such as the promotion of the nuclear family, a redefinition of relationships within the household, increasing restrictions on interaction with neighbors, more separation of work from residence and private from public space, and the introduction of new ways to organize and use space. People do not accept all these distinctions and changes that were embedded in the housing project but instead try to reconstruct their individual dwellings and negotiate the use of shared spaces with neighbors and others. Many feel that the new units are superior to their previous housing in Bulaq. Only some financially capable families, especially ex-owners who "could not stand living" in the housing project, have managed to buy apartments or houses outside the project. The majority of the population, however, have not had any alternative but to continue to live in the housing units allocated to them by the state.

Over the past fifteen years, residents of the project have been actively trying to accommodate themselves to the new apartments and to transform several aspects of the new units to meet their needs and visions. In fact, people's willingness to conform to the modern units began even before they were moved. They expected that they were moving to superior housing units and tried to prepare themselves for the move. Those who could afford it bought new furniture and replaced many of the objects that they had, while others repainted their old furniture and fixed the broken parts. They were preparing for a new life. As one woman explained, even the governor and his men were surprised when they saw the new furniture that people were packing. "They thought that we were just a bunch of beggars, but they quickly discovered that we had nice and good things. They even stopped paying the money that they promised to support the needy. They said, 'Look at what they have. They are not poor and do not deserve the support we planned to give them.'⁹ They came with many policemen supported by the Central Security force [al-Amn al-Markazi] because they expected us to resist, but we did not. We simply took our belongings out, placed them in the truck we rented, and moved."

People's active appropriation of the housing project as a collectivity is manifested in their usage of new concepts to describe their housing units after relocation. Words such as *bilook, saala,* and *murabba',* which were not used in Bulaq, are used currently in daily conversations and cultural expressive forms (such as jokes and songs). The people, however, are not passive actors who have absorbed uncritically the new organization of space. One example can be seen in how they have collectively redefined state attempts to introduce a new way of designating housing units. Each new *bilook* was given a number that is still used for mail and some other government-related purposes such as paying the rent and utility charges. These numbers, however, are rarely used in daily life. People gave new names to each *murabba'.* One is called *murabba' al-mi'iiz* (goats square) because its residents have many goats, another is called *murabba' al-itikeet* (whose people identify themselves as polite and dress nicely), and still another is called *murabba' al-is'af* (the square where the first aid unit is stationed). These names are used to identify the different *murabba'at,* and then names of the family members are used to identify the specific block and apartment.

Individual units have also been appropriated in various ways that were not intended by the state planners as indicated in the design and division of the housing units. Since the modern apartment is not total and finished, people always find methods and ways to redefine the internal and external design and to transform how it is used. Before I discuss these changes, a brief discussion of the role of the housing unit in daily life may be a necessary background for readers not familiar with Cairo and al-Zawiya.

The Housing Unit in Daily Life

The centrality of the housing unit to the reproduction of the family as a physical and social unit is clearly manifested in marriage arrangements. The apartment enables the couple to engage in sexual intercourse and to start having children. While a couple may be married legally, the marriage is not consummated and socially acknowledged until they have their own space, whether their own apartment or a separate section of an apartment shared with parents. According to Campo (1991), the word *dukhla* (the word commonly used to refer to the consummation of the marriage) means that the groom enters the bride and that the bride enters a new house, both of which take place at the same time.

Generally, families prefer that newlyweds live in their own separate apartments. Not only is available space limited, but sharing the residential unit with in-laws is perceived as threatening to the stability of the marriage and deprives the bride of her own furnished space, which is a major source of her pride. A newly married woman enjoys guiding her female guests throughout the apartment to show them the furniture, the appliances, and the clothes that she has accumulated. Gender distinctions are embedded in spatial organization from the moment when the parents arrange a marriage. The groom, who is the wage earner, is the one who should secure the apartment and provide the furniture of the bedroom where sexual intercourse takes place. The bride's role as a homemaker is highlighted by her responsibility to furnish the living room, the center of social interaction, and to obtain most of the kitchen utensils.

Women in particular are sensitive to the importance of the housing unit in the presentation of the self in everyday life. The apartment, its physical features and furniture, embodies messages that manifest the family's financial abilities. If one knows how to read spatial signs, it is possible to learn many things about the unit's residents, such as their religious identity and socioeconomic status. Blankets or clothes that women hang outside the apartment's balcony, for instance, are read by other women as indicators of the family's ability to invest in accumulating household goods, and they update the neighbors on the latest changes in the family's private life, such as the arrival of a family member from abroad, the birth of a child, or the marriage of a daughter. The apartment is not only important to a woman's own identity but also central to how a woman views other families. Women inspect apartments that they visit and construct elaborate narratives to describe their impressions of the apartment and its occupants. Visiting other apartments provides a powerful way for women to gaze at others and scrutinize their activities and identities. I felt this power when I became the subject of informants' inquiries when they visited my apartment. As a married woman, I was expected to invite women to visit my apartment and to inspect my furniture. Such visits, which I tried to coordinate and organize as much as I could, took a lot of time and effort. In addition to preparing an expected sumptuous meal, I had to rearrange the apartment to match the expectations that my interaction with people created. During these encounters, people not only questioned me about life in Garden City (the neighborhood where we used to live), our foreign neighbors, the situation in Jordan, and my education in the United States but also examined every room and every piece of furniture in the apartment. Children played with computers, looked through drawers, and rummaged through every box they saw, while mothers helped in the kitchen, took baths in our bathtub, and watched my wedding video and other videotapes that they brought with them. After each visit, the visitors constructed elaborate narratives about their visits and described our "big" apartment, its furniture and organized use of space, and the food we served them. "We visited her, met her husband, and saw her apartment" became a common phrase used when introducing me to others, indicating closeness and familiarity.[10]

SIGNS OF DISTINCTION

The housing unit is thus important for the representation of the self and for showing the family's distinction. As "active users," people have employed various strategies that have transformed the standardized spaces into personalized homes and diversified the homogenous housing project. These strategies localize change in durable forms so that it is easy for the eye to observe and measure the financial ability of the housing unit's occupants. At the relocation time, all the apartments were identical in the shape and division of space when the people moved to them. They did not manifest the socioeconomic differences between the people. For instance, several ex-tenants and ex–house owners moved to apartments similar in size, number of rooms, design, and location. This similarity made it crucial for financially capable families to signal their social distinction through other means. In addition to consumer goods such as

VCRs and color TVs, families with sufficient resources introduced various physical changes to the modern apartment to signal their distinction. Most of these changes were marked by their high cost, afforded only by those with relatively high incomes, often families with male relatives working in the Gulf. The residents of each block examine changes that other families have introduced to their physical structure of the housing units and select what is suitable given their budgets, planned activities, and the messages that they would like these units to embody.

These physical changes introduced to the individual unit include adding balconies, removing and adding walls to expand the living room or to separate it more from the kitchen, adding windows and doors, rearranging and replacing the old washbasin with a ceramic one, renewing sewage connections and replacing the old toilet with a porcelain one or with a flush toilet, remodeling the kitchen and adding wood cabinets, installing water heaters, and repainting the apartment using oil paint.[11] Here, it is meaningful to note that people use the word *hadad* or demolition to describe many of these changes. This word indicates that people saw certain aspects of the internal design of the apartment as so unfitting for their needs that they had to be destroyed. Before and after "we demolished" become two distinct stages in the history of the apartment and the life of the family in the unit. People also refer to the apartment that has been changed as *muwaddaba* (arranged), and its price increases substantially compared to other apartments of the same size but without the same changes. Due to the complexity and diversity of these changes, I will discuss as an example the changes introduced to the balcony, which are the most common and visible to the public and express the socioeconomic status of the family.

ON THE BORDER BETWEEN THE PRIVATE AND THE PUBLIC

The "eye" is a product of history.
Pierre Bourdieu, *Distinction*

The balcony, which overlooks the public land in the middle of the square, has been changed in various ways over the last fifteen years. In the original design, it was open to the outside, and a wall separated it from the living room. Over time, capable families removed this wall and covered the balcony with heavy wooden or metal shutters (see Figure 5). More recently, families who could afford it have shifted to a more expensive

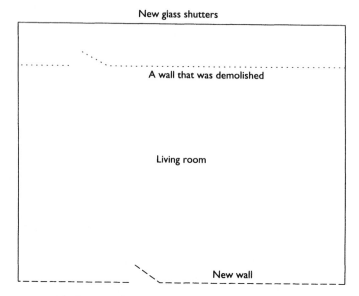

New glass shutters

A wall that was demolished

Living room

New wall

FIGURE 5: Better-off families remove the wall that separates the balcony from the living room and install new glass shutters. These shutters become signs of distinction that convey to others the financial means of the family.

kind of balcony covering, which consists of wide glass shutters with aluminum frames. With the removal of the wall that previously separated the balcony from the living room, the two become one entity that mediates the interaction between family members and outsiders.

The social significance of these changes becomes clear if we examine the role of the balcony in daily life. The balcony is a "stage" (Goffman 1959) that is used to communicate with others and to present the self in public. Women often read the news of other families, such as the birth of a child or the arrival of a family member from abroad, from the objects and clothes displayed on the balcony's laundry ropes. On the balcony, young men and women subtly exchange love messages. They whistle, signal with hands, and communicate verbally to arrange meeting with one another. The balcony is also the stage where neighbors exchange standard insults when fighting. From her balcony, a woman, Um Sabri, follows the news of her daughter, Hanan, who defied her family's will and eloped with a neighbor and then moved to live with her mother-in-law. Um Sabri tries to provoke Hanan's mother-in-law by using a tape recorder to play songs meant to challenge and degrade her. Um Sabri also displays the new clothes and blankets that her husband sends from Saudi Arabia to show his ability to provide for her. The new, expensive aluminum-framed glass shutters, therefore, frame people's interaction with outsiders and attempts to communicate their desires and frustrations.

The alteration not only expands the living room but also allows a new way of observing and seeing others. From the vantage point of the couch, which is usually placed in front of the glass shutters, men and women engage in various popular activities in al-Zawiya al-Hamra: socializing with others, listening to music, or watching television (which is always placed in the living room) while observing what takes place in the middle of the *murabba*ʿ and other apartments. This couch is the preferred seat that family members compete over and the one that is usually offered to guests. Moreover, the alteration gives more flexibility in controlling who sees whom and when. The new glass-fronted balcony in combination with curtains allows those inside the apartment to see others without being seen or without showing more than their eyes or face. Such an arrangement is not available to families who cannot afford to change their balconies. The moment they step onto the balcony, they are under the gaze of others. So rather than providing a platform for scrutinizing the community, the balcony, which remains separated from the living room, gets used for storing some household items or keeping domestic animals. This is one of the main reasons why Majda (whose family could not afford such alterations) used to go to her neighbors' apartment to communicate with her boyfriend without being seen by others in the *murabba*ʿ. As Gilsenan (1982) argued, "Seeing without being seen is knowledge, perhaps even power" (190). Hence, the new glass shutters not only express the financial ability of the family but also reinforce the symbolic power that the balcony secures for its members. At the same time, a certain resistance to being exposed to the gaze of others is manifested in balconies that have been covered with wooden shutters that do not allow passersby to peek inside the unit (see Figure 6).

While the better off use relatively expensive material, needy families resort to clay, old wooden boxes, and other cheap materials. Some families, for instance, build small shacklike rooms (especially when living on the ground floor) to sell some groceries to the neighbors or keep their domestic animals. Others turn the lower part of the staircase into a small shop to provide services such as ironing or to sell groceries and candy. Alternatively, such items may be sold from a kiosk placed next to a block. In these cases, the sellers have to negotiate such changes with neighbors

FIGURE 6: The original design of the balcony can be seen on the second and fourth floors (the left side of the photograph). The most expensive alterations are on the third and fifth floors. Notice that to ensure visual protection, balconies on the ground floor are covered with wooden shutters. Photograph by Farha Ghannam.

and must obtain permits from local authorities. This rejection of the separation between working and living space has also manifested itself in the many apartments that are turned into clinics, offices, and shops. As will be examined further in chapter 4, integrating the workplace within the residence area enables family members, especially women, to cooperate in taking care of the new investment.

The Daily Use of "Modern" Space

> *The blanket that Bourdieu's theory throws over tactics as if to put out their fire by certifying their amenability to socioeconomic rationality or as if to mourn their death by declaring them unconscious, should teach us something about their relationship with any theory.*
> Michel de Certeau, *The Practice of Everyday Life*

Contrary to such strategies, which localize change in visible forms and physical transformations, "tactics" are based on shifting meanings and functions of space over time to satisfy a particular purpose. The daily use of space does not simply follow the prescriptions embedded in the housing unit. To use is "not simply to apply, to put into practice, but to evade the prescriptions embedded in 'official' textuality" (Frow 1995: 48).

The shifting meanings and functions of space are clearly manifested in how the various rooms are furnished and decorated. Except for single-room apartments, most housing units have a similar division of space. As previously mentioned, the unit is usually divided into a place for socialization and receiving guests (*saala*), a place for sleeping, a place for cooking, and a place for personal hygiene. The *saala* is usually a small room near the entrance to the apartment. It is the locus of most daily activities, ranging from socializing and watching TV to preparing food and serving it to family members and guests. It is a space that is typically furnished by the bride, who is responsible for receiving guests as well as serving them drinks and food. Currently, the bride's family buy a standard set of furniture for this room, called *antireeh* (from the French *entrée*, which indicates an informal sitting room). The set usually consists of one couch with two matching armchairs and a coffee table. Older married couples still maintain their old furniture, which consists of two or three high wooden couches that are placed along the room walls. Many families utilize one or more of these couches for sleeping at night.

The *saala*, which is open for visitors, is one of the main spaces used to display the social distinction and the religious identity of the family. It has the television set and the VCR if the family has one. Quranic calligraphy, religious items, calenders, clocks, posters of singers and actors, and pictures of family members may decorate its walls. Better-off families usually have a glass-fronted cabinet where they display china cups and glasses that are not used daily. They also have a small high table that is moved from one side to the other to serve drinks (tea and soft drinks) to guests. The pieces of furniture do not always stay in a fixed place. They are moved from one room to another depending on the occasion and the social function of a particular space. Suad, a newly married young woman, for example, moved the *antireeh* from the *saala* to one of her two bedrooms in order to protect it from the neighbors' children. As she explained, mothers come to visit and bring their young children with them, who not only jump on the furniture but also spill tea and water and sometimes accidentally urinate on the couch and the carpet. She furnished the *saala* with a straw mat and placed some mattresses on the sides for people to sit on. This space is used for receiving the neighbors, while the *antireeh* is saved for her husband's friends and relatives who visit from outside the neighborhood.

The preferred seat depends on the activities conducted in the *saala* and the nature of the socialization process. The seat that faces the apartment's door, which is usually closer to the window or to the balcony, is preferred when people are chatting or listening to music. It allows the person to see who is coming into the apartment and observe the outside world, an activity that people enjoy very much. When people are watching television, there is competition over the seat that faces the TV set. Families try to keep the *saala* clean and organized during the daytime to be ready to receive guests. At night, many families turn it into a sleeping place. Visitors are not required to remove their shoes before coming into this room, which is usually covered with a plastic mat or a carpet (during the winter or special occasions). Women, however, tend to enter the *saala* barefoot because they usually prefer to sit on the floor or on the couch cross-legged or squatting. Except for a very few cases of extreme religiosity and when the visitor is a total male stranger, there is no sex segregation in this room. Sisters, mothers, or wives fix the sweet strong tea that is usually served to guests. When the visitor is a stranger, the brother, the husband, or the son takes the tea from the female relative at the door and serves it by himself. With male visitors who are close to the family, young women may chat, joke, and sit in the same room. Male visitors are, however, quite restricted in their movement within the housing unit. They do not enter other rooms without invitation, while female visitors can freely follow the hostess to the kitchen and bedrooms.

As opposed to the state's original design, people do not worry about separating, ordering, and labeling spaces. The private kitchen was emphasized in the state public discourse as necessary to avoid personal injury and conflicts between neighbors who shared the same kitchen. In the new unit, however, preparing food is not limited to the kitchen. Women do not separate what is seen as "work" (preparing food, for example) from pleasure (such as socializing and watching television). In fact, the more the task is seen as time-consuming work (as is the case with stuffing vegetables and making *ruqaq* [thin bread] for the Sacrifice Feast), the more it is made an occasion for a festive gathering where women exchange stories and jokes, listen to music, and drink tea. A woman may feel very comfortable sitting on the bed near a window on a sunny day during winter to sort rice, to shell peas, or to peel garlic. She may bring the gasoline burner to the living room to fix tea or prepare mint syrup while chatting with others and warming the room at the same time. She may squat in the staircase to hollow out and stuff eggplants and squash with the help of some neighbors. Thus, women's daily activities continually cross the boundaries that state officials and planners projected in the new apartments as central to modern housing.

Through practices, discourses, and rituals, people define and redefine the meanings of space and protect it against evil spirits. The bathroom, for example, which was emphasized in the state discourse as a sign of a modern and healthy family, embodies contradictory processes and activities. People use it not only for personal hygiene, bathing, and washing clothes but also as a place to perform ablution, an essential prerequisite for praying. It is also seen as the place where *jinn* and *'afarit* can possess (*yalbis*) the body and cause the person harm and pain. The person's body is vulnerable in the bathroom, making it easy for a *jinn* to control it. This is the reason why one should not speak or mention the name of God in the bathroom and why one repeats before entering the bathroom: "God protect me from evil and defilements" (*'a'uzu bi-llaah min al-khubs wa al-khaba'yis*). By the same token, in a Friday sermon, a *sheikh* describing the rules for dealing with space strongly recommended to mention God's name whenever one enters a place, especially if it is dark or deserted. This is necessary to pacify the *jinn* and dislocate the devil that inhabits these places. Transforming a place into a safe and blessed one was also done ritually when women slaughtered ducks and chickens on the door step of the new apartment and let the blood run down. Through such rituals and prayers, various spaces are cultivated with meanings and signification.

But What Shall I Do with My Chickens?

> *Last night, I had a dream. We went back to Bulaq. I was very happy and said, "Now I can buy some chickens."*
>
> (Um Hassan, a fifty-five-year-old woman who was relocated fourteen years ago, reporting on a dream of hers in 1994)

As is clear from the previous discussion, women are the main daily users of the housing unit. They spend much more time than men in the apartments and are responsible for decorating, cleaning, and arranging their housing units.[12] As manifested in Amal's story, cleanliness is highly regarded and socially rewarded. The time and effort that women invest in cleaning and organizing their housing units is related to the social prestige attached to their units and their role in maintaining them. The attention paid to the cleanliness of the apartment increases drastically when people expect visitors. This is especially noticeable during certain occasions such as the two Eids (Muslim feasts), when every corner of the unit is carefully cleaned and new covers are used for the couches and beds. Cleanliness is also one of the things that women celebrate when remembering the past. "Yes, we used to live in one room. But it was like *el-qishta* [cream]." This comparison refers mainly to the white color of cream, which indicates in this case the apartment's ultimate cleanliness. They always refer to the amount of time and effort they spent every day securing enough water from the public tap to clean the dwelling unit, bathe the children, and take care of their household chores and then carrying the dirty water to the public drain. This effort and this appreciation of cleanliness frame women's positive reaction to the piped water, electricity, and separate bathrooms available in the new housing units.

Women are main agents in negotiating the requirements of the modern space with their families' economic realities and daily needs. The water heater at Um Magdy's apartment was paid for by her son who works in the Gulf. The heater increased the electricity cost and necessitated more bargaining with the unmarried sons who live with her about how to pay the bill. Um Magdy tries to monitor the monthly expenditure closely and seeks to control when and for how long the heater is used. When the charges increase, Um Magdy refuses to pay the whole bill and insists that her working sons contribute. Rather than allowing the expenses of the new apartment to grow, women also employ several tactics to reduce them. Thus, they use the gasoline burner to heat water for laundry and to cook foods that take time and that require women to stand for lengthy periods. This is the case when they fry fish and potatoes or when they prepare *ruqaq* (thin bread that is used in cooking for the Sacrifice Feast). These practices are not seen as being in contradiction with modernity. On the contrary, they are viewed as "smart" practices that express the skill of the woman and her ability to save some money for the family and to physically relax, by sitting on the floor, while cooking. Women are also active in physically transforming the structures of their apartments. A woman usually saves the money, finds a contractor, and helps in the performance of the work. She also takes care of the "privatized" land under the control of her family, waters the plants, and looks after the domestic animals.

Women, however, greatly miss many of the spaces in their old neighborhood, such as the rooftop, the narrow lanes (too narrow for cars), the open area around the public tap, the corniche of the Nile, and the local shrines, which were important sites of socialization and where women used to "eat together," a signal of closeness and strong relationships. Spaces that were used to raise domestic animals not only represented sites for economic investments but were also the locus of interaction between women. Raising poultry and sheep at home not only provided meat, eggs, and milk for the family but also secured a surplus to exchange with the neighbors and to take as gifts to sick people and new mothers. While taking care of their domestic animals in the morning and evening, women used to meet on the rooftop to discuss daily affairs, the latest news of the neighborhood, and national and international news.

Many women complain about the time needed and the restrictions on mobility that are imposed by raising domestic animals (for example, women need to provide food and water to the poultry on regular basis). But they still choose to continue raising poultry and refer to this process as "*tasliyah*" (entertainment). "It is nice to raise chickens and ducks on the roof and sit under the sun while watching the poultry," Um Khalid comments. "You can feed them the leftovers so that you secure meat and eggs for the family." In addition to its economic and social roles, raising chickens and ducks is rooted in an ideology that assumes that *baladi* (or locally produced) food products are tastier and better for the health and the body. Women insist on serving such products to new mothers and to sick people to strengthen them. Some even believe that non-*baladi* (farm-grown) chicken is not pure (*taher*) because it is fed fodder (*'alaf*). Freshness, a highly regarded quality of food products, is also secured when domestic animals are kept at home.

The freshness, goodness, and purity of *baladi* products are all behind the efforts, time, and creativity of women in finding spaces to raise poultry. Such spaces range from the area under the bed, rooftops, and balconies to a small shack attached to the apartment (when living on the ground floor) or a balcony that is added specifically for this purpose (when the family lives on other floors), and the garden in the middle of the *murabba'*. The use of these spaces is not only informed by women's experience in Bulaq but also reinforced by the prevalence of this practice among people in *el-ahali* in al-Zawiya.

It is important to note that members of the same family understand and react differently to the modern apartment. Young women tend to prefer more privacy in their future homes and like the idea of being separated from others so that their activities will not be scrutinized. They endorse having separate entrances to kitchens and bathrooms and disapprove of their current apartments, where the *saala* is in front of the kitchen and the bathroom so that the latter is usually accessible only by going into the former. Such an arrangement means that strange men who need to use the bathroom have to enter the kitchen, while women have to pass in front of the *saala* on their way to the kitchen and the bathroom. This is why several families use a curtain or add a wall or a door to the kitchen to separate it from the *saala*. Another example can be found in the attitude of younger men and women to raising poultry at home. The younger generation, which is more educated than the parents, seems more willing to accept the dominant class's definition (as mainly circulated in the media) of modern furniture and spatial arrangements of the housing unit. Many young women, for instance, emphasize that they will not raise chickens inside their future apartments but will keep them only if they have extra space outside the housing unit. Using arguments about beauty, order, health, and hygiene, they try to prevent their mothers from keeping animals inside the apartment.

As a result, mothers have to negotiate their desires with the preferences of husbands and children. Um Hassan, who described her dream in the beginning of this section, brought many chickens and ducks when she moved to her new apartment. They were big and healthy. In Bulaq, she had had plenty of space on the rooftop to let the chickens and ducks eat and move more freely. After relocation, she would throw the chickens from the balcony of her apartment on the fourth floor, and they would land in front of the apartment and spend the whole day outside in the open space around the block. The chickens would return only in the evening to sleep on the small balcony, adjacent to the kitchen. When she bought new chicks, they did not grow because they were locked inside a cage kept in the apartment. Um Hassan shifted to pigeons, but soon her husband and children started complaining about the dirt the pigeons left over the place. Little by little, Um Hassan slaughtered all the chickens and pigeons that she had brought with her, and her family members refused to allow her to keep any more poultry on the balcony after they repainted the apartment and remodeled the kitchen. The mother still dreams of going back to Bulaq. The first thing that she would do upon her return would be to buy some chickens to keep on the rooftop. She and other neighbors could not convince the widow who lives on the top floor to open a hole[13] that would give them access to the roof. Given this, Um Hassan was planning to add another balcony to the back of the apartment adjacent to the kitchen. The new balcony, she hoped, would be used for her chickens.

Meanwhile, she managed to successfully negotiate with her children a place in the kitchen to keep the sheep for the Sacrifice Feast (*Eid al-Adha*). To save some money, determine how fatty the animal should be, and secure its "purity," the mother decided to buy a small sheep two months before the *Eid*. She would feed and take care of it until it would be slaughtered during the feast. When the decision was taken to buy the sheep, the children started complaining about the smell, the noise, the dirt, and the work needed to care for it. The mother promised that she would take the

FIGURE 7: Domestic animals are kept on rooftops, in shacks in front of buildings, and in cages on balconies. During the two months before the Sacrifice Feast (*Eid al-Adha*), some families keep sheep in the kitchen during the night and in the shared space in the *murabba'* during the day. Photograph by Farha Ghannam.

sheep down to the public space that was shared by the people of her *bilook* during daytime, but she emphasized that at night the sheep should be kept in the apartment (the kitchen or the balcony) or it could be stolen (see Figure 7). She promised that if she kept the sheep in the apartment during the night, she would bear the sole responsibility for taking it up and down and for cleaning after it.

Dreams and Realities

The way Um Hassan and other women use their apartments and outer shared spaces is part of a larger set of spatial practices. One important thing to notice about these practices is their multiple meanings and consequences. The visible changes that I examined here (such as those introduced to the balcony) aim primarily to communicate social meanings and display the status of the family to neighbors and visitors. In the next chapters, I will examine other meanings and analyze how they transform the project and the neighborhood at large. These practices and processes are not easily classified as oppositional or affirmative to the state plans. This means that they should be examined within their specific contexts to explore who is implementing them, what meanings are attached to them, and how they change the individual housing unit as well as the overall project. Privacy, for example, was emphasized in the state public discourse when justifying the relocation project. Separating gender groups and attaching activities to designated areas were seen as central components of modern housing that were needed to avoid moral transgression and produce a healthy family. Several families expressed their amazement when recalling the past, at how they used to live in one room in Bulaq, although, as they emphasize, that one room was big enough to carry out most of their daily activities. Since relocation, they have been adding small rooms to apartments on the ground floors and big balconies (to be used as kitchens or sleeping areas) to apartments on other floors. In addition to the separation of activities, adding large balconies to the housing units is disrupting the appearance of homogeneity that the project aimed to create (a point that will be discussed further in chapter 6). Other changes and uses of space transform the distinctions between private/public and work/residence areas (for more on this, see chapter 4), which were highlighted in the state discourse and design of the project as signs of modernity. Therefore, even though these changes may be informed by official views of spatial use and organization, they still challenge and transform the individual units and the project at large. Their transformative power will be addressed further in the next chapters.

As reflected in Amal's story, desires and aspirations are abundant, but the means to fulfill them are few. The flow of information (mainly through the media) creates desires and dispositions that are hard, if not impossible, to translate into concrete realities. The pain expressed in Amal's story is shared by many young men and women who dream of fancy cars, spacious villas, and various consumer goods. How do these dreams and changes shape the group's identity? How is the past constructed in light of these changes? How did relocation reorder relationships within the group, and how are its members being situated in al-Zawiya? In the next chapter, I show that although many of the relocated group view the new housing as an improvement and a valuable gain, especially for ex-tenants, there is a general feeling that relocation negatively shaped their location in Cairo's physical and social space.

CHAPTER 3

Old Places, New Identities

---

*Should the modern city wish to resume the old colloquy with the
sacred Nile, and, in the interests of hygiene and beauty, push the
industries of Bulaq off to the outskirts, this quarter might undergo
profound transformations but its soul would never be entirely
changed.*

(Fernand Leprette, *Egypt: Land of the Nile*)

A favorite topic for Abu Hosni, a driver in his mid-fifties, is the changes
that have been transforming both his village of origin, Cairo, and Egypt
at large. Women in the village are becoming "lazy," he complains. "They
do not even bake bread at home any more." Television, he continues "is
absorbing everybody's time. People do not visit each other, and farmers
go late to their fields because they spend most of the night watching soap
operas and movies." Women and their practices are always central to Abu
Hosni's accounts. "Look at women here in Cairo. They imitate *el-mooda*
[fashion] without consideration to our social norms and traditions. They
simply see some actress on television with a hairstyle or a particular dress,
and the next day they blindly follow her." One of his narratives focuses on
his friend Mohammad, an Egyptian man who worked in the United
States for a long time and ran a successful big horse farm. Over the years,
Mohammad interacted with many American women, and he could have
married any one of them in a "blink of an eye, as you know," Abu Hosni
pointed out, addressing me. Instead, Mohammad chose to marry a
woman from his own country. As a faithful son, he rejected the "global

West" and went back to his own village, to ask his father to arrange for his marriage. Mohammad's father selected his brother's daughter. The bride, according to the description, had been living in the village all her life. She did not interact with foreigners and did not speak any English. In short, unlike cosmopolitan Mohammad, she was what anthropologists would traditionally consider to be the "authentic isolated local." The experienced husband took his new wife to the States and taught her English and all the basics of etiquette. Over time she became like *el-khawaagiat* (Western foreigners). She had two daughters and a son. To teach them about their religion, Mohammad used to drive for hours to take his children and wife to pray every Friday in a mosque in another city. One weekend, the father discovered that his son, by now a teenager, was having a relationship with a young American woman who followed them to the city where they prayed. The American woman argued that the son should spend *el-weekend* with her (Abu Hosni said "weekend" in English). The father could not believe that all his efforts were being wasted; he felt that he was going to lose his children. When he turned to his spouse and discussed his concerns with her, she accused him of backwardness (*takhalluf*). At this point, the husband realized that it was time to go back to Egypt. He sold his farm and asked the buyer to grant him one month before moving out. He bought tickets for his children and wife, left them money to last for one month, and asked them to join him in Egypt if they chose to.

Mohammad found an apartment for the family in the popular (or *sha'bi*) quarter of al-'Abassiyya in Cairo.[1] The apartment was big (a sign of wealth) but very dirty and without electricity or water. Abu Hosni, presenting himself as the savior of the family, persuaded the man to repair the apartment and install utilities before the arrival of the family. Mohammad told Abu Hosni that he was financially capable of providing a fancier place with all the modern facilities for his family but that he wanted to get back at his wife, who had forgotten her *'asl* (origins). In a month, Abu Hosni went with Mohammad to the airport to pick up the wife and the children. It was very clear that they came against their will and resented being in Egypt. Mohammad continued his punishment of the wife by going every morning to a nearby restaurant to buy some *ful* (a traditional Egyptian dish made of broad beans) that became the family's daily breakfast. With time, the father took his son and daughters to show them different parts of Egypt, and he bought a car for one of his daughters when she started college. The three children got used to living in Egypt, and they all speak good Arabic now.

Such narratives that describe the interaction between "the local" and "the global" and that tend to depict women as vulnerable to changes brought about by the outside world are common in al-Zawiya al-Hamra. They are repeated in daily conversations, national newspapers, and weekly speeches in local mosques and on religious audiotapes circulated in the area. While these narratives celebrate men's economic success and their hard work to maintain religious and cultural traditions, they try to "localize" women and restrict their movement. Women are viewed as negatively influenced by traveling abroad, acquiring consumer goods, and consuming global images and discourses. Restrictions on women's movement are depicted as important to maintain the family solidarity and religious identity. Such multilayered narratives, I argue, should not be detached from their immediate context and simply conceptualized as a rejection of the West, the global, or the outside. Rather, they should be examined within the larger frame of the continuous struggle to define "local" identities and reinforce gender distinctions. The growing globalization of cultural signs, this chapter shows, challenges notions that structure people's interaction (even between a husband and a wife) and identifications. Mohammad could not control and discipline his family (especially his wife) while he was outside the local context that enables certain structuring principles (such as the notion of '*asl*) to work effectively.

In the above narrative, Mohammad's struggle to maintain the Egyptian and Muslim identity of his family required several returns to various sites representing "the local." It is important here to remember that as a theoretical concept, "the local" should not be confused, as Massey (1994) and Lash and Urry (1994) correctly argued, with the concrete, the empirical, the autonomous, or the spatially bounded entity (see also Urry 1995; Hannerz 1996; Tsing 1993). As indicated in Abu Hosni's narrative, the local shifted from Mohammad's village in Egypt to a mosque in the United States to a popular neighborhood in Cairo. Although geographical space is used as a point of reference for several local identities in Cairo, these different contexts share a set of social relationships and identities that include those who are like us (local people) and exclude people who are not like us (outsiders). Thus, when people identify the relocated group as "those from Bulaq," they are trying to exclude them from another collective identity that includes people who have been living in al-Zawiya al-Hamra and identify primarily with it. This chapter first maps the identities that are attached to, and formed by, the relocated group to show how national policies and global processes are shaping communal feelings. Relocation and the disruption that it caused are important because they shape how men and women remember the past, how they are situated in the neighborhood, and how they view the city. In addition to relocation, the discussion pays particular attention to the various global discourses and images that are reshaping life and identities in al-Zawiya.

Dislocating the Local

To understand the local identities formed in the new area, it is important to remember, as discussed in the first chapter, that the project started by separating and stigmatizing the targeted population to justify the state policies that aimed to "modernize" and re-integrate them within the nation. Central to this process was the presentation of negative impressions of Bulaq and its population. The state's negative constructions of the group drew on Bulaq's ambiguous representation in the popular discourse and the media. Bulaq is usually represented as the real, authentic popular (*baladi*) neighborhood, whose people are seen as generous, brave (*gid'an*), and kindhearted. It is also known for its role in resisting French and British colonization. In a competing representation, however, Bulaq is a "tough" neighborhood and a center for drug trafficking and other illegal activities (Early 1993: 32). Rather than drawing on the positive aspects of life in Bulaq, the state discourse homogenized the group, emphasizing the negative aspects of the area and its residents.

The people were represented as criminal, unhealthy, and isolated others who did not contribute to the construction of the mother country. These representations were part of the "symbolic violence" that the state used to justify the relocation project. In addition to physical force (manifested in sending the Central Security force or *al-Amn al-Markazi* to move the people), "symbolic violence," which is "a gentle, invisible violence unrecognized as such" (Bourdieu 1990: 127), was central to the relocation process from the beginning. Presenting negative images of the group for itself and for others was important to secure the participation of the people and the legitimacy of the government's actions.

Such images have been internalized by the old residents of al-Zawiya al-Hamra and have structured their views of the relocated population. After resettlement, these publicized images fostered a general feeling of antagonism toward the newcomers. In addition to repeating the same words that were circulated in the media, such as *qiradatia* (street entertainers who perform with a baboon or monkey) and drug dealers (*al-Ahram*, December 27, 1979: 3), residents of al-Zawiya have added other stereotypes to describe this group, such as *labat* (troublemakers), and *shalaq* (insolent), as well as thieves and alcohol abusers. Women in particular have been singled out (as discussed in chapter 1, they were also singled out by the Minister of Housing, who described them as dancers/prostitutes or *Ghwazi*): they are described by *ahali* residents as rude and vulgar and are linked in daily conversation with bad manners. Thefts in the market, for example, are blamed on women from the relocated group. Abu Hosni also described how a woman from this group came into the mosque wearing a low-cut sleeveless dress that revealed her bosom. She was scolded by the mosque attendees, who explained that she should not enter the mosque dressed like that. Abu Hosni ridiculed her justification that she left the house in a rush because she was worried about her missing child. As in the state public discourse, old residents in al-Zawiya al-Hamra refer to "the moral transgression" (*inhiraaf*) of the children of this group because they used to live in single rooms and small *'ishash* close to each other. "Children must have seen their parents engaged in sex, and they grow up thinking that it is legitimate to engage in sex with anybody," as one man explained. "These children must have imitated their parents with other people in the crowded and narrow areas where they used to reside."

Although some old residents of al-Zawiya think that members of the relocated group were "cleaned" (*nidifu*) or were developed and evolved (*'ittawwiru*) after relocation, they still believe that they are thugs (*baltagia*) and troublemakers (*labat*). Some even try to disassociate the relocated population from Bulaq and the positive qualities that are linked with its authentic identity as a *baladi* area and emphasize instead that most of them were newcomers to Bulaq. The old housing conditions are also used against the group in conflicts with others. It is said, in a negative way, that the group *'itmaddinu* (became civilized). One woman, who lives in *el-ahali* but across the street from *el-masaakin*, described how her father-in-law feels very angry because "these people who used to wait in line to use the toilet in Bulaq became civilized after relocation. They are currently owners of apartments with separate bathrooms that they do not know how to use, which causes sewage to flow and leak into the houses of their neighbors in *el-ahali*."

As I mentioned in the introduction, the importance and prevalence of these negative views became clear to me as soon as I started my fieldwork. Informants who lived in private housing (*el-ahali*) repeatedly warned me against coming to know any member of the relocated group. One of my informants in *el-ahali* cautioned me against going to the housing project alone and offered to send her son, a policeman, with me if I insisted on going. Even the few who know members of the resettled group from working together, going to the same school, or attending the same mosque and know that these constructions are not correct still insist that the general idea is valid and that the "good" people they know are merely exceptions. These views are reproduced by young children, men and women, as well as by inhabitants of *el-ahali* and the old housing project. They are repeated in front of members of the group itself, especially in conflicts and rejections of marriage proposals.

Members of the relocated group contest these negative images and have different strategies to deal with them. For instance, they argue that in this group, as in any other, only a small number can be labeled as drug dealers and troublemakers. There are also those who separate themselves from the "bad" people by emphasizing that all the thugs, troublemakers, and thieves were moved to 'Ain Shams. Others emphasize that members of the relocated group are skillful, strong, and brave (*gid'an*) but that they are misunderstood by others. Other differences and hostilities are invoked to explain the reproduction of the stereotypes. "They do not like us because we [from Bulaq] are *Sa'idies* [immigrants from Upper Egypt] and they [*el-ahali* residents] are *Fallahin* [immigrants from Lower Egypt]," a young woman who was born in Bulaq asserted.[2] She added that *Sa'idies* were "brave and do not accept being insulted. They prefer to take their rights with their own hands. They are real men who are ready to die, if necessary, to defend their honor and to protect their women." On the other hand, the *Fallahin* were "opportunists, unattractive, boorish [*rikhimin*], submissive, cowards, guileful [*kahiinin*], and deceitful [*makkaaren*]." These *Fallahin*, according to the woman, could not understand the courage of the *Sa'idies* but saw it as rudeness and viewed the *Sa'idies'* rejection of oppression and humiliation as troublemaking.

It is important to note that reactions to the negative images of the group are gendered, in that while women tend to resent and try to refute these images, men's reactions are more ambivalent. Young women in particular express frustration with these stereotypes that color their interaction with others, interfere in their friendships, and reduce their chances of marrying outside their group. Bulaqi men, however, as a young man explained, are "weak" in al-Zawiya and think that emphasizing their reputation as tough and willing to fight back ensures that they will not be challenged and threatened by others. This reputation became significant after the conflicts that erupted following relocation with the older residents of *el-ahali*, which led in one occasion to the death of a young Bulaqi man. Currently, young men pride themselves on the fact that they stand as a collectivity when a conflict erupts and involves others from outside the group, whether from *el-ahali* or *el-masaakin*. Commenting on a fight that broke out in a coffee shop called *Nejoum Bulaq* (the Stars of Bulaq), a young man was very proud to tell me that all of them rushed to the aid of their fellow Bulaqi against the other man, who was from another group that resides in *el-masaakin*.

The negative constructions of the relocated group are supported and perpetuated by the physical segregation of their housing project from the rest of the community. Their public housing is clearly defined and separated from the old housing project and private houses. It is referred to by others as *masaakin el-Turguman* (the first neighborhoods to be removed).[3] As was mentioned in chapter 2, public housing is characterized by a unified architectural design (the shape and size of the buildings, the number of stories, and the colors of walls and windows). The unity in design and shape sharply defines and differentiates public housing from private houses; this makes it easier to maintain boundaries that physically and socially separate the relocated from other groups. Thus, neither the state's public discourse nor the shape and location of the housing project enhance dialogical relationships between the relocated group and other groups in al-Zawiya al-Hamra. After fourteen to fifteen years of resettlement, the relocated group continues to be stigmatized, and their interaction with the rest of the neighborhood is restricted.

Remembering Bulaq

> *Even newly established collectivities quickly compose histories for*
> *themselves that enhance their member's sense of shared identity,*
> *while solidarity is fortified by a people's knowledge that their*
> *communal relations enjoy an historical provenance.*
>
> James Brow, "Notes on Community, Hegemony,
> and the Uses of the Past"

Because of their stigmatization in the state's public discourse and the hostility that they encountered from the residents of al-Zawiya, the relocated population reimagined a common history and identification with the same geographical area. When people used to live in Bulaq, they identified more with their villages of origin and/or with their particular *hara* (a social unit that consists of the residents of a narrow lane).[4] After relocation, Bulaq became an anchor for the group's sense of belonging and took precedence over other identifications. The disruption of their "rootedness" in a particular geographical and social space and the inequalities produced in this process created the grounds for a new collective identity that links them to the old place. It is important to emphasize that I am fully aware of recent critiques of using words such as *rootedness* to describe people's attachments to particular places (see, for example, Malkki 1997). While I am sympathetic to this critique, especially the danger of naturalizing relationships between people and space, it is also important to be careful not to glorify and legitimize displacement by equating it only with positive values linked to fluidity and hybridity. I would like to continue to use the word *rootedness* because it best captures the sense of rupture caused by relocation. It indicates a gradual and long process of settlement in the same space and conveys the strong value that people attach to the security and sense of community produced over a long time of settlement in the same area. As will soon become clear, this process has been very important in structuring people's practices and identities.

The attachment to the old place is not single or one-dimensional, and Bulaq is remembered and related to differently by gender and age groups. For men, its central location secured easy access to other parts of Cairo. They emphasize more changes in their relationship with the city and how relocation has altered their accessibility to work (many still go to work in Bulaq or places very close to it) and to other facilities such as entertainment centers and transportation stations. For women, the old location provided them with access to the corniche of the Nile, shrines, local markets, and cheap goods. Food, its superior quality and lower prices, in particular plays an important role in how women remember Bulaq. "The days of Bulaq are the days of *el-hana* [well-being and happiness]," one woman explains. "Those were the days of honey and sugar. We ate so much there." In fact, food continued to attract women to Bulaq for years after relocation. Because the meat and fish sold there are perceived as fresher and tastier, for example, some women still go to Bulaq to buy meat for special occasions such as weddings. The smell of food is also used by women to signify important transformations in the relationships within the group. In Bulaq, one woman repeatedly emphasized, the food smelled much better. "When our neighbors used to cook something, you could smell from afar how delicious their food was. They used to either send us some or ask me to share the food with them. Here we do not smell anything."[5] For women, life in Bulaq also meant more work, especially in bringing water up and down from the housing unit. People's memories of the negative aspects of life in Bulaq are closely related to the housing conditions. One woman summarized this condition by saying: "We were poor [*ghalaaba*] who used to live in ruins [*kharaaba*], and above all that we had to listen to the talk of jealous critics [*al-'awaazil*]."

In addition to gender differences, there are variations between parents and their children in how they relate to the past and the current location. The older generation, who remember many of the difficulties they had in Bulaq, tend to have less interaction with other groups outside the mosque, while the younger generation have more opportunities to interact with other members of the community, especially in schools and workplaces. Although members of the former generation do emphasize their association with Bulaq, they tend to articulate their identities in terms of the new location. They try to focus on the positive aspects of the relocation and the similarity between Bulaq and al-Zawiya al-Hamra. The younger generation, who moved when they were a few years old but have been experiencing more the hostility and stereotypes of other groups, tend to emphasize more their strong attachment to Bulaq and highlight the differences rather than similarities between the old and the new locations. Sammer, a car tinsmith in his mid-twenties, moved to al-Zawiya when he was twelve years old. His work takes him into different parts of the city, and he is always happy when he meets a co-worker from Bulaq. They eat together and support each other against other workers and superiors. He states: "I am partial to [*mitahayyiz*] everything related to Bulaq. I always say that I am from Bulaq [*min Bulaq*] but live [*ba'ish*] in al-Zawiya."

Despite these differences, Bulaq is of great significance for most of the group in reimagining their communal feelings. Through recalling the past and emphasizing its positive attributes, the displaced people attach their belonging to the old place. For most of the population, especially the needy, Bulaq meant a sense of security and a support system that was formed through lifelong relationships. Being rooted in the same area provided them with social capital that they drew on for moral and material support.[6] While people criticize the old housing conditions and generally see in the current apartments a big improvement, they highlight the positive aspects related to social life in Bulaq, especially the strong relationships between neighbors. When talking about Bulaq, many refer to how their units were organized so that they opened out into shared spaces, which created more interaction between the people. In al-Zawiya there is more separation, and people do not need to cooperate. As will be discussed further in the next chapter, in *el-masaakin* neighbors can avoid each other for a long time. A thirty-five-year-old woman described her feelings about the new settlement and her old place: "In Bulaq, people used to cooperate, and their hearts were together. They used to ask about their neighbors and care for each other. Here it is like a prison, every person is limited to his own cell [*Zay al-sign kul wahed multazem bi 'anbaruh*]. We were very sad to move" (Um Ahmad, a housewife and the daughter of an ex-owner, relocated when she was twenty-one years old).

The feelings of belonging to Bulaq are objectified in the name that connects them with the past: *Ahali Bulaq* (people of Bulaq) appears as signifying a collective reference to the group in signs that support the president, the National Democratic Party, and local representatives in the Neighborhood Council. At the same time, stores and coffee shops are named after Bulaq, and people express their strong attachment to it in songs and daily conversations. Other groups call them *Bituu' Bulaq* (those who are from Bulaq) and call the housing project after one of the most stigmatized parts of Bulaq (*masaakin al-Turguman*). The relocated group's current connections with Bulaq are thus partially self-constructed and partially labeled by others.

Although relocation reordered relationships within the group and destroyed a major part of their social capital, the old neighborhoods still structure some of people's current interactions. The group still refer to the people who used to live in Bulaq as "*min 'andina*" (from our place). This not only creates a common ground for identification but also indicates certain expectations and mutual obligations. Obligations are even stronger between people who used to live in the same *hara*. Work (especially in machine and car repair), marriage, shopping, and socialization still connect the relocated people with Bulaq. At the same time, Bulaq is the point of reference for their identification with those who moved to 'Ain Shams, which is one hour by the city bus from al-Zawiya.

Symbolic Capital and *Baladi* Identity

Through relocation, the group lost, among other things, a major part of its "symbolic capital." This is manifested in two important aspects related to the identification with the old location. First, Bulaq is located on the other side of the Nile, opposite to an upper-class neighborhood, Zamalek. This neighborhood, inhabited by foreigners and upper-class

Egyptians, secured jobs for women as servants and for men as domestic workers.[7] The location empowered Bulaqis through their association with Zamalek. Young men and women, as emphasized by the people themselves and documented in a famous old movie (*A Bride from Bulaq*), could even claim that they were from Zamalek because only "a bridge separates" the two neighborhoods. Although the Nile and a huge socioeconomic gap separate Bulaq from al-Zamalek, people focus more on the bridge that connects the two areas. Some also describe how they lost the pleasure of looking at the beautiful buildings of Zamalek. Um Mohammad recalled on several occasions her happiness when she first visited Zamalek. She compared this happiness with the feelings she would expect to have if she suddenly were to meet her deceased mother. "When I saw the high buildings and beautiful streets, I felt as if I met my mother who died immediately after I was born." The pleasure of looking at the beautiful Zamalek was, according to one young man, even greater "since residents of Zamalek were humiliated [*min zulluhum*] each time they saw Bulaq with its shabby and old houses."

Second, Bulaq is defined as a *baladi* area, and people perceive their relocation to al-Zawiya al-Hamra as moving down the social ladder. *Baladi* is a complex concept, and its meaning has shifted over time. According to El-Messiri (1978), before the twentieth century, *ibn el-balad* (literally meaning "the son of the country") was used to differentiate the indigenous Egyptian population from the foreign ruling class (Turco-Circassian) and other non-Egyptian groups (such as Sudanese and Syrians).[8] During the eighteenth and early nineteenth centuries, *awlad el-balad* (plural of *ibn el-balad*) included Cairo's 'ulama, merchants, and masses. This concept acquired negative connotations under the British colonization in the late nineteenth and early twentieth centuries and became used to refer mainly to lower classes. During this time, the Egyptian elite (previously considered part of *awlad el-balad*) identified more with the dominant Western lifestyle and distanced themselves from *awlad el-balad*. With the end of the British colonization and the 1952 revolution, *baladi* generally became used to indicate authenticity and traditionalism in opposition to *afrangi* or Westernized upper class (see Armbrust 1996; Early 1993; Campo 1991; El-Hamamsy 1975). Currently, *baladi* is an ambiguous concept. On the one hand, *ibn el-balad* is seen as "authentic," generous, and brave. On the other hand, upper and upper middle classes associate *baladi* people with "ignorance, illiteracy and dirtiness" (El-Messiri 1978: 54). These views informed the negative constructions circulated in the media to legitimize the relocation project.

Despite the multifaceted associations of the term *baladi,* Bulaqis in al-Zawiya currently identify Bulaq as a *baladi* area (or *hita*) primarily in reference to a quarter that has been formed gradually over a long period of time. The rootedness of a group of people in the same place over many years creates familiarity between the residents and provides them with open social relationships and a sense of trust and security. The phrase "They eat in the street around the same *tabliyya* [round table] as one family," is often used to describe the close bonds between the inhabitants of Bulaq and other *baladi* areas. In Bulaq, "people used to live close together separated only by narrow lanes," several informants repeated, so "that even if one coughed, the neighbors could hear him." This physical proximity[9] and the need for moral and material support from others secured direct knowledge of neighbors, which fostered mutual support and guaranteed social control. This knowledge and social control was especially important for the movement of women and children within the neighborhood. As will be discussed in chapter 4, because parents used to know each other well, they allowed their daughters and young children to move relatively freely outside the house.

People's feelings of loss over their *baladi* identity are related to the strong relationship between identity and the place of residence. Generally, *baladi* as a cultural identity is associated with the residents of certain old neighborhoods such as Bulaq and old Cairo. "It is as if the quarter had a reality of its own that bestows on them certain values and patterns of behavior" (El-Messiri 1978: 77). Many examples can be found in how the media have represented those who leave their authentic popular quarters as abandoning their people, traditions, and identity. In *Arabisc,* a soap opera (starring Salah el-Sa'dani and Hala Sidqi) broadcast during Ramadan in 1994, for instance, the people of an old quarter are celebrated as representing "authentic" Egyptians. When a young ambitious woman decides to leave the old quarter to pursue her career, she is criticized and attacked by her neighbors and relatives for "trying to wear a dress that is not hers." By moving from that neighborhood, she becomes exposed to bad men and women who try to seduce and exploit her, and she brings misery to herself, her family, and the neighbors. A move back into the authentic neighborhood (just like the move back to Egypt made by Mohammad to save his family in Abu Hosni's narrative) is the cure for the problems that are created by leaving it. Similarly, in *Kalam Rigalla* ("Men's Talk"), actor Hamdi Ahmed (incidentally, a native of Bulaq elected as its representative in the parliament at the time the group was relocated), who plays the role of a civil servant, finds himself facing several serious problems: He is pressured to take a bribe, his son becomes a thief, and his greedy wife helps the son in selling the stolen products. The wife in particular has stopped listening to him, tries to imitate upper-class women, and pressures him to acquire more money. He finds that the only solution to his problems is to go back with his son to his "authentic" neighborhood, go back to his old work, and eat the food that he used to eat before. He successfully manages to attract the rest of the family, including his wife, to join him, and all their problems are solved.

Social Capital and Local Identities

In contrast to Bulaq, al-Zawiya al-Hamra is a relatively new neighborhood. As stated in the introduction, it was mainly agricultural fields until the 1960s, when the area started to expand rapidly with the construction of the first public housing project. This project housed a big number of families from different parts of Cairo who could not afford to live in more central locations. Immigrants (mostly Muslims) from different parts of the countryside also moved into private dwellings in al-Zawiya. More displaced families from various parts of Cairo, including Bulaq, were relocated to a second housing project during the early 1980s. The heterogeneity of al-Zawiya's population is often used by its residents to indicate that al-Zawiya is not "an authentic popular quarter" or *mish hayy sha'bi 'asiil*. Compared to the old usage of *baladi, sha'bi* is a broader recent concept that has been used since the 1940s but that was only publicized by the 1952 revolution (El-Messiri 1978: 46). It was first used by the media and then penetrated the daily language. *Sha'bi* is derived from the word *sha'b,* which means "people" or "folk." While the word *hayy sha'bi* is used to refer to Bulaq, but always with the word *asiil* (authentic or real), *baladi* is never used to refer to al-Zawiya al-Hamra.

Here we do not see the dichotomy between *baladi* and *afrangi* or *raaqi* areas as presented in the analysis of *baladi* identity (see, for example, Early 1993; Campo 1991). The *baladi* (and *sha'bi 'asiil* or authentic) and *raaqi* (upper class) are mediated by neighborhoods such as al-Zawiya. Al-Zawiya is seen as located between *baladi* and *raaqi* areas, which places it, as described by a male informant from Bulaq, in a tedious or annoying (*baaykh*) position. In short, people see al-Zawiya as missing both the authenticity and close relationships of *baladi* areas and the "modernity" and privacy of advanced (*raaqi*) neighborhoods. Al-Zawiya is thus geographically and socially marginal compared to Bulaq.

A key word for understanding the differences between what are seen as "authentic" *baladi* neighborhoods such as Bulaq and "less authentic" newer neighborhoods such as al-Zawiya is *lama*. *Lama* is from the root *lamm*, which means "to gather or collect." Variations of the same root can also mean "to mix with people below one's status" (*lamlim*), "the crowd or mob" (*lamma*), and "the riffraff or rabble" (*limaama*). In al-Zawiya al-Hamra, the word *lama* refers to the rapid gathering of people with diverse backgrounds in the same area. People from different quarters, towns, villages, and religions are coming to live in the same neighborhood, hang out at the same coffee shops, visit the same market, and ride the same bus. These spaces are defined as *lamin,* compared to more "homogenous" places such as the village and the *baladi* quarter. The homogeneity of these places is not based on similar economic activities, a common place of origin, or the absence of differences among their inhabitants. Rather, it results from the familiarity or intimacy (*ulfa*) created through the gradual rootedness in a specific place over a long period of time. Cairo is *lama* compared to the village, al-Zawiya is *lama* compared to Bulaq, and *el-masaakin* are *lama* compared to *el-ahali*. The familiarity between residents of a particular locality secures social capital that facilitates mutual understanding and the formation of many social relationships. This is a familiarity that is based on gaining knowledge of others — their current condition and previous situation. It is a familiarity that enables people to "place" each other (Stewart 1996: 201). Knowing others and being able to place them is central to vital economic and social processes such as forming savings associations (*gami'yyat*) and arranging marriages. Marriage, for instance, is preferred between families who "know each other." This means that the family of the bride is familiar with the economic conditions as well as the character, manners, and reputation of the groom and his family. This familiarity became critical for Abu Subhi when Hassan, a man from another neighborhood, proposed to his daughter. When Abu Subhi asked about the groom, Hassan's boss emphasized that he was "like one of his sons." This reassured Abu Subhi and his family, who accepted the proposal and had a big engagement party. The family, however, had to break the engagement after they discovered that the groom was selfish, greedy, irresponsible, and a gambler. *Gami'yyat,* which are rotating savings associations, are impossible between people who do not know each other. The leader of an association selects only people that he or she knows and trusts from his or her neighborhood and other areas. Mirvat thus formed a savings association that included neighbors from *el-masaakin,* her cousins in Bulaq, and ex-neighbors who currently live in Dar il-Salam in southern

Cairo.[10] She knows all these participants very well and knows that they will pay their shares on regular basis.

The negative connotation of the word *lama* does not mean that people do not like company. To the contrary, people prefer streets, buildings, and neighborhoods that are *wanas* (abundant with life and activities) over quiet areas. This is clearly manifested in their attitude toward upper-class areas, which are seen as empty, quiet, and scary.[11] Furthermore, spaces that are not inhabited or used by people (such as vacant apartments, streets at night, and uninhabited mountains)[12] are seen as unsafe. These spaces are usually occupied by jinn and demons (*ginn* and *'afarit*), which make them potentially dangerous spaces. Such spaces can be transformed ritually by saying "Peace be upon you" (*'s-salaamu 'aleekum*), repeating the name of God, and reading the Quran.[13]

Lama, however, indicates the mixture of a heterogeneous population that brings good (*el-hilw*) and bad (*el-wihish*) together. The relocation of thousands of families simultaneously from different parts of Cairo (including Bulaq) to the same housing project makes it difficult to maintain social control, acquire enough knowledge of the people around, and recreate the social support and trust that existed in Bulaq. The history of Bulaq clarifies this point. Immigrants from the countryside continued to come to Bulaq over the years. Usually, however, they came in relatively small numbers and were already linked to relatives or people from their villages. Not only did this facilitate their immediate integration into the existing social network, but the presence of the relatives and village connections in Bulaq made it obligatory for the newcomers to abide by the rules of the community.

The same comparison applies to *el-ahali* and *el-masaakin*. While the former have continued gradually to attract residents from various parts of the countryside since the 1960s, *el-masaakin* were formed in a short time and have combined people from different parts of Cairo and Egypt. This difference is manifested in the labels used to refer to these two forms of housing. *Masaakin sha'biyya* is the full expression that formally refers to the housing project and can be roughly translated as "housing for the folk or the people." The word *sha'biyya,* with its positive connotations that refer to authenticity and rootedness, was dropped from the name, and people use only the word *masaakin* (shelters or dwellings) to refer to the project — a word that simply refers to the physical structures of the housing units. In comparison, the term used to refer to private housing is *biyuut ahali,* which can be translated as "houses of the people." The first word, *biyuut* (houses) is usually dropped, and *ahali* (people) is used to refer to private housing. The words that were dropped indicate the inferiority of *el-masaakin* compared to *el-ahali*. The former are usually identified as *lama* because of the mixture of their residents. *El-ahali* in comparison are characterized by a sense of homogeneity that is the outcome of their gradual formation and the integration of their residents over a long period of time. The distinction between *el-ahali* and *el-masaakin* demonstrates how people differ from the state in their construction of the relationship between space and cultural identities. While the state public discourse tends to assume that modern space is capable of transforming people's practices and identities, residents of *el-masaakin* and their neighbors give more power to social actors, who are seen as the source of the positive or negative identities of various spaces. Thus, *el-masaakin* are looked down upon not because the physical structures are not appealing to the people but because the mixture of their residents makes them socially inferior to *el-ahali*. This inferiority is reflected in how inhabitants of *el-masaakin* are perceived. The sixteen-year-old Jihan expressed to me more than once her anger at her friend Samia, who lives in *el-ahali,* because she refuses to pass through their residential area (*el-masaakin*) and instead chooses longer routes to reach school.[14] She also resents the reactions of her teachers and friends at school who continuously express their amazement when they find out that Jihan lives in *el-masaakin*. They cannot believe that a person who is so nicely dressed and well-mannered is *tarbiyyat* (brought up in) *masaakin*.[15]

Raaqi versus *Sha'bi* Areas

The identities of Bulaq and al-Zawiya al-Hamra are usually constructed in comparisons and contrasts through time and space. Through time al-Zawiya is compared to Bulaq, and through space it is compared to other *baladi* as well as *raaqi* or upper-class areas such as Zamalek, Heliopolis, and Ma'adi. Relationships between neighbors and commitment to the collectivity are central to the distinction between *sha'bi* and *raaqi* (refined or upper-class) areas. *Sha'bi* people see themselves as willing to sacrifice for the benefit of their neighbors and help the needy — a characteristic similar to what Weber (1978) called "common feeling," which "leads to a mutual orientation" of the actions of social actors to each other (42). They are *'isharin* or sociable and fond of company. They would interfere to correct a misbehavior, stop a fight, protect a woman, or help in an accident. In contrast, *il-wasalin* (those who arrived) or *awlad al-zawat* (sons of the aristocracy) do not know the occupant of an adjacent apartment and are not willing to help even those in need.

Life in the street is central to the distinction between *raaqi* and *sha'bi* areas. In the latter, the street is central to many activities, including weddings, death observances, playing, socializing, and selling various foods and goods. Similarly, the shared space between *murabba'at* in *el-masaakin* is the site of extensive social interaction that ranges from women selling vegetables and fruits while taking care of their domestic animals to men conducting various economic activities in small workshops that spill out from the first floor of many residential units. In *raaqi* areas, "There are no people in the street, and nothing is sold there." Women in particular expressed fear because they do not feel safe walking in empty streets. While upper-class neighborhoods are silent (*huss huss*), people in al-Zawiya prefer *zeeta*. The word *zeeta* literally means noise, but this usage signifies the noise that accompanies joyful atmosphere created by intensive interaction. "To have fun," laugh, dance, sing and sit for hours cracking jokes are central to the daily life of *al-sha'byyin*.

It is interesting to note that the differences between upper-class and *sha'bi* areas, the United States and Egypt, al-Zawiya al-Hamra and Bulaq, and Cairo and the village are constructed in similar ways. While relationships between people in *sha'bi* areas are intense, direct, and personal, relationships between upper-class people are seen as impersonal and superficial. There is a striking resemblance between how people imagine (largely based on information presented on TV and videotapes) *raaqi* areas and how they construct the United States, where each person *fi haalhu* (minds his own business) and does not help or care for any one else. Like American life, *raaqi* areas are desired and resented at the same time. The spacious villas and clean streets are liked, but the empty streets are feared, and the separation between neighbors is not appreciated. Young men more than women and older men have the chance to tour the city with friends and visit *raaqi* areas. These visits create expectations and dreams that are not easily fulfilled. Ali, a worker in a shoe factory, walks with his young male friends talking about their dreams and feeling happy while touring the city. It is only when they reach one of the rich neighborhoods such as Zamalek or Misr al-Jididah that they all "feel depressed" (*binhis b'ikta'ab*). "We cannot believe how different life is in these areas compared to al-Zawiya." Gaining access to life in upper-class areas remains a frustrated dream. "We always imagine that one day while we are walking, an old woman will adopt us and bathe us. For some reason, we always think that she would first bathe us as if we were mangy [*garbanin*]."

'Asl, Space, and the "Authentic"

> *To be modern . . . is to experience personal and social life as a*
> *maelstrom, to find oneself in perpetual disintegration and renewal,*
> *trouble and anguish, ambiguity and contradiction: to be part of a*
> *universe in which all that is solid melts into air.*
>
> Marshall Berman, *All That Is Solid Melts into Air*

Since Sadat started his open-door policy, Cairo has witnessed the introduction of new forms of communication, more emphasis on international tourism, an increasing importance of consumer goods, and a growing flow of ideas related to civil society, democracy, and political participation. These transformations have been shaping the lives and identities of people in al-Zawyia. The flow of information through various channels, especially television, and the experiences of rubbing shoulders with tourists and foreigners, working in oil-producing countries, and acquiring consumer goods are contributing to more awareness of the socioeconomic activities that differentiate social groups in Cairo. Describing the difference between al-Zawiya al-Hamra and upper-class areas, a male shop owner who works in al-Zawiya (but lives in another middle-class neighborhood) explained: "Here in al-Zawiya, you will not find Pizza Hut and Kentucky Fried Chicken. Such places can never profit in areas like this. People are poor, and the money they would pay for one meal in one of these restaurants would feed the whole family for a week, if not more." In addition to the presence of certain global restaurant chains, satellite dishes are spreading on the roofs of various buildings, another way to identify upper-class neighborhoods. Young men also identify upper-class neighborhoods by the consumption of whisky and heroin, comparing it to the cheap beer and hashish that low-income earners in al-Zawiya al-Hamra can occasionally afford. New symbols, desires, dreams, and expectations are continuously produced by the growing globalization of Cairo. All these changes challenge various mechanisms used to regulate relationships and structure identities. One example can be found in the notion of *'asl* and how its role has changed in positioning people and structuring relationships.

In Abu Hosni's narrative, when Mohammad returned to Cairo, he tried to punish his wife because she "forgot her *'asl*," became like a foreigner, and accused her husband of backwardness when he tried to protect their children. Similar to its usage in Morocco (Rosen 1979), the usage of *'asl* (origin) here refers to the process of upbringing (*tarbiyya*), which is closely shaped by the social relationships assumed to exist in a particular setting. Whereas some other groups, such as Awlad Ali, tend to associate *'asl* with blood (Abu-Lughod 1986), *'asl* in al-Zawiya is assumed to be shaped primarily by economic conditions, residency, and social relationships, and it in turn structures the individual's manners, feelings, and actions. *Kul wahid bi yi'mal bi'asluhu* indicates that each person acts according to his or her origin or breeding. Thus, *'asl* shapes and is externalized in the actions of people. Knowing the person's *'asl* provides useful information about the manners and relationships that connect the self with a particular place.

One's place of birth (a village, a town, or a neighborhood) plays a prominent role in shaping one's *'asl.* Those who are born in the village differ from those who are born and raised in Cairo. A forty-five-year-old woman who was born in the countryside and has been living in al-Zawiya al-Hamra for more than twenty years, but who still thinks of herself as a "stranger," explains that she prefers to befriend women who were born and raised in rural Egypt. She trusts them more than those who were born and raised in Cairo. *Fallahin,* according to her, do not play games; they respect traditions, are loyal to their friends, and can be relied on. "People in my village," she emphasizes, "are honest. We do not know *ilawwa'* [how to play games]. Women of Cairo act deviously and change colors all the time. You can never trust them."

'Asl by itself is not always sufficient to organize practices. The social context is necessary to enable the individual to manifest his or her *'asl.* Again, this can be seen in how people perceive the difference between the village and the city. In the village, the *'asl* can be clearly detected and can indicate how a person is going to act. Kinship and direct knowledge of each other in the village make it difficult for individuals to escape social control. "In the village," as one woman explained, "no matter where you go, you will find someone who knows either you or a member of your family. If you do something that violates the norms, someone is prone to report what you did to your relatives and neighbors." In comparison, the anonymity of the city, especially in areas such as al-Zawiya al-Hamra, secures freedom for its inhabitants that makes it harder to control their actions and pressure them to conform to certain collective norms.

At the same time, *'asl* is not fixed. As in the case of Mohammad's wife, and many other cases, people "forget their *'asl*" and behave in ways that others do not think is appropriate considering their origin. It is because one can forget his or her *'asl* that the move from one locality to another (village to city, Bulaq to al-Zawiya, or Egypt to the United States) is seen as threatening to the identity of the individual. Some changes in people's behavior are seen as positive, especially when they are needed to respond to a new social environment. For instance, women who come from the village describe the many transformations in their dialect and interaction with others that were necessary for them to be able to live in the city. Similarly, learning English and living in the United States were not threatening for Mohammad's family. It was only when Mohammad noticed that his wife had "forgotten her *'asl,*" that he felt the need to go back to Cairo. The return was to an authentic *sha'bi* area and entailed feeding her *ful* (Egyptian traditional food largely associated with the poor) every morning. This was important to "force" her to remember and act according to her *'asl.*

A person without origin or *ma-luush 'asl* is not to be trusted. To be able to decode the information that is related to a particular *'asl,* one should know well where the person is coming from. In Bulaq, the flow of information and direct interaction between neighbors ensured enough knowledge that enabled people to depend on the notion of *'asl* in enacting marriages and building support systems. But relocation, as discussed above, divided neighbors, separated kin, and brought many strangers to live in *el-masaakin.* It became hard to accumulate the information necessary to judge a good husband, to trust a neighbor with one's savings, or to allow children to mix with others.

Relocation, one manifestation of global processes that have shaped the state's plans to restructure the urban space, is not the only force that is informing people's identities. While women are usually presented in the popular discourse, as indicated in Abu Hosni's narrative, as more vulnerable and susceptible than men to changes brought by global flows, there is more realization that every person and place in Cairo is exposed to various discourses and processes. Television, for instance, shapes people's practices and lives. Parents try (often unsuccessfully) to control the programs that their children watch. Wives struggle against husbands who try to play pornographic movies. Several women have succeeded in convincing their husbands that God will not accept their prayers or help their children in passing their exams if they play such movies at home.

All these various changes challenge notions such as *'asl* and limit their role in providing the ground for social interaction and mutual trust. They create uncertainties about how people are expected to interact with others. When her daughter's wedding approached, Um Hilmi cried for hours to convince her husband and daughter that the consummation of the marriage should be *baladi.* The reason was that her daughter's mother-in-law had traveled outside Egypt and "had seen the world [*shafit el-Dunya*]." She was *qadra* (strong or capable, including the ability to make up stories). Um Hilmi was worried that one day the mother-in-law might claim that the daughter was not a virgin. Um Hilmi insisted that her son-in-law use his finger to deflower his bride, after which she finished the job herself by soaking a white cloth with blood before showing it to everyone. What was striking about Um Hilmi's account of her daughter's wedding was not her insistence on a *dukhla baladi*. This form of defloration is common when there is reason for people to doubt the virginity of the bride, as is the case if the groom has visited the bride's family often or if the father of the bride is dead or works in the Gulf. To remove any doubts, the woman's virginity is displayed in front of a midwife and some female witnesses. What was striking about Um Hilmi's description was her strong feeling toward her daughter's mother-in-law and how she linked that with traveling outside Egypt. Like many men in al-Zawiya al-Hamra, Um Hilmi felt that the woman who travels abroad is strong and a potential threat.

It is not incidental that women are usually depicted as more vulnerable than men to such changes. While the narratives of many men and older women celebrate the positive effects of the growing globalization of the city on men, women are often viewed as negatively influenced by traveling abroad, acquiring consumer goods, and appropriating global images and discourses. In the next chapter, I will examine how these narratives and other restrictions imposed on women's access to public spaces are part of men's attempts to reproduce their power and to reinforce gender distinctions. These attempts are motivated by a desire to control, not only women's bodies, but also their minds and the information that they may acquire outside the domain of the family and the neighborhood. The discussion will pay particular attention to how uncertainties brought about by relocation and other global forces are shaping people's views of various public spaces such as the coffee shop and the vegetable market.

CHAPTER 4

Gender and the Struggle over Public Spaces

The distinction between the social and the political makes no sense in the modern world . . . because the struggle to make something public is a struggle for justice.

Seyla Benhabib, "Models of Public Space"

Karima is a sixteen-year-old woman. She is the youngest daughter of eight children. Karima, an older single sister, and two of her unmarried brothers live with their mother. Since the father is dead, Karima's movements are monitored by her mother, the two brothers, and, to a lesser degree, by her unmarried sister. Sami, the youngest brother, feels that it is his duty and right to closely monitor Karima's movements. In fact, because he is the youngest son, he cannot exercise any real power over his mother or older siblings. Hence, Karima seems to be the only member in the family that is subject to his attempts to exercise some power. They frequently fight over many issues, ranging from his attempts to forbid her from looking at passersby from their balcony to arguments about fixing his food and doing his laundry. Controlling Karima's movements at this stage of Sami's life is central to the construction of his masculinity and his role as "the man of the house." Sami's attempts to control his younger sister intensify when he is temporarily unemployed or when there is a tension between the two.

This tension was manifested in a conflict during an *Eid* (one of the main Muslim feasts). During one Sacrifice Feast, Karima and Sami were not on speaking terms. Despite their mother's and my efforts to reconcile them, they both insisted on not talking to each other. During the two major Eids, young women are given more money and are allowed more freedom to go out with other female friends and relatives, eating at restaurants and visiting national attractions such as the pyramids, the zoo, and various public parks. When one of her friends proposed a visit to an amusement park in another neighborhood, Karima accepted immediately. Since the mother and the sister were outside at the time, Karima did not inform any family member of her plan. When Sami noticed her absence around 11 P.M., the mother tried to cover up for her, but soon he realized that his mother did not know where Karima was. He was very upset and, as his mother described, kept on going up and down the stairs anxiously waiting for Karima. When she came back around midnight, the mother warned her that Sami was very angry and that she should hide under the bed until her mother was finished with her bath. Karima did not take her mother's warning seriously and sat down in the living room to watch television. When Sami came back, he immediately attacked her and started hitting her in the face. Then he dragged her by the hair from one side of the apartment to the other and hit her head against the wall several times. The mother, who heard Karima's screams, came out half naked from the bathroom and, with the help of their next-door neighbors, managed to calm him down. They all said that Karima was mistaken and that Sami had the right to discipline her. However, they scolded Sami for his brutality and questioned his method of punishment because he could have caused her permanent physical injury. When Karima told me the story in private, she emphasized that her brother was right and that she was not supposed to stay out that late, even with a close friend, without telling her mother. Even though she refused to talk to him for months, she repeatedly expressed appreciation for her brother's concern and affection.[1]

This is an extreme example of the attempts of males to control their female relatives' access to public spaces. On the one hand, it shows the failure of Karima in negotiating her access to public space; on the other hand, it exemplifies how physical force (and more often the threat of its use) is employed to secure the compliance of women to their families' rules. This case also conveys that struggles over space are not limited to those between the people and the state, the subject of discussion in the previous two chapters. Gender, age, and religious groups also continuously struggle with each other and with the state over space and how it should be used and organized. As my following discussion of the workplace illustrates, such struggles are central to the attempts of men (and old women) to reinforce gender inequalities. The attempts to control women's access to the workplace, I argue, are not limited to the desire to control the female body and female sexuality. There is also a strong desire to control women's minds, the knowledge they have access to, and the kind of solidarities they may form. Then I focus on the social meanings attached to the coffee shop and the vegetable market to analyze how these meanings are negotiated, how they are linked to the increasing tendency for people from different groups to mix in the same area, and how they are related to the state's efforts to maintain current power structures.

The Private and the Public as Objects of Study

> For the Arab, there is no such thing as an intrusion in public. Public means public.
>
> Edward Hall, *The Hidden Dimension*

Life in the Middle East has been often viewed in terms of a clear dichotomy between the private world of the woman and the public world of the man, such that men, seen as dominant and powerful, monopolize the public domain, while women, viewed as subordinate and powerless, are secluded and confined to the private sphere. Women's segregation has often been seen as central to men's sense of honor, and seclusion has been analyzed as a mechanism to control women's sexuality, which is perceived by the society as powerful and potentially destructive (Mernissi 1987; MacLeod 1991; Hessini 1994).

The distinction between the private and the public has been viewed as a separation between "two different worlds" (Abu-Lughod 1986; Mernissi 1987). Mernissi (1987), for instance, argued that "space boundaries divide Muslim society into subuniverses: the universe of men (the *umma,* the world of religion and power) and the universe of women, the domestic world of sexuality and the family" (138). To cross the boundaries that separate the public from the private, women need to protect themselves and prevent any potential social disorder or (*fitna*) by wearing the veil. Women thus can "enter men's public space only by remaining shielded in their private space," and the veil is seen as a "symbol of interiority" (Hessini 1994: 47) that renders the woman "invisible" in the street (Mernissi 1987: 143). Such studies, though they have much to offer to the study of the politics of sexuality, usually limit their discussion to women's access to paid work and limit the complex relationship between space, knowledge, and power to the control of women's sexuality. In addition, in these studies the meanings of *public* and *private* rest on gender-biased notions, and the public in particular has been conceptualized from a male point of view (Gilsenan 1982; Gerholm 1977; Ossman 1994). Focusing usually on the marketplace and the mosque, the public realm has been viewed as consisting of the "main places where men interact, where they see other men and where they themselves are seen" (Gerholm 1977: 165). Women's practices continue to be seen as part of the private domain even when they are conducted outside the housing dwelling — in the alley or the *hara,* for example (Nadim 1985; Abu-Lughod 1987). Therefore, while men sitting on the side of the street are considered as part of the public, women who fetch water from the village well are perceived as part of the private (Gilsenan 1982). In short, women are constantly viewed as privatizing the public. At the same time, men are often viewed as a unified category, with little attention to how young men's access to various public spaces may be restricted by their parents and/or the government.

The dichotomy between the private and the public has been criticized by several scholars (Nelson 1974; Altorki 1986; Hegland 1991; Fraser 1992; Benhabib 1992). Feminists in particular have shown that the distinction between the private and the public "has been part of a discourse of domination that legitimizes women's oppression and exploitation in the private realm" (Benhabib 1992: 93). More theoretical studies have shown how the notion of "public" has changed over time (Sennett 1977; Calhoun 1992). Currently, as Fraser (1992) showed, *public* is used to mean "state-related," "accessible to everyone," "of concern to everyone," and "pertaining to a common good or shared interest" (128). *Private* usually refers to private property or to "intimate domestic or personal life, including sexual life" (Fraser 1992: 128). There is a need, therefore, to continuously question who is defining what is "private" and what is "public" and how the distinctions between them shift over time and are being negotiated by gender and age groups.

My aim here is not to deny the gendered nature of the separation between the "public" and the "private." Rather, I argue that by assuming a rigid dichotomy and fixity in the separation between "the world of men" (always equated with the public) and "the world of women" (always equated with the private), the analysis fails to account for the continuous struggle to define the boundaries between the private and the public and how their definitions are central to the reproduction of power relationships and the reinforcement of gender inequalities. In this chapter, I want to show that we should go beyond emphasizing the gendered character of public space to examine which, when, why, and by whom certain public spaces are closed or opened to age and gender groups. This examination is a necessary step to understand how the meanings of various spaces are constructed. While women are encouraged to frequent some spaces, such as the mosque, other spaces — for example, the workplace and the vegetable market — are constructed in negative terms. Even though women are subjected to more restrictions, young men also have to struggle with their families and with the state to secure access to public spaces such as the street and the coffeehouse. Before proceeding to discuss the gendered character of public space, I will examine the notion of "privacy" and how the housing project introduced new ways to separate the private from the public.

Privacy and Modern Housing

> *Men have, through modernity, established a firmer claim on urban space but the city is ultimately possessed zonally, fleetingly and sometimes randomly and not by a particular gender, group or tribe.*
>
> Chris Jenks, "Watching Your Step"

According to *Merriam-Webster's Collegiate Dictionary*, *privacy*[2] is defined as "the quality or state of being apart from company or observation," "freedom from unauthorized intrusion," "a place of seclusion," and "secrecy." Like some other societies, people in al-Zawiya do not have a specific word that designates the English meaning of "privacy." Similarly, Arabic-English dictionaries such as *al-Mawrid* tend to present a limited sense of the meaning of *privacy*, which is translated as *'uzla* (seclusion and solitude) or *sirriya* (secretiveness), while the *Oxford English-Arabic* dictionary adds to the meaning the words *wihda* (loneliness) and *khalwa* (retreat).[3] Not one single word indicates a desired, positive temporary separation of the self from others. No one in al-Zawiya would ask, "Do you want to be alone?" No one would say, "You invaded my privacy" or "I need some privacy." Stories often describe how Egyptians did not understand the need of their foreign visitors to be alone, especially when they were sick (see, e.g., Rugh 1984). In fact, people feel sorry for those who live on their own. I was pitied because I was childless and did not have company when my husband was at work. Women therefore not only encouraged me to visit them to avoid being alone but emphasized the importance of having a baby to entertain me (*yisallani*). Similarly, when Nadia's husband traveled to work in Saudi Arabia, she moved to stay with her parents for more than two years. She feared living on her own and felt that it was safer and more enjoyable for her and her child to be with her family. Being with others is very central to people's daily life, and being on one's own is seen as dangerous and scary.

The absence of an equivalent Arabic word for the English concept of privacy does not mean the absence of concern about family life, domestic affairs, and bodily functions in al-Zawiya. This concern was manifested in the state public discourse and continues to be central to how people conduct their daily life. As discussed in the first chapter, the state discourse placed great emphasis on the need to separate nuclear families and conduct intimate actions related to the body, such as bathing, in designated areas away from others. Children should not see their siblings bathing or their parents engaged in sex. At the same time, each nuclear family was to occupy its own separate unit.[4] The contracts given to families when they were relocated make a clear distinction between the spaces that are controlled by the individual family and other spaces that are to be collectively used. The enclosed space of the apartment belongs to the family, while spaces outside the units such as the staircase and the rooftop are to be jointly managed. The contracts call upon people to form an owners' union (*itihad mulak*) to regulate the use of these spaces. The project created a dichotomy between the domain of the family and the rest of the community. For instance, rather than seeing the rooftop as an extension of the whole building and viewing it as open to all the residents, the current view is that the rooftop belongs to the families who live on the top floor. They have the right to use and regulate who has access to it. As reported for the Algerian housing project discussed in chapter 2, "The outside now corresponds exactly to the opposition between the family nucleus and the neighborhood, between the apartment and the rest of the building" (Bourdieu 1979: 89). With the absence of the previously shared spaces such as the roof and the bathroom, many (especially the better off) can afford staying apart from their neighbors for days. This absence features prominently in narratives about the past and the current lack of cooperation between neighbors and decrease in exchanges of goods (especially of food) and services. The new apartments, and their doors, make it possible to have little interaction with others and to avoid neighbors.

OPEN DOORS, CLOSED HOMES

> *I was only seven years old when we were relocated. I remember a*
> *Christian friend of my mother who described how happy they were*
> *with the new housing units that they moved to in al-Zawiya al-*
> *Hamra. We all were so excited about moving. My friends and I*
> *used to talk for hours, imagining how life was going to be in the*
> *new apartments. We used to picture the new bathrooms and count*
> *the number of showers that we would take in the morning and*
> *evening. We were very happy while we were helping my mother pack*
> *our belongings. It was only when I saw them removing the door of*
> *our room that I felt deep sadness, pushing me to weep very hard.*
> *Without realizing it, I found myself holding the door tight*
> *screaming, "I do not want to leave, I do not want to leave," but*
> *of course my parents and siblings would not allow me to stay. We*
> *all were crying when we moved.*
>
> A twenty-two-year-old woman describing her feelings
when her family was relocated

The "door," as noted in chapter 1, had a special significance in Sadat's *infitah,* or "open-door policy." This policy, as stated by Sadat (1981) himself, aimed to "open the universe . . . open the door for fresh air and remove all the barriers and walls that we built around us to suffocate ourselves by our own hands" (12). While Sadat's policies aimed to open the door to the outside, at the local level doors were utilized to enclose and separate nuclear families from each other. The modern family was perceived as a nuclear family that occupied its own separate apartment and had a door that enclosed its activities and defined its separate boundaries. Doors have a special significance in how people depict attachment to the old location and current interaction in the new project. As the above narrative reveals, the door mediates the relationship between the social actor, the housing unit, and the larger community. The door is recalled when people remember the past and point to how space connected them in Bulaq while it separates them in al-Zawiya. Many used to live in rooms that opened on a common hallway (*fasaha*), and the building (*bayt*) had one door that enclosed them as a unit. The statement "We did not use to close our doors" is made to signify a complex set of relationships, manifesting security, closeness, trust, and honesty, that is said to have characterized the old location. In comparison, *el-masaakin* are formed of residents who come from different parts of Cairo and various Bulaqi alleys. The security that was guaranteed through long-formed relationships was disrupted, and the basis for leaving doors opened was shaken. Simultaneously, the new housing units provided families with the possibility of closing their door to reduce contacts with their neighbors and the rest of the community. The door has thus made it possible to separate the self from others and has allowed the control of interaction between social actors. As Bourdieu (1979) described for the Algerian rehousing project, "The outside world begins at the front door" (89).

Since relocation, the door has become more important in mediating the interaction between the family and others. It has become the entrance to the family's life, its exit to the outside world, and the gate that is used to communicate with others, establish or restrict relationships with neighbors, and express solidarity with the rest of the community. In short, it is the "gate" that regulates the inclusion and exclusion of others from the family's life. This is not to say that the gate is rigid. In fact, because the rules that regulate this gate are flexible and change according to the context, the door becomes the locus of tension with others. Closing the door can be translated as separating your world from others when there is tension between neighbors, especially in *el-masaakin*. The door symbolizes and reinforces the distinction between "us" and "them" when there is tension between neighbors.

The special importance of the door is revealed on a daily basis because it functions like a thermometer that indicates the fluctuation of the relationship between neighbors. The families of Um Mahmmod and Um 'Emmad are two of the few families that continued to live next to each other after the relocation. Their memories of their life in Bulaq have created a sense of closeness between the two families and openness between their apartments that is not common in other blocks. The two women think of themselves as sisters, a fact that is manifested in how the children of each family call the other woman *khalti* (mother's sister). Although physically the two apartments are separated and have their own wooden doors, there is a continuous flow of news, objects, and people between the two units. The doors are usually open (especially in the summer) from morning until late at night. This changes, however, when there is tension between the two families. The number of visits decreases rapidly, and some members who are directly involved in a conflict may stop talking to each other. In this context, the door gains more significance. How one opens and closes the door signals feelings of anger, disrespect, and frustration. When a young woman of the two families slaps the door hard while one of the neighbors is passing, she is making a clear statement about her anger. If she closes the outer door of the apartment while her neighbor's door is open without looking and asking for permission from anyone near the door, a conflict erupts between the neighbors because this action is seen as disrespectful. Only when neighbors are not on talking terms do they close the door without asking for a permission. Um 'Emmad laments the days of Bulaq when she and Um Mahmmod would settle their problems without delay and would check on each other if one of them did not see the other for a few hours. In *el-masaakin*, however, she says, one could "die while the door is closed and without anybody knowing." This is a common expression that is used to express the extreme condition of isolation that people feel in the new apartments compared with the old ones. It signifies the rigid distinction that has been created between the domain of the family and the rest of the community.

The door and the ability to enclose the family's life introduce a new definition of privacy. Families' reactions to this new possibility vary depending on their members' education, economic status, and religious views. There is especially a marked difference between the better off and the needy. The needy (such as Um 'Emmad and her family) see in the door and the growing separation from their neighbors not a positive change that protects the family but a barrier that reduces interaction and cooperation within the community. The relatively better-off families (such as Um Mahmmod's) see in the door a welcome development and tend to introduce physical changes to their units that secure more visual protection. This can best be exemplified by the wall that has been introduced to create a space that mediates the interaction between those who are standing at the door and those who are inside the living room.

SEEING AND PRIVACY

As mentioned in chapter 2, the living room is the main space where family members interact with each other and with visitors. They eat, drink tea, and watch television in this room. Like the *maglis* in Lebanon (Gilsenan 1982) and the *mafraj* in Yemen (Gerholm 1977), the *saala* is on the border of the private and public. During daytime, it is public and open to visitors (both men and women), while at night it is privatized and used as a bedroom for family members. Both men and women tend to secure their privacy in this space by dressing modestly. In addition, when the doors of opposite apartments face each other, families who can afford it have added a new half-wall that separates the living room from the kitchen and creates a space called *turqa* (corridor or hallway). Without this wall, the *saala* is exposed to the eyes of the neighbors when the door is open (see Figure 8). The new *turqa* makes it possible for the person who

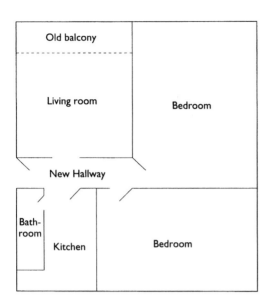

FIGURE 8: Families who can afford it add a new half-wall that separates the living room from the kitchen and creates a space called *turqa* (corridor). This wall blocks one's view of the living room from the apartment doorway or from other rooms in the apartment and provides visual protection for family members, especially when they sit on the floor to eat.

answers the door to have full control over the interaction with the visitor. Here it is important to notice that there is a strong relationship between seeing and the sense of privacy. The new arrangement allows Um Walid to secure the protection of certain actions. She needs visual protection, for instance, to avoid certain undesirable social obligations, especially sharing food, with neighbors. Um Walid not only closes the apartment door before serving the food but also hides the meat under the rounded table (*tabliya*) until the time for its distribution (usually toward the end of the meal) to her family members. If neighbors see the meat, they should be invited to have some. It is the act of seeing (and not smelling, for instance) that makes it obligatory to share the food. Privacy in this sense "appears as an escape from the demands and burdens of social interaction" (Moore 1984: 14).

Central to the regulation of the relationship between the self and others is the control of what, when, and how the self is to be seen by others. Here it is important to point out that regulating acts of seeing does not mean a total shielding from the eyes of others, as argued in relation to "the Islamic city" (see Abu-Lughod 1987). Rather, it is the attempt to control who sees whom and under which conditions. Thus, while young women are encouraged, and in many cases required, to wear the scarf to have access to the workplace and other public spaces, they are allowed to dress in fancy clothes, wear full makeup, fix their hair, and dance in front of male and female guests in weddings and birthday parties that often take place in the street. This is a celebration of their beauty, sexuality, and skills as dancers. As long as it takes place under the gaze of the family and the rest of the community (men and women), dancing is not stigmatized or prevented.

At the same time, sharing a bed with a sister, a mother, or a female visitor is accepted. Daughters may prefer to sleep in the same bed with their mothers in winter to keep warm or simply because they feel lonely when sleeping in separate beds. But, the apartment, which may be the most private space, becomes more "public" for women at night. Female members wear pants under their long dresses (*galaliib*) because the rooms where they sleep are accessible to their male relatives, and mothers describe how the presence of children prevents them from wearing revealing nightgowns or using makeup. The body becomes the most intimate space that should be protected from the gaze of others. Similarly, sexual relationships change to a large extent after the birth of the first baby. Since children are not required to ask for permission before entering their parents' room (when the parents have their own separate room), intimate relationships between couples are exclusively limited to nighttime and only after the children are completely asleep. Many women reported that they have not seen their husbands' naked bodies for fifteen to twenty years. The body in this context becomes the most intimate space that should be protected and regulated. This protection is central to the meaning of privacy in al-Zawiya.

Rather than a separation between two domains, this notion of privacy rests on regulating encounters between the family and outsiders as well as among its members. This regulation is crucial to the negotiation of changes that people introduce to their units and that threaten to violate the privacy of others. This can be elaborated through revisiting the changes that people introduced to the main balcony, briefly examined in chapter 2. Over the last fifteen years, this balcony, which overlooks the public land in the middle of the square (*murabba'*), has been changed in various ways that enable family members to see what happens in the center of the *murabba'*. Because these balconies open on the middle of the *murabba'*, they are not seen as violating the privacy of other families. No negotiations are required between neighbors to implement such changes. The situation is different when one family opens a new window that may expose the bedroom or the kitchen of another family. In this case, negotiations are needed, and families who are threatened by the gaze of the neighbors can prevent such changes. "Our neighbors allowed us to open a new window in the bedroom because they know that my sons are well-mannered and that they will not look at their apartment," Um Hassan explains. This window, which overlooks the bedrooms in the opposite block, remains closed most of the time and is opened only in the night when it is hot to cool the bedroom or when Um Hassan lowers her basket to buy some groceries from the kiosk that is attached to their block. A certain resistance to being exposed to the gaze of others is manifested in balconies (usually on the ground floor) that have been covered with wooden shutters that do not allow passersby to peek inside the unit.

Privacy is a relational concept that is context bounded rather than a rigid dichotomy between two separate domains. Privacy here indicates all the actions that should be protected from the gaze of others (whether family members, neighbors, or officials). This makes it important to examine the role of social actors in negotiating and redefining the meaning of privacy. For example, domestic violence is considered "public" in that people are expected to step in to stop a fight between family members. Neighbors who fail to do so are blamed. Tension may escalate and relationships may be temporarily severed because one family did not interfere to mediate a conflict in the next-door apartment. This was painfully expressed in a story told by a female informant. One man used to beat his wife, but as soon as she started screaming, the neighbors rushed to help her. To avoid this interference, the man shifted to removing all his clothes before beating his wife. In this way, the man "privatized" an action that is considered public and managed to prevent others from helping the wife. Using his naked body, which should not be seen by others, the man managed to discourage others from helping his wife.

Engendering Public Space

> Rather than a fixed boundary dividing the city into two parts, public and private, outside and inside, there are degrees of accessibility and exclusion determined variously by the relations between the persons involved, and by the time and the circumstance.
>
> Timothy Mitchell, *Colonising Egypt*

Public spaces are gendered in that they "both reflect and affect the ways in which gender is constructed and understood" (Massey 1994: 179). While men have more freedom touring the city and enjoy less restricted access to various public spaces, women's movement is structured by several factors such as age and dress code and is restricted to certain times (for example, day or night and times of the absence of menstrual and birth blood). Men and women are expected to perform differently in the street. As men walk, they scan the area around them, ready to mediate in fights or to help in any emergency. Their masculinity and reputation are contingent upon their ability to interfere to protect a woman, correct a misbehavior, or help in rescuing people in an accident. While teasing and making comments that target young women from outside their immediate surroundings are perceived as a source of enjoyment and entertainment, young men should refrain from targeting women from their *murabba'at* or streets. In contrast, a young woman who is walking alone should show modesty by taking a serious posture that is manifested in walking fast and avoiding looking at men or responding to their comments. As one man emphasized, a young woman who answers back risks being insulted further, attracts more attention to herself, and may cause a conflict between her male relatives and the man who harasses her.

While men can and often do go out almost at any time (day and night), women do not usually go out late at night without being accompanied by a male relative or a female friend. They usually prefer to walk arm in arm. They are more relaxed when walking in a group, laughing and chatting loudly. When they are walking with a male relative, he assumes full responsibility for their safety. Sometimes conflicts may erupt if the male relative feels that other young men are being offensive in their comments or the way they look at the female relative. In contrast to the young, older women have more freedom and can walk alone without the threat of harassment. The power older women acquire over time is manifested in more mobility and more confidence while in streets, stores, and marketplaces. So they can talk in loud voices, can address strange men directly, and can answer back verbally and physically if they feel they are being treated disrespectfully.

Men, as manifested in the story of Karima, try to regulate the movement of their sisters, wives, and mothers. The realities of daily life, however, make men's attempts to restrict women's access to public space an ideal more than a practical possibility.[5] More often, women take charge of their families, due to the absence of the husband (because of his death, old age, or employment in Cairo in more than one job or in one of the oil-producing countries). Women thus not only take care of their family affairs in the "domestic sphere" but also are the main agents in negotiating the daily needs of their families, bargaining in the market, and forging social support networks. Above all, they have the time and skills needed to negotiate and follow up on matters related to the Egyptian bureaucracy.[6] Employing a set of strategies that range from pleading, entreating, and invoking blessings to offering money, cigarettes, and food to officials, women often manage more successfully than men in negotiating their families' needs. For instance, people in al-Zawiya usually install a wire from the road electricity to light up the street during wedding celebrations. Um Mukhtar, a widow in her late forties, was not lucky during her daughter's engagement party because some officials saw the connection and imposed a fine of three hundred pounds. She was not lucky again because the officials talked to her younger brother (a teacher in his mid-twenties), who "did not know how to handle them," as she explains. "I could have given them thirty pounds and offered them soft drinks and some food to overlook the wire. My brother just took the ticket. He was too proud to argue with them. I talked to some officials who told me that it was too late to do anything about it. Well, I will try again with some other officials to at least reduce the fine."

While women who go often to the market, the mosque, and government offices to attend to the affairs of their families are not restricted, their movement is closely controlled when it is motivated by socialization or is leisure oriented. Women, especially the young, like going out (fusha). Fusha implies going out to the open space to enjoy fresh air and the company of others. The most preferred visits are to the seaside during the summer and to local attraction centers such as parks and the local zoo during the winter.[7] The further the trip is, the more restrictions are put on the woman to be with other women or male relatives. Permissions for visits inside the neighborhood are usually easy to obtain, and young women often simply inform the mother that they are visiting a friend or a neighbor. Traveling to other parts of the city, however, demands more negotiation and preparation. The verbal permit to travel inside the city and outside it can be granted by various family members — the father, the mother, an older sister, or a brother, depending on the context. A clear yes is needed when the trip is outside the city; on such occasions, the father is usually involved in the decision, with mediation from the mother or older siblings. When the mother agrees to allow a daughter to go on such a trip, it is difficult, if not impossible, for the father or the brothers to reverse the decision.

It is important to remember that women's access to public space shifts and changes over time. Many factors — age, marital status, economic need, the number of children, and the background of the "social guardian" (education, age, job, gender, and regional culture) — shape women's access to public space. Although women enjoy relative freedom under the supervision of their mothers while they are single (including the possibility of working outside the home), their movement becomes more restricted after marriage. In his attempts to assert his power as the "man of the house," the husband tries to restrict the movement of his wife to a large degree, especially during the first few months after marriage. Most husbands argue (often without success) that their wives should wait for them at home until they come back from work. A man may not allow his wife to visit her parents, even when they live nearby, without notifying him first. These restrictions stimulate desires for consumer goods, especially TV and tape recorders, to keep the woman entertained while the husband is absent. At the same time, some of these modern appliances, such as the phone, highly desired by young women, are being manipulated in men's attempts to restrict women's movements. Mona quickly learned to resent the phone that enabled her groom to call every hour from his shop (which is two hours by bus away from home) to make sure that she was at home. The husband's restrictions are usually relaxed when the wife becomes pregnant and has their first child. However, the presence of children often restricts women's movements. The birth of a child ties the mother down for a while and reduces her long-distance mobility, such as visits to other neighborhoods or to her home village. Still, over time, women become more mobile and free to move inside and outside the city.

The "right" of a husband to regulate his wife's movements is usually accepted by men and women in al-Zawiya and is strongly supported by religious discourses circulated in the mosque and through audiotapes. Rather than directly debating this right, which would lead to physical violence and social condemnation, women tend to cooperate with each other and employ various tactics and strategies to escape the control of the family on their movement. Um Mohammad, who lives in *el-ahali*, has a short-tempered husband who tries to control her movements and determine which neighbors she can visit. He decided that one neighbor, Um Fathi, "was not a good woman" because she always fights with her neighbors and swears by using the usually male-designated phrase *'alyya italaq* ("May my wife [or husband in Um Fathi's case] be divorced"). Abu Mohammad especially forbade his wife from visiting Um Fathi after she had a big fight with one of their neighbors. He feared that such visits might cause a conflict between his wife and their neighbors. Um Mohammad, however, likes to visit with Um Fathi. She tries to do that during the daytime when Abu Mohammad is at work. When she needs to visit Um Fathi during the night while her husband is at home, Um Mohammad coordinates with another neighbor, Um Walid. They may pretend that they are going to a local store or visiting a sick friend. Then they choose a route that will not make Abu Mohammad suspicious of their destination and discreetly look back to make sure that he is not watching. This process is facilitated by the several multiple crowded lanes in *el-ahali* that allow Um Mohammad to disappear in one of them without being easily observed. Such strategies provide women with flexibility to satisfy their own preferences while avoiding conflicts with husbands and showing compliance with social norms.

Symbolic Violence and Struggles over Public Spaces

> *But inside and outside are not situated side by side, each one constituting a separate domain; indeed, on the contrary, they are reflected in each other, and it is only by this opposition and this complementary nature that they reveal their true meaning.*
>
> Pierre Bourdieu, "The Sentiment of Honour in Kabyle Society"

In addition to physical violence inflicted occasionally both on young men and women, symbolic violence is central to controlling their access to public space. Like other forms of domination, men's domination presupposes "a doxic order shared by the dominated and the dominant" (Krais 1993: 169). This order is internalized by social agents, structuring their practices and perceptions of the world around them. It is this order that men (and older women) try to maintain through their attempts to restrict women's access to some public spaces. Rather than seeing this system as imposed on them by others, women accept this as part of the taken-for-granted domain. Notions such as love, solidarity, care, and modesty are interwoven with power inequalities between family members in such a way that, when her brother beats her, Karima feels that it is because he cares for her. This is exemplified also in women's insistence that if a man really loves his wife, he will not allow her to work outside the house. In short, "patriarchy seated in love may be much harder to unseat than patriarchy in which loving and nurturance are not so explicitly mandated and supported" (Joseph 1994: 58). Limiting women's access to public space is often justified in al-Zawiya al-Hamra by the need to protect them from the evils of the outside world. But it should be remembered that notions such as protection, fear, and love are part of the symbolic violence that is utilized to control the production and circulation of cultural meanings and social representations. This symbolic violence facilities the naturalization, internalization, and reproduction of gender inequalities. It is within this framework that one should examine the social attitude toward women's work outside the home.

THE WORKPLACE AND WOMEN'S ACCESS TO PUBLIC LIFE

Um Rida has a twenty-two-year-old daughter, Halla, who works in a sewing factory. She leaves early in the morning and comes back late in the evening. The mother knows that her daughter needs the job to be able to buy the rest of her *gihaaz* (trousseau). Although Halla is not engaged yet, she has been working on and off for the past four years, investing her money in buying clothes and household appliances and saving money to buy her part of the furniture (usually a set for the living room) for her future home. Even though Um Rida trusts her daughter very much and rarely questions her movements, she often expresses her resentment at Halla's job. The mother emphasizes that, since she started working, Halla has learned *qillit il-'adab* (bad manners or impoliteness). "Not only does she refuse to help in the household chores," the mother complains, "but she also answers back when I talk to her. She even stopped praying." The mother describes how proud she was of her daughter who (like the mother) decided to wear the *khimar*[8] and used to perform her religious duties on regular basis. Halla tries to explain to her mother, often without success, that since she started to work, she comes home very tired and without any energy to help with the housework.[9] At the same time, there is no place for her and her female co-workers to pray in the factory. Her neighbors and mother have encouraged her to approach the manager to ask him to designate a separate place for prayer where they cannot be seen by male workers.

Halla accepts the social definition of women's work outside the home and emphasizes that she will not continue working after marriage. For one thing, the pay is very low and the hours are very long. She is forced to work overtime and does not receive any benefits such as health insurance, paid holidays, or compensation when she is sick. More important, she knows that her future husband will not want her to work. Many men prefer to work in two jobs to secure the expenses of their families rather than allowing their wives to work outside the house. There is a widespread view that links a woman's work after marriage with the inability of the husband to provide for her. Men from Halla's hometown in upper Egypt are especially known for their unwillingness to allow their wives to work. As her mother emphasizes, "They prefer to die out of hunger rather than allowing the wife to work." Even if the husband agrees and the wife works, her relatives will interfere and take her away from her husband, saying, "If he cannot feed you, we can." Halla also knows that even if her future husband allowed her to work, he would not help with the house-work, which would mean that she would end up with two jobs, inside and outside the house. Married women usually do not work outside the home unless there is a great need, as is the case when the husband is very ill or very old and cannot work or when the husband marries another woman.

But in addition to these social conventions, there is a strong associa-tion between "bad manners," as stated in Um Rida's narrative, and women's work outside the domestic sphere. "Bad manners" are mani-fested in being able to answer back and challenge the mother's author-ity or being assertive and addressing other men directly. In the work-place, Halla meets other young women from different parts of Cairo, and the site seems to foster solidarity among them, bringing them together to exchange stories about their lives. Young women often feel and see the suffering of other female fellow workers, and their discus-sions bring part of the family's power into question. They "eat together," a notion that usually designates strong solidarity between people, and their relationships extend beyond the workplace to include the home and occasional trips to areas around Cairo. They may also meet their future husbands through one of their female co-workers. The relationship between female workers was nicely described by a factory worker in Cairo: "Friendship here [in the factory] is stronger than outside. We talk about nearly everything that occupies our minds. . . . If we see a fellow worker poorly dressed whose husband is taking her salary, we show her the unfairness of it and encourage her to ask for her rights" (Ibrahim 1985: 299).

Thus, working not only provides women with some income that makes it possible for them to feel a sense of limited independence but also allows them to be part of a collectivity of women and to know more about the condition of others. Similar to other "subaltern counter-publics," workplaces become "parallel discursive arenas where members of subordinated social groups invent and circulate counterdiscourses to formulate oppositional interpretations of their identities, interests, and needs" (Fraser 1992: 123). Halla tells stories about other friends at work who suffer physical and verbal abuse by family members. Unlike her reactions when she is the subject of such inflictions, Halla's reactions to the experiences of her fellow workers are strongly critical of the social system. Halla especially voices her criticisms when one of her colleagues is about to be forced to marry against her will. With this in mind, it becomes clear that limiting women's access to the workplace not only is motivated by notions of shame and honor and the desire to control women's sexuality but also aims to limit their access to knowledge and experiences that potentially challenge current power inequalities. In short, the struggle over access to the public sphere is part of the struggle over what Bourdieu calls the "doxic" (1977), or the taken-for-granted domain that is central to any domination system. This, and not *only* the fear of women's sexuality, is a major source of the anxiety of parents in al-Zawiya al-Hamra who allow their daughters to work and of those husbands who do not let their wives work or who hesitate to allow them to visit their families, often until after the birth of their first child.

WOMEN'S WORK AND THE USE OF PUBLIC SPACE

The attempt to restrict women's access to information explains why many women work in various activities that do not take them away from the neighborhood. The fact that these activities contribute to the income of the family does not challenge the masculinity of the husband or bother the neighbors or the relatives of the wife. Women sew and embroider garments, make bead necklaces, and sell clothes. They utilize the empty land next to each *murabba'* to sell cooked foods, sugarcane, roasted corn, and fresh vegetables and fruits. Women also use this space to promote some of their seasonal home-based industries. Some women, for instance, set up ovens on the side of the lanes between the *murabba'at* to bake the *ruqaq* (thin bread) that is widely used during the Sacrifice Feast and get a specific amount of money per kilo of flour that they mix and bake. Through this utilization of space, women simultaneously publicize their activities, interact with others, and supervise their children who play nearby (see Figure 9).

The public space around the *murabba'at* is also used to integrate the workplace with the residence area. This not only secures extra income for the family but also enables its members, especially women, to take care of the new investment. Having a small shop next to the housing unit, for instance, enables Um Su'ad to take over while her husband is outside the neighborhood. These additions are also used as an economic safety

FIGURE 9: Women manage family investments around the housing units. Some families have placed small grocery stands next to housing blocks to sell soft drinks, candy, and ice cream. Through this use of space, women simultaneously publicize their activities, interact with others, take care of some domestic animals, and supervise their children who play nearby. Photograph by Farha Ghannam.

buffer for the family when the working male relative is unemployed due to illness or being laid off. Sahar and her husband resorted to this option when he was diagnosed with diabetes, which prevented him legally from resuming his previous work as a bus driver. They managed to get the approval of the neighbors and a permit from the local authorities to start the new project. Next to the entrance of their neighbors' block that faces the bus station, they placed a *batriina* that consists of a glass-fronted cabinet and some shelves to store and exhibit his merchandise. In addition to candy, chewing gum, chocolate bars, and biscuits, Ali sells various cold juices that are prepared by his wife in their apartment during the summer and spicy boiled chickpeas in the winter. Recently, Ali got a job as a driver for an upper-class family in another neighborhood, and Sahar took over the *batriina*. Ali's new job is not guaranteed — he and his wife are not sure whether he will continue working for that family. Sahar's role is thus vital for the future security of the family. She is currently not only adding to the family's income but maintaining the right of her family to the space and the *batriina*. If Ali loses his new job, he can reclaim the *batriina* and resume his work there. These additions therefore enable women, especially married women whose work outside the home is negatively viewed, to participate more actively in the economic activities of the family and provide them with the chance to socialize with others and expand their social networks.

At the same time, these activities encourage the presence of people between the different *murabba'at*. Immediately after relocation, these spaces were "empty," dark, and potentially dangerous. Such empty spaces are often equated with evil spirits, who may attack and harm the vulnerable passersby. This makes it unsafe for women and young children to be outside, especially at night. The continuous presence of human beings in these spaces ensures the pacification and dislocation of evil spirits. It also secures help when one is in trouble. People are always ready to help in stopping a fight or protecting a child. At the same time, being seen by others provides social control that allows more freedom of movement for women and legitimizes their interaction with men. The same is clearly manifested during Ramadan, when women are allowed more freedom to stay outside late at night. The presence of many people and the increase in street lighting facilitate women's access to public space during this month. Paradoxically, the presence of others also restrains women's movements because they become more visible to others, especially when they try to "sneak" outside without the knowledge of their families. The power to restrict women's access to external spaces is thus scattered across the community, a fact that makes women feel that they are under the gaze of their families all the time. The presence of others who may tell their families (or at least start gossiping) makes it hard for women to feel outside the control of the family. The threat of the gaze of others frames women's ambiguous feelings toward the relatively wide and often well-lit passages between the different *murabba'at* that replaced the old narrow lanes in Bulaq, where they could walk between homes with some degree of invisibility.

The view of the *murabba'at* and the spaces between them is influenced by the shuffling of neighbors and mixing of people from different parts of Cairo. The new setting is structuring both the interaction of family members with others and the way they view public space. This shift is exemplified by the growing restrictions on the access of women and children to various spaces. In Bulaq, male children were allowed to stay outside until late hours. "My parents did not use to worry about me," a man in his mid-twenties explains. "I was only seven years old when they allowed me to stay outside until midnight. My parents knew that if I got in trouble, there were many people who knew them and who would help me. Here, in al-Zawiya it is harder for parents to allow their children to be outside because they do not know the people around them." Similarly, in Bulaq, several men and women emphasized that mothers did not hesitate to allow their daughters to play with other children because they knew them and their parents. Currently, they are selective in interacting even with the neighbors.[10] One woman said, referring to her current neighbors, "Are these neighbors that I should allow my daughters to interact with? No, they are not good people. Their children steal from others and their mother is rude and vulgar (*lisanha tawil*). It is better to keep away from them."

These reactions are part of a larger system that defines the social meanings attached to various public spaces. While children are encouraged to go to school, mothers often feel frustrated because they cannot totally control the upbringing (*tarbiyya*) of their children when they mix with others in "the street." A "good mother" tries to keep her male and female children "under her wings," as one woman explains. Mothers try to keep their children away from the street, which is associated with "dirty language" and "bad manners." I often witnessed struggles between mothers and young children over the latter's desire to play outside. Mothers bribe, beat, scold, and even lock up their children to play at home rather than in the street, where they might interact with others who would teach them bad habits.[11] These restrictions are directly linked to the knowledge that social actors are expected to acquire in different public spaces and how this knowledge is central to the social meanings attached to various spaces and who has access to them. In the previous chapter, I examined the word *lama*, which sums up people's reactions to the increasing mixing and gathering of a heterogenous population in the same housing project. This heterogeneity informs the social construction of space. Public spaces such as the coffee shop and the vegetable market are considered *lamin*. The presence of a mixed group of people in the same space makes it a site where social norms can be challenged or questioned. In addition, these spaces are subject to state intrusion and control, which also shape their role in the life of young men, parents, and women.

YOUNG MEN IN THE COFFEE SHOP

Although there are coffeehouses in other parts of Cairo where women are allowed, in al-Zawiya coffee shops are open only to men.[12] They gather there to drink sweet tea[13] and to play chess, cards, and dominos inside the shop during the winter and in front of it during the summer. For many young men, the coffee shop (*qahwa*) is one of the few spaces where they can socialize with their male friends away from their families.

The coffeehouse in al-Zawiya al-Hamra is perceived ambivalently by both men and women. First, coffee shops, especially those attended by young men, are targeted by the police. There are informants (*mukhbirin*) who report to the police any activities in the various coffee shops. As one man explained, "The government fears that we gather in one place and that we may discuss politics." Second, police will target visitors to a particular coffeehouse if they suspect that a thief, a drug user, or a fugitive attends it. When the police raid a coffeehouse, they usually detain all the attendees. Young men in particular are dragged outside, slapped in front of people in the street, and beaten in the police station (*qism*), which was upgraded from a small police post (*nuqta*) after the 1981 clashes between Muslims and Copts.

Almost every young man that I met had a story to tell about himself or a close friend or relative who was taken to the police station for questioning because he happened to be in a *qahwa* during a raid. Young men and their parents dread "visits" to the police station not only because they believe that they can be framed for crimes they did not commit but also because torture has led to the death of a few suspects in the police station. In one case, the police claimed that a man charged with theft committed suicide by throwing himself from the window of the police station. The family of the victim and their neighbors did not accept these claims and publicly protested the incident, claiming that he was thrown from the window by the investigating policemen. To avoid being taken to the police station, young men keep a watch, and as soon as they feel or hear the police coming, they run in different directions. Such experiences and fears frame the negative views of the coffeehouse.

Although police intervention may restrict the utilization of the coffee shop as a site for the production and circulation of discourses critical of the state, the experiences of young men in this space and in the police station shape their views of the government and its policies. For example, the reactions of young men to the news circulated in the state-controlled media about "terrorism" and attacks by Islamic groups differ from those of their fathers and female relatives. Young men draw on cases of their friends who were allegedly framed for crimes they did not commit to argue that the same is done to others who are accused of conducting terrorist attacks.

The possibility of detention is in itself the source of anxiety of many parents. Still, mothers and fathers fear another danger that challenges their attempts to raise their children according to their ideals: the presence of strangers who cannot be trusted. Like the workplace and the street, the coffee shop brings together the good (*el-hilw*) and the bad (*el-wihish*), which means that young men may interact with others who teach them to gamble, smoke, use drugs, or drink alcohol. Coffeehouses frequented by young men are stigmatized by parents, and older men avoid patronizing them. They are also losing their prior function as places for potential employers to find and contract workers. The coffeehouse, especially attended by young men, is increasingly viewed as a space where only unemployed and worthless men gather.[14] Young men therefore struggle not only with the government but also with their families to secure access to the coffee shop and other public spaces.

THE SOCIAL CONSTRUCTION
OF THE VEGETABLE MARKET

> *Opinions — about people and about politics — take shape in*
> *the network of communications in the suq; even the most severe*
> *government censorship cannot stand up against the whispered*
> *asides which pass from person to person in the suq.*
> Robert Fernea, "Suqs of the Middle East"

There are at least two entities that people call market (*suq*) in al-Zawiya al-Hamra. One of these markets is located between the old *masaakin* and *el-ahali,* while the other is in the *ahali* area but close to the new *masaakin.* The actual market is hard to define physically. One of these structures was built by the government in 1985. It consists of several wooden booths encompassed by a concrete wall. One part of the market has a roof, while the other part is not covered. Although the roofed market has been a main feature of Middle Eastern cities, traders here do not like the roofed space allocated to them by the government. There is a continuous struggle between the merchants and government officials over where the former can sell their products. The officials try to force the merchants to stay within the bounded market. Merchants, however, refuse to stay within the boundaries of this structure and take their goods to the nearby streets. Only a few traders with heavy loads or hard-to-move goods stay inside the formal "market", but they stay in the uncovered part. The rest take their fruits, vegetables, cheese, and other products into the nearby intersection. Sellers feel that the street is more spacious, allows them to exhibit their goods to a larger number of people, and is more convenient for customers who can obtain their daily needs while passing by. The intersection and part of the main street become very crowded, and merchants compete over the space that they want to control to display their goods. The word *suq* is used to refer to both the official structure and the intersection where the goods are displayed.

The vegetable market is full of movement. Women from nearby villages bring big baskets of seasonal products, some breast-feeding their babies while older children play around; merchants move their goods to allow a car, whose driver is honking madly, to pass; a man tries to force his horse, that is pulling a lettuce cart, to proceed through the crowd; trucks try to unload; small children sell lemons, parsley, and other goods; and a man carries a tray with tea glasses to be sold to the traders. Products are piled on carts, and their sellers loudly describe the taste of the fruit, announce the prices of vegetables, and call upon people to inspect their merchandise and compare prices. Fresh and frozen fish are being sold on the corner of the street, while on the other side there is a shop with an immense woman selling internal organs, legs, and heads of water buffalo. A woman sits next to a cage with several chickens, waiting for customers who select one or two, which are then weighed, slaughtered, and dipped in the boiling water to make it easy to pluck the feathers. Another woman squats with a big basket of rice, and a group of women stand around waiting for her to weigh the amount they requested. One woman screams at one of her female customers who tries to pick a piece of cheese from the metal container. Flies continue to fly in and out of the container, but the merchant is only bothered by the fact that her other customers may feel disgusted if they see the female client putting her fingers into the container. Around the area that is defined as the market, there are shops that sell spices, fabrics, clothes, shoes, and miscellaneous household equipment.

Most of the studies of the market (conducted mainly by male anthropologists) focus on the *bazaar* or the central market, which is dominated by men (Gilsenan 1982; Geertz 1979; Gerholm, 1977). Studies of the *suq* also tend to focus more on the merchants than on how the people, especially women, interact and view it. Little attention has been devoted to the study of local vegetable markets that women visit to buy their daily vegetables and fruits.[15] Unlike the central markets and bazaars that have attracted the attention of researchers, the suq in al-Zawiya al-Hamra is dominated by women. They are the majority of the sellers and buyers. Although there are other closer options that could save them time and effort, such as peddlers and women who sell vegetables and fruits on the corner of the street, women normally prefer the more distant local markets to secure lower prices and fresher products.

In the market a woman compares prices, checks the quality and freshness of the vegetables, and then decides what to buy for the day. She checks with the merchant to make sure that the advertised price is the same as the price that he is charging. She bargains to see if the price can be reduced and reads the reaction of the merchant to ascertain when she should leave or when she should increase the offered price. Although she may know some sellers by name, she does not try to maintain a commitment or a strong relationship to a specific merchant, for if she did, she would not be able to maintain the broad bargaining space that allows her to compare and select what is suitable for her budget and needs. She picks up every single vegetable and examines it closely to make sure that it is fresh and not damaged. Then she hands the plastic bags, which she brings with her to avoid paying extra for them, to the man or the woman who is selling the vegetables. She keeps a close eye on the merchant to make sure that the weights used are correct and that he does not add any bad products. She carefully calculates the total cost and counts the change. Meanwhile, she keeps her eyes open for lettuce leaves or other vegetables that can be fed to her chickens and ducks. Some merchants do not mind if she collects some of the green leaves that they have thrown away. If she does not find anything to take back to her poultry, she may buy them some old cheap vegetables.

A central feature of the woman's interaction with the male or female merchant is suspicion and distrust. Merchants, whether those who reside in al-Zawiya or those who come from villages around Cairo, are not to be trusted because they may try to cheat on the weight, the price, the quality of the food, and the change they give back. Because women expect to engage in such arguments and disagreements, special verbal skills are taught as part of women's socialization, which includes visits to the market from early childhood. Young girls accompany their mothers to the market during school vacations and are sent alone to buy some simple things as they grow older (around ten and over). Before reaching this stage, they are taught "the language of the market" and how to be assertive so that they can bargain and answer back if the merchant tries to cheat them. Women's assertiveness in this context, unlike their assertiveness in relation to the workplace, is highly regarded and celebrated.

The relationship between clients and sellers is not the only potential source of conflict in the market. Women view the relationships between buyers as a more serious threat. They view the market as an unsafe place where one should be very careful because, like the coffee shop, it is *lamim*. The fear of the market is not related to a threat of vengeance or the threat of the use of weapons, as is the case in some other, male-dominated markets (see Gilsenan 1982). Rather, the presence of a mixture of strangers, as the word *lamim* indicates, who do not know each other and who are not subjected to the same social obligations makes visits to the market potentially dangerous. Women always tell stories about incidents when the money, jewelry,[16] or purchased goods of unsuspecting women were stolen by other shoppers. The relocated group is usually singled out as the source of troubles in the market. "They pretend to get into a fight near the market," one man from *el-ahali* explains. "When you get closer to observe and your attention is directed to the people fighting, one of them steals your stuff without your noticing it." Just like the coffee shop and the street, the vegetable market brings together people from different areas in the neighborhood. This makes it an ambiguous space that is visited every day to get the best and cheapest products but that is feared and resented for the threats it poses to its visitors.

Like the coffee shop that shapes how young men view the state, the vegetable market is the main site that shapes women's opinions of government policies. Even though their visits to the market are usually short and goal oriented, women still hear complaints about prices and new regulations related to the market and observe the struggle between the merchants and government officials. Women's efforts to secure their daily food with limited budgets makes them experts on the changing prices of vegetables. They monitor increases in the price of tomatoes, the availability of onions, and the freshness of fish and link them with the policies and projects of the government. For instance, women were very concerned when the governor decided to relocate *Rod al-Farag* market (the major vegetable market in Cairo). They thought that the relocation of the market outside the city would cause large increases in the prices of vegetables and fruits. When I visited al-Zawiya in December of 1994, women considered the increase in vegetable prices and the shortage in some supplies to be a natural outcome of the relocation of that market.

Public Spaces and Collective Identities

Young men have more mobility and freedom to tour the city and visit various public spaces. Still, they have to struggle with their families and government officials to secure access not only to the coffee shop but also to

other spaces. Young men are the first to suffer when a crime is committed in the neighborhood or an armed attack is carried out in Cairo or else-
where in Egypt. They are rounded up in mosques, markets, streets, and
city buses. In addition, the street, the coffee shop, and the workplace have
a common feature: they bring different groups together and therefore
potentially threaten the ability of the family to control the kind of knowledge acquired. The fact that people in the neighborhood come from
different places produces anxiety over the habits, actions, and language to
which young men and women are exposed. The negative constructions
of the coffee shop and the vegetable market are largely related to the
mixed population assumed to be present in these sites. In this, both the
coffee shop and the market serve as continuous reminders of the state
policies that brought many people from different parts of Egypt to live
in the same area. Relocating a large number of families to the same area
over a relatively short time brought the good (*el-kwayyis*) and the bad (*el-
wihish*) together. It is the anxiety over what children would learn in the
street, what young women would learn in the workplace, and what
young men would learn in the coffeehouse that structures the attempts
of parents, spouses, and siblings to restrict the movement of daughters,
wives, and brothers. As will be discussed in the next chapter, this anxiety
also informs the reactions of men to various modern appliances such as
the TV set. Many men argue that TV is making women "lazy," teaching
them new ideas, and stimulating their desires for new products and consumer goods.

In contrast to the market and the coffeehouse, the mosque is viewed
in positive terms by people in al-Zawiya. In Abu Hosni's narrative in
chapter 3, Mohammad's attempts to maintain the identity of his children
in America led him to the mosque. Not only in the United States but also
in al-Zawiya al-Hamra, the mosque is a powerful space for creating a collective Muslim identity. Unlike the coffee shop and the vegetable market,
the mosque is depicted as a safe space that brings members from different
groups together on equal terms under controlled conditions. The decline
in social control, which ensured the compliance of individuals to collective norms in Bulaq, and the increasing flows of information and consumer goods to the neighborhood have paved the way for religion as a
powerful basis for structuring and shaping people's interaction in al-
Zawiya. In addition to relocation, in the next chapter I examine other
major transformations that have been sweeping Cairo and Egypt at large
and that reinforce the role of religion in creating a sense of certainty in a
world where all that is solid melts into air.

CHAPTER 5

Religion in a Global Era

Islam as the object of anthropological understanding should be approached as a discursive tradition that connects variously with the formation of moral selves, the manipulation of populations (or resistance to it), and the production of appropriate knowledges.
Talal Asad, *The Idea of an Anthropology of Islam*

My fieldwork in Cairo required me to be a frequent rider of the city buses that connect different quarters with the center of the capital. The bus was very crowded late one night when I returned from al-Zawiya al-Hamra to al-Tahrir Square. But this time, unlike other times, there was a strong male voice reciting the Quran. A young bearded man, dressed in a white T-shirt and white pants, proceeded to talk about religion and what it meant to be a "good Muslim." And in this instance, unlike encounters in the mosque, a dialogue ensued between the bearded man and the other passengers. One man in his fifties protested by stating that the bus was not the right place for preaching and referred the bearded man back to the mosque. The man's protest against the sacralization of this public space was countered by others who supported the bearded man because, as one woman said, he was just asking people to obey God and follow his commands. With a strong and confident voice the bearded man commented, "The people who go to the mosque know all the things that I am telling you now. It is the people who do not go to the mosque that we need to address. It is the duty of those who know to tell those who do not." Faced with all of the support that the bearded man had garnered, the man who protested stated that he was just worried that the police might arrest the bearded man. The repressive power of the state and its attitude toward Islam were thus brought into the minds of the passengers. The message was clear: just because the man was asking people to follow Islam, he could be arrested by the police.

The dialogue between the bearded man and some young men on the bus covered the questions of how to define Muslims and their duties, the legitimacy of the use of violence against "nonbelievers," and pressures of the West on Muslims, especially women, to abandon their religious practices (such as the Islamic dress). The bearded man ended his talk by introducing himself as Mohammed Ibn Abdullah (the Prophet's name) and by announcing that he was working for the faculty of engineering in a well-known Egyptian university. He attacked the state's description of *al-Sunniyin* (defined in the popular discourse as strict followers of the Prophet's traditions) as *siyya'* (people who are good for nothing). *Al-Sunniyin,* the man emphasized "are the best and purest people in your country. No, we are not *siyya'.* We are educated people. We know, and it is our duty to let other people know." He got off the bus before the last station and disappeared into the crowd in the street, and the bus driver treated us to a loud song by Um Kulthum, the popular Egyptian female singer.

Not only the city bus but mosques, schools, shops, universities, and streets are used by Islamic activists to interact with people in different parts of Cairo. As stated by the bearded man in the bus, these activists are aware of the importance of various spaces and the potential audience present in each space. Mosques are visited by most of the population at least once a week and by many on a daily basis. The majority of daily visitors to the mosque are housewives, youngsters, and retired men. In contrast, virtually all working men and women take the bus to work every day. The man in the bus preaches to those who cannot visit the mosque on a regular basis and to those who do not have access to the discourses of *al-Sunniyin* as circulated in the mosque. Such efforts by Islamic groups that aim to establish an Islamic community (*umma*) are important in consolidating the basis of a collective religious identity in al-Zawiya al-Hamra.

The growing importance of religious identity, I argue, is a striking example of how global trajectories, especially a hegemonic discourse of modernity and the flow of images facilitated by new systems of communication, shape the identities of the relocated group. I focus on the mosque and the relationships between Muslims and Copts to show how religion is facilitating the creation of a sense of community that is based on "a subjective feeling of the parties, whether factual or traditional, that they belong together" (Weber 1978: 40). Religious identity, the discussion shows, has been consolidated by the uprootedness of the group and the daily struggle of its members to appropriate what they perceive as positive aspects of modernity and relinquish what they view as negative.

Ruptures and Dislocations

> *Hegemony is not the disappearance or destruction of difference.*
> *It is the construction of a collective will through difference. It is*
> *the articulation of differences which do not disappear.*
>
> Stuart Hall, "Old and New Identities,
> Old and New Ethnicities"

The discussion so far showed how relocation rearranged local identities and added to the old identifications: people are now identified with a village (the place of origin), as locals of Bulaq (where they resided for generations), as occupiers of the stigmatized *masaakin,* and as inhabitants of al-Zawiya (known for its poor reputation in Cairo). We also saw the significance of Bulaq for how the relocated population imagine their communal feelings, especially in regulating relationships inside the group. The stigma and stereotypes linked to this identity, however, do not facilitate the group's interaction with the residents of *el-ahali* and other parts of *el-masaakin.*

Despite the differences that separate the relocated group from others, most members of this group share with the old residents a religion.[1] Religion has become a powerful discourse in articulating and socially grounding the various identities: displaced families, *ahali* and *masaakin* inhabitants, people of Bulaq and al-Zawiya, rural immigrants, *Fallahin* (peasants who come from various villages in Lower Egypt) and *Sa'ides* (immigrants from different areas in Upper Egypt), who are largely pushed from their villages to Cairo in their search for work and a better life, as well as residents who have moved from other areas of Cairo, can all find commonality in religion. With the absence of the old guarantees secured by rootedness in the same area and the increasing mixing of strangers from various parts of Cairo in the same housing project, religion promises[2] to provide a strong basis for trust and social control. At the same time, religion has become central to what Jean Comaroff (1985) called "the social relocation of the displaced" (176). Emphasizing the reli-

gious identity of the relocated group legitimizes its presence in al-Zawiya
and furthers the interaction of its members with others. In short, religion
facilitates the creation of a sense of belonging and promises to create a
unified community out of a fragmented urban fabric.

NATIONALISM AND RELIGIOUS IDENTITY

There are several factors that make religious identity strongly compete
with other identities, especially with nationalism, in articulating the
presence of the group in al-Zawiya al-Hamra. First, although people
strongly identify themselves as Egyptians, the state's definition of "modern Egyptians" is exclusive. Different groups are not seen as contributing
positively to the construction of the country. Rather, and as shown in the
previous chapters, the official discourse has presented the relocated group
as isolated and plagued with many social ills and as people who needed
to be "civilized" and reintegrated within the nation to be able to contribute to the development of Egypt.[3] To summarize the preceding discussion, the project destroyed old neighborhood relationships and stigmatized and physically segregated the relocated population. Second,
Egyptian nationalism is closely linked to religion. As argued by several
authors, the Egyptian government has been using religion since the
early 1970s "to consolidate power and mobilize society" (Ansari 1984: 398;
see also Gilsenan 1982; Dessouki 1982; Ibrahim 1982; Ahmed 1992; Abdel
Fattah 1997). Sadat in particular presented himself as *al-Ra'is al-Mu'min*,
or "the Believing President," and strategically used religion to support his
rule. He also used religious groups to weaken the Nasserists, Marxists,
and radical students (Waterbury 1983). The government continues to
appeal to religion in its attempts to counter the growing number of
Islamic movements (Hanna 1993). More emphasis, for example, has
been placed on religious education in schools and the media. Religious
institutions affiliated with the government (such as al-Azhar and the
Ministry of Endowment) have been intensifying their activities to show
that the government is "the guardian of the true Islam" (Hanna 1993: 26;
see also Starett 1998). These policies have been strengthening the role of
religion in mobilizing both Muslims and Copts and in empowering religious leadership for both sides (Abdel Fattah 1997). Third, the growing
identification and pressure of various religious groups in Egypt in general,
and in Cairo in particular, are reinforcing religious identity. As the
encounter in the bus and other encounters in the mosque show, Islamic
activists are communicating with people in different parts of Cairo and are

working to reshape people's practices and to empower the religious basis of collective identities. Finally, in addition to their stigmatization, physical segregation, and the negative construction of *masaakin*, the group was relocated to al-Zawiya during a time when tension between Muslims and Christians was escalating rapidly. This tension culminated in the bloody clashes between Muslims and Christians in June of 1981. These clashes created strong opposition between Muslims and Christians and strengthened the religious basis of collective identities. I will briefly examine these clashes to show how religion was used to mobilize Muslims and Christians to control 180 square meters of land (*Egyptian Gazette*, June 21, 1981: 1) and how the clashes shaped the identity of the relocated population. Before proceeding any further, it is important to point out that my description of these clashes is largely based on data from Muslim informants. As stated in the introduction, the fact that I am a Muslim limited my interaction with Christian families.

RELIGION AND THE STRUGGLE OVER PUBLIC SPACE

According to Muslim accounts, the dispute was over a piece of land that was owned by the government and was designated to build a mosque for the workers of the Animal Feed Factory.[4] Part of this land was utilized by a Christian man, 'Aziz, to store construction-related material that he sold in his nearby shop. After years of using the land, 'Aziz tried to register it in his name.[5] Muslim informants emphasize that he bribed a local official who issued him a fake deed (some say that 'Aziz was only given a promise but never received any documents to support his claims) confirming his ownership.

When Muslims opposed 'Aziz's attempts to take over the land, he tried to mobilize Christians by announcing that he would donate it to build a church, something that was supported by many Christians inside and outside al-Zawiya. It is worth mentioning here that the construction of a church or even the renewal of an existing one requires a permit from the Ministry of the Interior (Hanna 1993). Restrictions on the building of churches are based on Ottoman laws that go back to 1856 (Hanna 1993). Until recently, a presidential decree[6] was needed not only to build a new church but also to fix and maintain existing churches (Hanna 1997). These restrictions have been the source of conflict between Muslims and Christians in different parts of Egypt since the early 1970s. They have been utilized by Islamic extremists to destroy and burn churches constructed without permits (Waterbury 1983; Hanna 1997). According to one writer, they were one of the main factors behind "the growing militancy of the church" (Ansari 1984: 398). Building churches was therefore a charged issue and the center of tension between Muslims and Christians in various parts of Egypt.

When Muslim activists saw a sign declaring the land as a site of a church, they countered the next night by posting a sign with the name of the mosque they intended to build.[7] This started a "war of signs," as described by one Muslim man. Christian activists would post a sign in the night stating the name of the church they planned to build, and the next night Muslim activists would replace it with another sign stating the name of the mosque to be constructed there. On one of these nights, Christians used paint to write the name of the church on the same sign that was used by Muslims the night before. Some Islamic activists took the sign to the police station and explained the situation to an officer there. They removed the paint used to write the name of the church so that the officer could see the name of the mosque. The officer decided that "the situation should remain as it is" (*yutrak al-hal 'ala ma hua 'alih*), meaning that the status of the land should not be altered. Muslims interpreted this decision as legitimizing the idea of building a mosque on the disputed land. *Al-Sunniyin* mobilized men and women who cleaned the land, built a fence around it, erected tents, and placed blankets on the ground for prayer. Christians felt that the police had sided with Muslims and denied them the right to build a church.

Tension escalated between the two sides when leaflets were distributed in other areas of Cairo calling on both Muslims and Christians to support their co-religionists in al-Zawiya al-Hamra. According to written sources, the National Democratic Party (NDP) played a strong role in intensifying the conflict (Hanna 1993; Ansari 1984). A leaflet was signed by the NDP secretary general, two representatives in the People's Assembly, and local committee members. This leaflet stated that the security forces had inspected in cooperation with officials from the NDP the claims of the Christian family and had found these claims groundless (Ansari 1984). The situation exploded when 'Aziz, outraged by the scene of Muslims praying on the disputed land, opened fire on them. The incident reconfirmed the fear of many Muslims who believed that Christians invested their money in buying weapons that they stored in their churches to be used in the future against them. These fears were nurtured by Sadat's pronouncements that Copts were fighting along the Phalangists in Lebanon and that they were trying to change the Islamic character of Egypt (Ansari 1984).[8] In addition, Muslims felt that Copts were becoming stronger economically because of their ownership of houses and management of successful businesses. All these factors enabled Islamic activists in the area to mobilize Muslims against Christians. Muslims, however, did not participate as a collectivity in the attacks on Copts. Many tried to help their Christian neighbors by protecting their property. This was done by either keeping it at Muslim homes or labeling it with *Allahu Akbar*. Some also assisted Christian men, who decided to return to their villages until the situation calmed down, to reach the central train station.

The Central Security Forces (*al-Amn al-Markizi*) interfered, using tear gas and implementing a curfew lasting for two months in order to maintain peace in the area. Clashes between the two sides led to the death of 17 people, the injury of 112, and the detention of 266 (Ansari 1984: 411).[9] In addition, 171 shops and public places were destroyed (411). But above all, these clashes created a deep split between Muslims and Christians. The name of the grand mosque constructed on the disputed piece of land manifests this split. The name *al-Nazir* (as pronounced by people) given to the mosque is derived from the verb *anthara*, which means to warn. This name not only signifies the victory of Muslims, but, as explained by one informant, continues to warn Copts against any attempt to challenge Muslims. It is a sign that, as described by one Muslim woman, provokes grief (*hasra*) in the hearts of Christians. For Muslims, *al-Nazir* is now a highly regarded mosque that attracts worshipers from different parts of al-Zawiya. It has a section for after-school classes and medical clinics with labs catering to many low-income families in the area. People pride themselves on the fact that most of the construction was conducted by private local efforts. Muslim men, women, and children helped in the collection of the money, the cleaning of the land, and the construction of *al-Nazir*. Stories are also told about divine help in the control of the land. One man recalled seeing a "very beautiful woman, who was not from this world, helping with her delicate hands in cleaning the location of the mosque." While reinforcing the distinction between Muslims and Christians, *al-Nazir* stands as a reminder of the solidarity and collective identity of Muslims who participated in the control of the land and the construction of the mosque.

The 1981 clashes have been seen by several writers as the beginning of Sadat's end. Sadat perceived these clashes as an attempt by Christian and Muslim leaders to "embarrass him" before his visit to the United States and to "ruin his external policies" (Ibrahim 1992: 38). He especially resented the reactions of Copts who protested in the international media before and during his visit to the United States (Abdel Fattah 1995). In the few months (especially early September) after the clashes (which took place in June of 1981), Sadat ordered the arrest of thousands of journalists, academics, political activists, and religious leaders (both Muslim and Christian). Tension escalated until Muslim extremists assassinated Sadat in October of 1981, four months after the sectarian conflict in al-Zawiya. The literature tends to link the relocated group directly or indirectly with these clashes (see Ansari 1984; Campo 1991). "The immediate cause of the sectarian conflict lay in the government's decision to use the little space left in Zawiya al-Hamra to relocate the inhabitants of slums in other parts of the city" (Ansari 1986: 225; see also Campo 1991: 136). These studies do not present any empirical data to support such general statements, and one should be careful in making such connections, generally based on unsubstantiated assumptions. The oral histories that I collected indicate that the relocated group was not involved in these clashes. Neither its members nor the old residents of al-Zawiya connect the relocated group with the clashes. The piece of land under conflict was relatively far from the housing project, and I did not encounter any members of the relocated group who said that they participated in any way in these clashes. In fact, it was Sadat who linked the group with the clashes (see the interview with Sadat in *Mayo,* June 22, 1981: 3).[10] Some informants expressed their anger because Sadat had falsely accused the group when he announced to the media in the United States that the clashes were initiated by "some riffraff (*shwayyet awbaash*) who were moved from shacks (*'ishash*) and resettled in *el-masaakin* in al-Zawiya al-Hamra."[11]

Rather than arguing that relocation caused the sectarian conflict, I suggest that relocation took place amidst growing tension between Muslims and Christians, not only in al-Zawiya but in other parts of Egypt, and that the 1981 clashes shaped the group's identity and how it has been situated in al-Zawiya. These clashes left a deep split in the neighborhood between Muslims and Christians. Since their arrival, Bulaqis have felt the tension of the polarized religious identities in the area. According to Early (1993), who conducted field research in Bulaq during the 1970s, relationships between Muslims and Christians were "excellent." She stated that Muslims and Copts in Bulaq "exchange social calls during each other's feasts, and visit and fulfill vows at each other's shrines" (Early 1993: 118). There are strong indications from the people that refer to how their relations with Copts were altered after relocation. A fifty-year-old woman, Um Hani, used to have close Christian friends in Bulaq. When she started going to the mosque in al-Zawiya, Um Hani heard about "the horrible things that Jews and Christians did to the Prophet." This left her with strong feelings that now prevent her from visiting with her Christian friends. She is also encouraged by her friends in the mosque not to buy her groceries and monthly subsidized products from Christian merchants.[12] I attended at least one lesson with Um Hani in a local mosque where the sheikh urged people to buy only from Muslim merchants. Another young man explained that Christians used to be nice (*kuwayyisin*) and kind (*'atufyin*) in Bulaq. After moving to al-Zawiya, he started feeling that they were mean and grew to dislike them. The move to al-Zawiya amidst the growing tension and polarization between Muslims and Christians shaped the views of Um Hani and her neighbors of their religious identity in general and their feelings toward Copts in particular.

Both Muslims and Christians are active in inscribing messages on the inside and outside walls of their houses that identify the religions of the residents. Muslims display their identity through inscribing *Allahu Akbar* on outer walls and decorating their shops and houses with images of mosques, pictures of Mecca and Medina, and Quranic verses. Similarly, Christians decorate their houses and stores with crosses and pictures of Jesus, Pope Shenoudaha (the Coptic Patriarch), and the Virgin Mary. Stickers in Arabic and English such as "Jesus is leading me" and "God loves you" are used to decorate cars and privately owned buses. Space, private and public, becomes a vehicle for showing and reinforcing religious identities. The body is also a space where religious identities are visibly inscribed. Muslims naturalize religious differences by emphasizing that Christians can be distinguished by their features and gestures but most importantly by the cross that is tattooed on the inner wrist of the right hand.[13] I also came across a few old women who had tattooed the cross on their chins. Muslim women distinguish themselves by wearing the *hijab* (a scarf that covers the hair), which can be also worn by old Christian women. Recently more Muslim women are shifting to the *kihmar* (a garment that covers the hair, the shoulders, the breasts, and the back), which is seen as the "real Islamic dress that Christian women would never wear."

Unlike the tension between Muslim groups (those who live in *el-masaakin* versus those who live in *el-ahali* or those from Bulaq versus older residents in al-Zawiya), friction between Muslims and Christians is supported by the belief of the former that the latter are economically superior. They own houses, run flourishing businesses, and operate many shops and stores in the area. While marriages between Muslims who live in *el-ahali* and *el-masaakin* are being facilitated by the mosque, marriages between Copts and Muslims are very rare. In the few cases where such marriages took place, the Christian partner had to convert to Islam. The opposition between Muslims and Copts is also marked by purity rituals.

Some Muslims, for example, will not eat food prepared by Christians, believing that it is not "pure" (*tahir*) because Christians do not invoke the name of God before preparing it. Others simply mention the name of God before eating food prepared by Christian neighbors.

Compared with stereotypes circulated about other groups, the opposition between Muslims and Christians is manifested not only in daily interaction but also in the popular imagination. This can be illustrated by people's construction of the *'afriit* (demon) that can *yalbis* (wear or possess) a person. The identity of the *'afriit* varies, but two kinds are clearly distinguished. One is a good *'afriit* who is identified as a Muslim because he or she reads the Quran and asks for simple things like a glass of lemonade or some water. This is a harmless *'afriit* who can be easily disposed of by sending him or her to pray in Mecca. The other *'afriit* is evil and can cause harm and sickness. He or she is hard to get rid of even through beating the possessed body. This *'afriit* is often identified as a Christian priest, as manifested in his or her name and the fact that he or she cannot recite the Quran.[14] Compared with the simple things that the Muslim good *'afriit* asks for, the Christian one demands costly things such as expensive foods and new music tapes.

The growing hegemony of religious identity is manifested in the increasing questioning and redefining of "traditions." Rather than being "Egyptian," traditions are being redefined in terms of their relationship to Islam. *Shamm in-nisiim* is, for instance, a celebration of the spring that both Muslims and Christians usually observe but that is increasingly becoming defined as "Christian." Muslims debate whether they should honor this occasion. In one session, women discussed the roots of the celebration, and one of them emphasized that she had heard on television that this celebration was "Egyptian" and not "Christian" because the Pharaohs used to celebrate it. Another woman, who was identified as knowledgeable in religion and who attended the mosque on a regular basis, countered by stating that the sheikh in the local mosque said that *Shamm in-nisiim* was Christian and that the fact that it was observed by the Pharaohs did not make it a "Muslim" celebration. She silenced the first woman by asking her: "Do you believe what you hear on television or what the sheikh says in the mosque?" Some Muslims even reinterpret the meaning of *Shamm in-nisiim* (take a breath of breeze): after the death of the Prophet Mohammed, they argue, Christians were very happy and expressed their relief (*shamu nafashum,* which literally means "they caught their breath") in this celebration. More Muslim families have stopped celebrating *shamm in-nisiim,* and some even do not leave the house or eat traditional foods associated with the feast like *fisiik* (salt-cured fish) that day. More traditions related to weddings and celebrations of the seventh day after the birth of a child (*subu‘*) are being redefined from an Islamic view. Community in this sense "signifies not just a distinctive political ideology but a particular set of values and norms in everyday life" (Gilroy 1987: 234).

The Mosque: A Space for Unity?

The growing importance of religious identity is clearly manifested and reinforced in the increasing centrality of the mosque as a space that brings members of different groups together, facilitates their interaction, and promises to establish a unified collectivity out of a heterogeneous neighborhood.[15] The mosque is open to all Muslims, and differences between people are at least temporarily dissolved through their gathering as equals in the same space. Compared with the market and the coffee shop, where people's interactions are characterized by distrust (as discussed in the previous chapter), the mosque is the most acceptable and safest social space where various groups can meet and interact.

The mosque is the "House of God" (*Baiyt Allah*) that both men and women are encouraged to visit. People are required to obey specific rules and perform certain rituals to have access to it. While women are not required to be purified and usually wear old dirty clothes before going to the vegetable market, they bathe, dress in clean nice clothes, and perform ablution before going to the mosque. The mosque is actively utilized to frame the interaction between members of different groups as well as to empower emerging meanings, identities, and relationships. Those who are labeled as troublemakers, rude, selfish, sneaky, or untrustworthy can be present in the same space and collectively identify themselves as Muslims. Mosques proliferate inside *el-masaakin* and *el-ahali* as well as on the borders between them. These can be grand mosques with minarets and different sections that provide services to the community or small mosques that are hardly differentiated from the surrounding residential units. Mosques are, at least in principle, accessible to all Muslims and potentially bring them together as equals. In fact, the word *gaami‘*, used to refer to the mosque, is from the root *gama‘*, which means "to bring together." The unity of prayers and the importance of communal feelings are manifested in the unifying discourse and the similar movements that are performed simultaneously. The *Imam* leads the prayer and coordinates the movement of all the attendees through his pronounced signals that indicate when one should bend forward on the knees, stand up straight, and so on.[16] Emphasis is placed upon standing in straight lines, very close to each other, so that no space is left through which the devil could enter among the devout and divide their collectivity.[17]

The feelings associated with being part of a collectivity were cited by many, especially by women, as one of the main reasons for going to the mosque. As was the case with many of her neighbors, relocation shattered most of the support system that connected the fifty-five-year-old Um Ahmed with friends and neighbors who were relocated to 'Ain Shams or to different parts of the new housing project in al-Zawiya al-Hamra. Um Ahmed explained that she goes to mosques because the presence of other people strengthens her will and provides her with more energy than when praying alone. Although she used to perform her religious duties on a regular basis in Bulaq, Um Ahmed's religiosity gained a different meaning in al-Zawiya.[18] In addition to adopting the *khimar* (a head garment that covers the hair and the shoulders), which is seen as the "real Islamic dress," Um Ahmed began attending local mosques on a daily basis. From the many mosques constructed around her housing block, she selects six mosques to perform four out of the five daily prayers, attend weekly lessons, and participate in Quaran recitation sessions (see Figure 10). For Friday prayer, she usually selects a large mosque that is located within the boundaries of *el-masaakin* but is also attended by worshipers from *el-ahali*. Um Ahmed explains that the big mosque brings many people together and that she likes being part of a large collectivity. She also visits two small mosques that are identified with *al-Sunniyin*. She attends these two mosques, which are located in *el-ahali*, to listen to weekly lessons and participate in Quran recitation sessions. For the afternoon prayer (*il-'asr*), she attends a mosque that is on the margin of *el-ahali* across the street from *el-masaakin*. Daily, she visits this mosque, which is operated by a charitable organization (*gam'iyya khayriyya*), to learn reading, writing, and mathematics.[19] Another mosque located next to the vegetable market in *el-ahali* is a convenient site for the midday prayer when Um Ahmed is shopping for the family's daily food. For the evening prayer, she chooses a smaller mosque on the edge of the housing project attended by a mixture of women from *el-ahali* and *el-masaakin* areas. She prefers this mosque, as she explains, because she meets "wise" women who like to talk to her. Over the last five years, Um Ahmed has formed strong relationships with other women from different parts of the neighborhood, especially from *el ahali*, who attend the same mosque. If one of

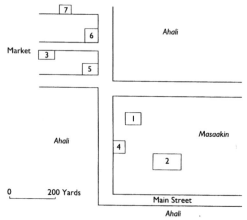

1 Um Ahmed's house.
2 The grande mosque she attends for Friday prayer.
3 Um Ahmed usually performs noon prayer in this mosque, which is located
   near the vegetable market where she shops.
4 This is a small intimate mosque that Um Ahmed frequents to perform the
   evening prayer.
5 Um Ahmed attends this grande mosque, which is managed by a charitable
   organization, for literacy classes.
6 She attends weekly lessons in this mosque, which is run by a charitable
   organization.
7 Um Ahmed occasionally visits this mosque, which offers Quran recitation
   sessions.

FIGURE 10. Through her daily trips to local mosques,
Um Ahmed crosses the boundaries between *el-masaakin*
and *el-ahali* and forges strong friendships with other
women from different parts of the area.

them does not come to the evening prayer, she goes with other women
to ask about their absent friend. She describes these relationships as *suhba
fi-illah* (companionship in God's love) that are not motivated by personal
interest. This provides such friendships with a special basis for trust.

Relationships between Um Ahmed and her friends are not restricted
to visits and confiding in each other when they have family problems.
There are also financial transactions that bind them together. One friend,
Um Sayyid, is a widow who lives with her only son and his family in *el-
ahali*. She keeps her savings with Um Ahmed because she fears that her
son may discover the money and waste it. When she needs cash, Um
Sayyid takes some from her savings and claims to her son that she bor-
rowed this money from Um Ahmed. The two friends agreed that Um
Ahmed can use any amount she needs from the money. In case Um
Sayyid needs a large sum of her savings, she gives a notice to Um Ahmed
beforehand to make sure that she has the requested amount.

Through her movement, Um Ahmed crosses the boundaries between *el-ahali* and *el-masaakin* and weaves the two areas together. Praying in the mosque is increasingly presented as the source of special rewards that await Um Ahmed and other prayers in heaven. The rewards associated with each step taken to the mosque are behind the long trips that are made to distant mosques. Thus, the mosque not only brings people together from the same neighborhood but also encourages people to move from one part of the city to the other. Young men and women, for example, tour the city in their search for the "truth."[20] Especially on Fridays, young men and women utilize the city bus to tour the capital in this search, in which "the truth" is usually linked with certain popular preachers. The notion of "truth" is complex and is related to various discursive strategies that publicly criticize the government without fear of its repression and that succeed in moving people emotionally and opening their hearts for more commitment to Islam. Through their movement in the city, young men and women hear about and may directly experience state oppression, encounter members of other social groups, and weave the city together as a lived entity. Visits to mosques in other parts of Cairo allow young men and women to feel part of a larger collectivity that extends beyond the boundaries of al-Zawiya. They also make their religious identity more visible in different parts of the city. Stories are told about how the police follow women who wear the *niqab* (a garment that covers the hair and face) and arrest their male relatives. Men also tell stories about how they became targets of police brutality because of their beards.

At the same time, older people are attracted to the mosque not only because they have more free time but also because they have lost many of the old spaces designated for socialization. With the removal of the rooftops, the corniche of the Nile, and local shrines, many have found a shelter in the mosque where they meet and interact with each other. The role of the mosque is being reinforced through opening it more to women, and a growing number of sheikhs are devoting short parts of the Friday *khutba* (*rukn al-mara' al-Muslima*) to answer questions related to women. Opening the mosque for women is perceived by Islamic activists in al-Zawiya al-Hamra as essential to counter other spaces that are open to women such as universities, the workplace, movie theaters, and nightclubs. As a female Islamic activist argued: "Is the university closed to women? Is the workplace closed to women? Is the movie theater or the nightclub closed to women? No, they are all open to them, and so should be the mosque." Women should go to the mosque to learn something that is useful for their families, one activist explained. In contrast, informal meetings of women outside the mosque are depicted by sheikhs, men, and often women themselves as "sinful" (*haram*) because they promote gossiping and backbiting (*namiima*). Um Ahmed said: "It is a waste of time to get together with the neighbors when I need to do my house-work. Gossiping and chatting with neighbors makes us forget to glorify God and forces me to participate in saying bad things about people who are not with us. This just helps in accumulating sins [*sayyi'at*] that will be severely punished by God, and this is why I avoid them. So when I have some free time, I prefer to spend it in the mosque."

By being part of the collectivity in the mosque, women forge friendships and create support systems that they can draw on during their daily life. More marriages, especially between residents in *el-ahali* and *el-masaakin,* are being arranged through these networks. Sheikhs (male and female) are also becoming more involved in solving conflicts between family members. One male sheikh was called upon to help in resolving a conflict between a mother and her daughter. Safa' is a nineteen-year-old woman. Her mother, who is in her late forties, started working as a washerwoman in a hotel in downtown Cairo after her husband's death five years ago. Safa's mother remarried a fellow worker, and Safa' and her siblings became very angry when they discovered that their mother was pregnant. Safa' felt ashamed of the fact that her mother was pregnant at that age, which publicly announced her active sexuality, and said that she would not talk to her until she got an abortion. Although some neighbors and relatives tried to reconcile the two, Safa' refused to talk to her mother. It was only when a friend of her mother took the daughter to talk to a sheikh in a local mosque that she accepted her mother's pregnancy. The sheikh convinced her that abortion is *haram* and that her mother did not do anything wrong by becoming pregnant. When the baby was born, Safa' took over the role of the mother, and she is now very attached to her two-year-old sister.

Discourses circulated in the mosque are addressing many daily con-cerns. Transportation, bureaucracy, corruption, unemployment, and social and gender inequalities are discussed by male and female preach-ers. In weekly lessons for women, for instance, female activists discuss many issues, including the shaping of the eyebrows, menstruation, sex-ual relationships, circumcision, pregnancy, abortion, domestic abuse, and relationships between spouses and neighbors.[21] During these lessons, women can directly ask questions about different aspects of their daily lives. They are also given directions about how to deal with changes in their lives. For example, a female preacher explained to us how we should deal with menopause. She scolded those women who celebrated the ending of their sexual productivity by slaughtering a sheep to express their happiness, even though they were also celebrating because, with the onset of menopause, they could perform all their religious duties, especially praying and fasting, without the interruptions caused by menstruation. This preacher emphasized that menstruation is from God and that women should therefore not celebrate its absence. The mosque thus is also a site for the construction of the meaning of bodies and the constitution of subjectivities. It plays a central role in people's daily life and the construction of individual and collective identities. It facilitates the interaction of different groups and promises to create a unified religious identity based on equality and solidarity.

While discourses circulated in the mosque may succeed in convincing women to comply with the Islamic norms in the short run, they are allowing women to question the interpretations of *shari'a* (Islamic laws and texts) by some sheikhs and the implications of these interpretations for various aspects of women's daily life. Nuha, for instance, is a twenty-three-year-old woman who has a high school diploma and works in a factory outside the neighborhood. Although she expressed enthusiasm for the application of *shari'a* in every aspect, she became more hesitant when she heard what that entails. She declared her amazement at one of the lessons that she attended. The female preacher told them about a woman's obligations and how she should obey her husband all the time. According to the preacher, "A wife should be patient, even when she is beaten by her husband. She should not answer back but should be submissive and obedient. Above all, she should never leave home without his consent." Even when living with the husband becomes totally impossible, she should not leave the house without his permission. When one of the attendees protested because that seemed like asking too much of the woman, the preacher said that the road to heaven was very difficult. Nuha emphasized that she would not accept such treatment from her future husband but expects respect and love.

Globalization and Religious Communal Feelings

> *A reinvention, to be authentic and creative, must make possible an expansion of the social and cultural universe. It must never be completed nor return endlessly to earlier material in a closed, ritualistic incantation.*
>
> Michael Gilsenan, *Recognizing Islam*

It is important to remember that complex local and national factors are juxtaposed with global forces to shape religious identity. State oppression, daily frustrations in dealing with the state bureaucracy, the fragmentation of the urban fabric, and the ability of Islamic groups to utilize various discursive strategies that mobilize people are as important as the economic frustration, the unfulfilled expectations and desires, and the need to have a voice in the global scene in understanding why religious identity is becoming hegemonic in al-Zawiya al-Hamra. Religious identity, I believe, should be analytically situated between the contradictory effects of the growing globalization of Cairo and its rapid urbanization.

The city bus is, for instance, a strategic site for the circulation of *al-Sunniyin's* discourses partially because it symbolizes the daily misery of low-income urban Egyptians and reveals the incompetence and/or indifference of the state.[22] It is mainly used by the poor, while people who can afford to spend more money use the smaller bus or the metro. Trips on the city bus are usually referred to as *akhir bahdala* (the utmost abuse or insult). These trips are very uncomfortable because the buses are old and very crowded. In addition to their physical condition, the buses have no fixed schedules and their routes are unpredictable. Given such conditions, it is no surprise that bus rides are associated with fights, insults, pickpocketing, and physical injury. In some cases, deaths have occurred while people were trying to jump to or from a bus that did not stop at all or simply paused for a few seconds. In short, the bus is a space that shows the government's inability to address a basic but seemingly solvable problem that causes daily misery for a major part of Cairo's low-income population. Thus, the hardships of daily life and state incompetence contextualize the discourse of the bearded man. For example, the bearded man utilized these hardships to remind us of hell, which as he emphasized, is thousands of times as hot as the crowded bus during Cairo's summer. This was used to frame his elaborate narration of the changing colors of the burning fire and to convey to us part of the horror of being grilled in *jahannam* (hell), the fate that is awaiting those who do not believe.

MULTIPLE STRUGGLES

It is important not to confuse my discussion of religious identity with "fundamentalism," "extremism," or "militant Islam," which has been the center of attention of many studies (Dessouki 1982; Ibrahim 1982; Kepel 1993). "Fundamentalism" especially has been the focus of studies that aim to examine the relationship between globalization and religion (see, for example, Turner 1994; Beyer 1994; Waters 1995; Watts 1996; Castells 1997). Such studies limit their discussion to the ideology of the leaders of some radical Islamic groups and tend to present these movements as "responses" or "reactions" to globalization. The role of ordinary people as active agents in negotiating religious and global discourses in their daily life and the formation of their local identities is largely neglected.

Central to the growing globalization of Cairo is the proliferation of discourses and images of modernity circulated mainly in the state-controlled media. Religious identity, I stress in this section, is closely linked to people's daily struggle to appropriate what they perceive as positive aspects of modernity and avoid what is considered negative. This entails a struggle on at least two fronts. First, people struggle against the state's attempts to copy Western modernity. Second, people also struggle against attempts by religious extremists who try to reject various aspects of modern objects and discourses and seek to live according to the time of the Prophet.

MODERNITY IS LIKE A KNIFE

There are different Arabic words such as *hadith*, *'asri*, and *madani* that refer to the notion of modernity. The common word that people in al-Zawiya use to refer to modernity is *tamaddun*, which was also repeated in the state discourse. *Tamaddun* indicates a process of becoming modern, civilized, or sophisticated. This word is from the same root as *madina* (city), and *al-tamaddun* is often related to the possibilities that are allowed by life in the city. Access to schools and health facilities and the use of new technologies, furniture, and buildings are aspects of *tamaddun* and urban life that are positively perceived, desired, sought, and embraced. Similar to the Western notion of modernity (see Giddens 1990; Berman 1988), *tamaddun* indicates progress or the movement from one situation to another. This movement is often perceived as positive. The move from Bulaq to al-Zawiya is seen by many people as part of *tamaddun* and *tatawwur* (development). The new apartments are seen as more modern than the previous housing units. A young woman explains that in Bulaq it was hard to have modern appliances such as refrigerators and washing machines. This was due to the absence of electricity and piped water and the fact that landowners did not allow tenants to acquire heavy appliances that threatened the shaky buildings. Some areas are also seen as more modern than others. Al-Zawiya is seen as more modern than 'ashwai'[23] or unplanned areas, but it is viewed as less modern than upper-class neighborhoods. Living in separate villas is seen as more modern than living in apartment complexes. In general, *tamaddun* refers to changes in various aspects of life such as taste for food, clothes, and colors. But above all, technological changes are collectively seen as signs of modernity. "*Al-tamaddun* is a blessing (*ni'ma*) from God," a man in his mid-forties says while referring to the phone, TV, and VCR.

While women tend to emphasize technological changes as central components of modernity, men (especially older men) tend to focus more on the negative aspects of modernity that threaten moral values and social relationships. The words of Abu Hosni summarize the general attitude in al-Zawiya: "*El-tamaddun* is like a knife with two edges; if not handled carefully, it can kill." Rather than the conventional opposition between tradition and modern, this metaphor presents a distinction between positive and negative aspects of modernity. There is a strong belief in the possibility of combining Western technological advancements with Muslim religious values and traditions.[24] Abu Hosni emphasizes the need to appropriate modern technologies and facilities such as TVs and cars. But for him, the other edge is of special importance because it is threatening to the community. This includes the weakening of solidarity between neighbors as well as the growing interest in accumulating money and acquiring consumer goods. Alienation and individualism are all seen as negative consequences of the project of modernity. Central to this threat, according to Abu Hosni and other men, are women's attempts to "blindly imitate" (*taqlid 'ama*) Western dress codes, makeup, and hairstyles. The practices of young men, such as wearing golden chains and listening to disco music, are also seen as negative aspects of modernity.[25] Similarly, in previous chapters we saw how people welcomed the housing units but had to struggle with the social and cultural consequences of this process. Just like the knife, relocation cut across the social networks that structured relationships in Bulaq, divided the group into two parts, and rearranged relationships between neighbors. As the woman in chapter 3 described, "In Bulaq, people used to cooperate and their hearts were together. They used to ask and care for each other. Here it is like a prison. Every person is limited to his or her own cell." The relocation of thousands of Egyptian families from different parts of Cairo to the same housing project created uncertainties about others and how to place them.

BEYOND WESTERNIZATION

> *We refuse to see authenticity* [asala] *through a backward look*
> *that glorifies* [tuqadis] *the past and rejects renewal* [tajdid].
> *Not every thing in the past is glorious for it has some elements*
> *of backwardness* [takhaluf]. *On the other hand, we refuse*
> *to distort our national character in the name of material*
> *or behavioral imitation of other societies.*
>
> Anwar el-Sadat, *The October Paper*

Abu Hosni and his neighbors are especially critical of the modernity of upper-class Egyptians and their imitation of the Western lifestyle. It is important to remember that Sadat's definition of modernity was closely linked to the West. He was fascinated by Western technology, production, administration, and lifestyle (Ibrahim 1992: 116). He wanted Egypt to "catch up with" the West and if possible "to become part of it" (116). As argued in Chapter 1, Sadat tried to rebuild Cairo according to Western plans, using Los Angeles and Houston as models. This imitation of Western modernity and the close links with the United States, which continued after Sadat's death, are criticized by many and have been used by Islamic activists to mobilize the people against the Egyptian government. Nuha, the twenty-three-year-old woman factory worker mentioned earlier, explained the conflict between the government and religious groups:

The problem is that the government has strong relationships with the United States which hates Islam and Muslims and is trying to spread its ideas and practices, especially wearing short clothes, the domination of science, and the destruction of religion. My cousin, who is a *Sunni,* explained to me that Americans have many methods to achieve their purposes, especially through schools. They try to prove that science is better than religion by using the comparative method. They bring, for example, a candle and a lightbulb and ask which is better. The first represents religion and the second represents science. Of course, one will choose the second. They also compare two pictures, one of a man wearing a *gallabiyya* [a long loose gown that the Prophet used to wear] with a beard and a rotten look [*mi'affin*)] while the second picture is of a handsome man who is shaved and looks very clean and tidy. Of course, anyone will choose the second. The whole idea is for science to replace religion and dominate the universe. Islam is compatible with science because one can find all answers in it if examined closely. Science should serve religion.

Abu Hosni and his neighbors are critical of a vision of modernity that completely accepts the Western model. They look at the West, especially the United States, in expressing their critique. Young men marvel at the technological advancement that they see in movies (such as *Terminator* and *True Lies*). They also point to the order of cities, the beauty of buildings, and the efficiency of the system in protecting the rights of individuals (for example, laws that prohibit intrusion on citizens without a search warrant, a sharp contrast to what they experience in their daily life, where young men can be arrested in streets and coffee shops). Americans are also credited for being honest and direct in their interaction. But people in al-Zawiya criticize the American society for "lack of solidarity and communal feelings." Each person in the United States, I was often told, "minds his or her own business and does not help or care for any one else." People often asked me with astonishment whether it is true that people in the United States do not know their next-door neighbors. They also asked about the willingness of Americans to help those in need. Is it true that Americans do not help when there is an accident? And that they do not bother when there is a fire next door? To avoid this individualism and lack of solidarity, Abu Hosni argues that unlike Americans, Egyptians should "hold onto" (*nitmasek*) their religion and should "not depart from it as foreigners do." Men and women use the same logic when critiquing the state's strong identification with Western modernity in general and the relocation project in particular.

Interestingly enough, both Sadat in his attempts to modernize Cairo and create a modern nation and the people in their attempts to live with this modernity resorted to Islam to legitimize their projects. When his open-door policy and relationships with the Israelis faced resistance, Sadat resorted to Islam to legitimize his efforts.[26] He emphasized that his rule was based on the "twin pillars of Imine (faith) and 'Ilm (science)" (Ahmed 1992: 217), and he presented himself as the modernizer, the Hero of Construction, and as the Believing Leader. He was often shown on TV praying, attending Friday *khutba,* and using his rosary to emphasize his religiosity. However, while Sadat's appeal to religion was a strategic choice to implement his policies, many people in al-Zawiya see religion as crucial to counter the disruption and negative changes that accompany the appropriation of modern technologies and discourses. Religion promises to provide the moral and spiritual resources that will enable people in al-Zawiya to reconcile their desire "to be rooted in a stable and coherent personal and social past" and the "growth that destroys both the physical and social landscapes" of their past (Berman 1988: 35).

The attraction of Nuha and her neighbors to a religious identity is part of making themselves subjects as well as objects of modernity. This emphasis on religion makes modernity in al-Zawiya different from the modernity that is depicted in Western social sciences, especially its emphasis on secularization (Habermas 1983; Harvey 1990; Turner 1990). This, however, does not make it an "inauthentic" or a "distorted" version of Western modernity (Sharabi 1988: 22). Modernity can no longer be viewed as a totality or a master narrative that entails similar changes in different societies, as modernization theory has argued.[27] Nor can it be seen as a whole that is either taken or rejected. As active social agents, people are able to selectively appropriate certain aspects of what they see as modern. Modernity stimulates desires. It motivates dreams. It causes joy. It causes disruption. It causes pain and suffering. It is struggled over and is reworked and selectively appropriated from specific locations in the social space.

MODERN DESIRES

In addition to their struggle against the state's attempts to copy Western modernity, people struggle against efforts of extremist groups who try to impose restrictions on how they appropriate certain aspects of modern life. Nuha expresses her religiosity in adopting the *khimar*, which is considered by many Islamic activists as the "real Islamic dress." She hears things on the radio, in the mosque, and from her friends and then lets her "heart and mind judge what to follow." At the same time, she opposes many of the restrictions that extremists try to impose on people, such as forbidding men to wear pants and prohibiting eating with a spoon because, as some argue, the Prophet did not do these things. She believes that had these things existed when the Prophet was alive, he would have used them. So it is not a sin (*haram*) to eat with a spoon, but if one chooses to eat with the hands, one will get extra rewards. Just like Nuha, many people continuously struggle to define the practices and traditions that are Islamic without threatening their religious beliefs or imposing unnecessary restrictions on their daily life.

The rejection of many of the ideas that are circulated by some extremists is clearly manifested by the struggle over some consumer goods such as televisions and VCRs, which are rapidly becoming signs of distinction. Many families try to solve Ramadan riddles (these are usually presented throughout the fasting month by popular Egyptian performers) and collect the covers of tea bags and chocolate bars to mail to the manufacturer in the hope that they may win a VCR, a washing machine, a gas stove, or better yet, a "dish," a familiar English word in daily life that refers to the

desired satellite dishes, which are spreading rapidly in upper-class neighborhoods. Among all the consumer goods that people use, the television
set is the one that Islamic groups most struggle against. This struggle can
be interpreted as a "rejection of modernity." But such analysis fails to see
how other aspects of modernity are being selectively incorporated in the
struggle of these groups. They use the fax machine, the tape recorder, the
computer, and many other modern goods to achieve their aims. Tapes, for
example, are used to circulate religious discourses to a wide range of audiences in Cairo. Especially to illiterate men and women, tapes provide a
powerful means of communication that brings popular preachers (i.e.,
those who are believed to tell the truth) from the mosque into the home,
the workplace, the taxi, and the street. These can be replayed until the
meanings become clearer to the listener. Young men and women can
gather to listen and discuss these tapes and pass them on to other friends
and relatives.

To understand the struggle over the television set, one should look at
how this medium is being used in people's daily lives. Except for very few
households with extreme religious beliefs, no housing unit is without a
television set. Each family, regardless of its income, owns a television set
(whether black and white or color, small or big) that is cherished by family members and visitors. The television set is a powerful medium that
conveys to viewers many experiences and stimulates new desires and
expectations. On the one hand, it connects people of al-Zawiya with other
Muslims whom they have never met and who are not assumed to be
duplicates of the self but are identified as Others closely connected with
the self. It brings them the news of Muslims who fight in Bosnia,
Afghanistan, and Chechnya. Young men who were frustrated with the
state's restriction on their participation in fighting with the Bosnian
Muslims circulated stories about God's help and support of the Bosnians.
People talked about invisible soldiers (angels) and about unidentified
white planes that bombed the Serbs. The television set brings global con-
cerns into the homes of Abu Hosni and Noha and communicates
Egyptian news and struggles to the rest of the globe. On the other hand,
television is blamed by Islamic groups for corrupting the people, silenc-
ing them, and distracting their attention from God as well as from what
happens in their country and the rest of the world. Some religious people subvert the word *tilifisyon* ("television" in colloquial Arabic) and pro-
nounce it as *mufisidyon* (from the root *fasada*, which means "to corrupt").
"The government does not want us to talk politics," Ali, a twenty-year-old
worker in a shoe factory, emphasized. "Sadat warned that he will send

anyone who talks politics to the sun. People are hungry, and when you are hungry you can only think of tomorrow's pound. You come back after working all day, sit and watch television for hours without talking to anybody. Television attracts our attention and does not allow people to talk. It is total silence. That is what the government wants. One is always worried because if he does not go to work tomorrow, he will not be paid. It is not like other advanced countries where people work just part of the day and then have time to think about politics. They can think and discuss the actions of the president, but we *al-ghalaba* [the poor] do not have the time to do that." But above all, television brings messages and discourses of the state into the homes of most of the people. Sadat and the current Egyptian government have been using TV to "delegitimize the Islamists while promoting a less governmentally-threatening version of Islam" (Diase 1996: 76). In short, TV supports the current power structure. With this in mind, and given the state's total control of what is broadcasted, trying to ban the television set is the only option to Islamic activists.

Despite Ali's feelings and views regarding television and its role in supporting the control of the state, he and the rest of his family spend many hours every day watching it. His mother tries to restrict her watching of TV to some soap operas and religious programs. Ali and his sisters prefer to watch music and dancing programs. This creates tension between them and their mother, who repeatedly emphasizes that it is *haram* to watch such performances. She expresses her embarrassment and guilt when she finds herself watching and sometimes singing or enjoying the music. The tension between what religious groups are calling for and how people feel about TV was clearly manifested when Samah, a woman in her mid-thirties, visited one of her friends in another neighborhood. Samah is very proud of her relationships with some women whose religiosity is manifested in wearing the *niqab* (a garment that covers the hair and the face) and their regular visits to mosques in different parts of Cairo. She tries hard to keep up with their recommendations regarding which sheikh she should listen to and which mosque to attend. But Samah came back bored and depressed from a two-day visit to one of these friends. "They do not have a television set," Samah kept repeating to us. "They think that it is *haram*. I tried to tell them that Quran and religious programs are played also on TV, but they did not listen. Thank God, I am back. I could not have taken it one more day." TV continues to be the main source of entertainment for Samah, especially while she is doing her housework, which takes most of her day.

Old Struggles, New Contexts

In many ways, these are not novel struggles. Egyptian intellectuals and writers have been debating these issues since the nineteenth century. Writers such as Qasim Amin asked: "How could Egypt duplicate Western achievements, without surrendering its Eastern identity?" (Rodenbeck 1998: 209). Similarly, in the late nineteenth century, Sheikh Muhammad Abdu raised the question: "Couldn't Muslims embrace useful Western ideas and still keep their identity?" (209). The main difference is that people in al-Zawiya are negotiating notions of modernity in their daily life. They have to deal with concrete realities and choices that confront their children, spouses, and neighbors. Religion here becomes a powerful force that helps people appropriate what is viewed as positive aspects of modern life while avoiding the alienation and disruption linked with this appropriation.

Religious identity in al-Zawiya encompasses members like Um Ahmed, whose religiosity is manifested in her "true Islamic" dress, strict performance of religious duties, and regular visits to the mosque. It also includes her son, who fasts during Ramadan but celebrates the end of the fasting month by drinking beer with his friends; her neighbor who prays in the mosque only on Friday; and another neighbor who prays only when she has exams and needs God's help to pass. Although religion brings people together and the mosque facilitates the formation of friendships and marriages, the stereotypes about Um Ahmed and her neighbors are still widely circulated and held to be true. Those who marry from the group or have strong friendships always refer to their spouses and friends as the exceptions to the rule. "It is true that my in-laws are very nice and kind. But the rest of the residents are really rude and vulgar." At the same time, although religion is a powerful force that shapes many aspects of people's daily practices and identities, it is not the only force that structures life in the area. The flow of information, money, and commodities into the area stimulates desires, fosters dreams, and introduces new expectations. How are these forces shaping the neighborhood and its spaces? What other strategies are used by Um Ahmed and her neighbors to situate themselves in al-Zawiya? How do they participate in the production of the neighborhood? This is the topic of the next chapter.

CHAPTER 6

Roads to Prosperity

The city becomes the dominant theme in political legends, but it is no longer a field of programmed and regulated operations.
Michel de Certeau, *The Practice of Everyday Life*

Dream 1

Hisham, a thirty-year-old worker in a leather factory, was growing more and more frustrated with his inability to find an affordable apartment in Cairo, a social requirement for the consummation of his marriage. Although he had been working hard and had tried to save as much as possible since he had gotten engaged five years ago, Hisham had not been able to save enough to pay the key money[1] demanded by the owners. Two years ago, Hisham and his family tried to put an end to his long waiting by adding a new unit to his parents' two-bedroom apartment, which had been allocated to them fifteen years ago by the government. The new unit consists of one bedroom, a small living space, a kitchen, and a bathroom with a separate entrance that opens onto a main street. Hisham's plan was easy to implement because his parents' apartment was on the ground floor. Still, he needed to discuss it with the other residents who were living on the same side of the building. Four families out of the five welcomed the idea. Only the widow who resided on the top floor did not want to add any extra rooms because she lived alone and did not have the required money. Cooperation of the neighbors was necessary for two main reasons. First, there was a need to pool resources to invest in the rather expensive foundation (*'asaas*) of the new addition. The neighbors agreed that the residents from the first to the fourth floor would make equal contributions to the cost of the foundation. The widow or one of her heirs was expected to pay a similar amount before making any future additions that would make use of the same foundation. Hisham and his neighbors found a local contractor, and they collectively agreed on the money needed for the foundation. After that, it was left to each family to negotiate with the contractor the shape of the expansion they desired, the amount of money needed, and how to pay it. The two options were to pay the whole amount or to pay an advance for the construction materials and divide the rest of the money on installments with interest. Second, and perhaps more importantly, the support of the neighbors was crucial to avoid the most serious threat — the removal of the additions by government officials. Not only do neighbors cooperate to collect money to pay off government employees to overlook such changes, but building the additions as a collectivity makes it harder for officials to demolish them. Unlike the "tricky and stubborn procedures that elude discipline" (de Certeau 1988: 96), the visibility and fixity of the changes that Hisham and his neighbors introduced to their units made them subject to the state's gaze.

Dream 2

I have never met Magdy. Although, since 1993, I have come to know his family very well, I have not had the chance to meet him face to face. A young man in his late twenties, Magdy has been working in Kuwait since 1992 and only visited Cairo twice over the past six years. Still, I feel that I know him. He is often the subject of discussions between his family members and their neighbors. His mother always talks about him with affection and describes his achievements with pride. His sisters and brothers always recall his jokes, retell his stories, and remember his tenderness and sensitivity. Magdy's fiancée and her family also describe his good manners and hard work to secure his future home. I also feel that I know Magdy through reading some of the letters and hearing some of the tapes that he sends to his family. Occasionally his mother has asked me to write to him on her behalf. When the family has gathered, often with some of Magdy's close friends, to record audiotapes for him, I have also greeted him and mentioned a few things about myself and his family.

But more important, I know Magdy because, in spite of his long absence, he still plays a significant role in al-Zawiya al-Hamra, where his family lives. Through tapes, phone calls, letters, occasional visits, and financial support, Magdy maintains connections that allow him to participate actively in decisions related to his family and to the formation of his neighborhood. Since my research started in 1993, I have followed and captured some of Magdy's dreams, preferences, and aspirations through the efforts of his family and fiancée to remodel his apartment, which he bought in Hisham's building in 1994.

One Building, Two Dreams

The cases of Magdy and Hisham direct our attention to several important issues that have been addressed directly and indirectly throughout this book. First, they communicate to us some of the new boundaries, differentiations, and social inequalities that are being produced, reinforced, and challenged by transnational connections. They show how global processes are producing new inequalities within the same city, the same neighborhood, and even the same family. In addition, they convey how access to and appropriation of global discourses and images are structured along national, class, and gender lines. Class in particular has been significant in regulating travel destinations, work plans, and access to information and resources. Magdy's case also directs our attention to other emerging hierarchies and power relationships that regulate interactions between cities other than New York, London, and Paris.

But above all, these two cases direct our attention to issues related to agency and the production of urban locality. They illustrate the active and creative role of city dwellers in the production and making of Cairo and its landscapes. Even though they differ in terms of the source of funding, size, shape, and organization of space, the apartments of Magdy and Hisham have a similar role in the construction of al-Zawiya. They both display in physical forms their active role in the making of the neighborhood. These forms, in addition to religion, facilitate the integration of the group and their housing project in al-Zawiya. As discussed in the previous chapter, religion is a powerful force in the formation of a collective identity. Religion morally situates the group in al-Zawiya and facilitates their interaction with other residents. In addition to religion, the many changes that people introduce to their housing units and the construction of new ones are strategies that allow the housing project to be physically integrated with the rest of the neighborhood. That is, the apartments of Magdy and Hisham are "techniques for the spatial production of locality." (Appadurai 1996: 180). Rather than stable, changeless, and spatially bounded, locality "is an inherently fragile social achievement" (Appadurai 1996: 179). As a structure of feeling, a material reality, and an attachment to a particular community, locality has to be continuously recreated and reinforced.[2] This process, as well as the task of studying it, is especially challenging with the increasing movement of peoples, goods, and discourses between different parts of the globe. How can we conceptualize the attachment of feelings to specific spaces while accounting for movement, fluidity, and travel (Malkki 1997; Gupta and Ferguson 1997)? How can we study the role of Magdy in his neighborhood without immobilizing him or depriving him of agency? One strategy, which I am proposing here, is to trace the logic of global trajectories through precise enactments. This strategy allows us to grasp how locality is produced through the interplay between dwelling and traveling, presence and absence, roots and routes, sites and feelings. Rather than seeing Magdy as "neither here nor there," the well-known phrase used to convey the uprootedness and mobility of migrants, this strategy allows us to see him as both here and there. It also enables us to follow individual and collective trajectories (which may take us to Kuwait, New York, or Sarajevo) and to analyze how global flows are articulated, transformed, and resisted in different contexts and by various social groups.

I will first share with you how I got to "know" Magdy through the flows that keep him connected with his family and neighborhood. I analyze Magdy's apartment, which he bought in the housing project, and the tapes circulated between him and his family as powerful techniques that keep him part of the life of his siblings and friends, provide him with moral support, and reinforce his attachment to al-Zawiya. Magdy's apartment, in particular, becomes a visible sign that objectifies and reinforces his active role in the making of his neighborhood in Cairo. In the last part of the chapter, I will place the active roles of Hisham and Magdy within a larger historical and spatial context and examine their wider social and cultural significance for the rest of the housing project and the neighborhood at large.

Egypt's Road to Prosperity

When Sadat started his open-door policy in 1974, he also relaxed the constraints previously imposed by President Nasser on migration from Egypt to other countries (LaTowsky 1984). However, while Sadat saw the road to development and modernization as going through the West, Arab countries such as Libya, Iraq, and Saudi Arabia became the sources of financial prosperity for many skilled and unskilled Egyptian workers. Since the mid-1970s, these countries have continued to inform the imagination of young men and to promise to fulfill their dreams of accumulating the funds needed for marriage, housing, and investment. Over the years, millions of Egyptians have worked abroad and sent money back home. In 1994–1995, the number of Egyptian labor migrants was estimated at 2.7 million and remittances from these workers at $3.3 billion (Economist Intelligence Unit 1996: 25, 52). The money sent by these migrants attracted the attention of policy makers and researchers. Although researchers in Egypt and other parts of the Middle East have been exploring the impact of labor migration on economic activities, gender inequalities, consumption patterns, and household structure since the mid-1970s, their focus has been mainly on the countryside (Brink 1991; Weir 1987; LaTowsky 1984; Myntti 1984; Taylor 1984; Khafagy 1983). Yet we know very little about how migrants from the city such as Magdy participate in the daily activities of their families and how they participate in the production of urban localities.

Magdy's Road to Prosperity

In the late 1980s, Jordan and Iraq were the first countries that attracted Magdy, who after nine years of education quit school to work in a printing company in Cairo. In his early twenties, Magdy traveled with one of his friends to Iraq and Jordan, hoping to find good jobs and reasonable income. During this trip, Magdy failed to secure the money that he desired. According to his sister, Nisma, Magdy and his friend suffered considerably because they did not manage to find suitable jobs. They had to work as street peddlers to secure enough money to be able to return with some gifts for their families. Magdy's next destination was Kuwait. Through an employment agency in Cairo, he managed to find a job as a security guard in Kuwait in 1992. He was hired for one year, but while there, he took an additional part-time job with a printing company to supplement his income. Before the end of the year, he had secured another contract that enabled him to stay in Kuwait as a full-time worker in the printing company. He has been working there for the past six years.

It is worth noting here that national boundaries are important in regulating Magdy's movement and participation in the social, economic, and political domains in Kuwait. Citizenship rights, social security benefits, and residency are still largely determined on basis of nationality. Labor migrants (from India, Pakistan, the Philippines, and various parts of the Middle East) are usually excluded from many aspects of life in oil-producing countries. They are often clearly segregated from the native inhabitants (see Nagy 1998), and they cannot attain citizenship no matter how long they work and live in these countries. Given these exclusionary practices, it is not strange that Magdy maintains strong connections with his neighborhood in Cairo and sends a major part of his income back to his family.

Magdy's letters and tapes do not include many details about the condition of his work. It is clear, though, that he works very hard, participates in *gam'iyyat* (savings associations), and sends a major part of his income back to his family. Over the past five years, Magdy has financed major reconstructions of his family's apartment. They have remodeled the kitchen and bathroom, expanded the living room, installed expensive glass shutters on their balcony, repainted the apartment with costly oil paint, and installed a water heater. When he sends money, Magdy also includes specific instructions on how it should be spent. Once he asked his mother to buy a new gas stove, a new carpet, and a wardrobe. Another time, he asked her to buy a table and some extra chairs. In addition to monthly allowances to his mother, Magdy also covers extra expenses during Ramadan and pays for the goat that they slaughter during the Sacrifice Feast. He also sends money to his unmarried sisters and younger brother to buy new clothes for the main Muslim feasts and other social occasions.

Magdy's short and few visits to al-Zawiya are joyful occasions. As soon as they know that he is coming, his mother and sisters spend days cleaning and arranging the apartment. They scrub the kitchen floor, carefully wash the bathroom, dust the furniture, and clean the walls and floor of the bedrooms and living room. Just before his arrival, they cover the sofas with brand-new covers, hang beautiful clean curtains, place a carpet in the living room, and spread clean sheets over the beds. They also cook his favorite foods. His sisters describe the excitement of waiting for his arrival from the airport and the joy, tears, and laughter that surround his entering their apartment. Once he is home, his married siblings, his friends, and the neighbors rush to greet him. Visitors and festivity continue until he leaves once again for Kuwait.

Like many other migrants, Magdy comes back to Cairo loaded with gifts for his family and close neighbors. He brings soap, shampoo, hair oil, whitening creams, clothes (such as underwear, training suits, pajamas, and *gallabiyyat*), fancy blankets, and electric appliances (such as tape recorders and food processors). These gifts are highly regarded and are displayed to visitors and relatives to communicate to them Magdy's success and commitment to his family. Some utilize their gifts in ways that Magdy did not intend. The Atari game that he brought as a gift for his young nephew, for instance, became part of his older brother's business. Magdy's brother attached the game to a small TV set and placed it in the small shop run by his wife. This game has become an attraction for many children who come to play for a nominal fee.

With this flow of money and goods from Kuwait to Cairo and meager wages at home, it is not surprising that many young men and their families view work in an oil-producing country as the only way to save enough money to secure an apartment and get married. Migrants' descriptions of their lives and work in oil-producing countries also support these views. Mothers and wives try to encourage their male relatives to stay in Saudi Arabia and Kuwait until they secure the money needed. For them, oil-producing countries are linked primarily with money and goods. Only the migrants themselves are fully aware of the difficulties associated with working abroad. They usually work for long hours and under difficult conditions. Ahmed, a construction worker who has been working in Saudi Arabia for four years, explains that, as an Egyptian worker, he is often at the mercy of Saudi contractors who take advantage of him and of other workers. Some contractors underpay (or refuse entirely to pay) their Egyptian workers. Ahmed emphasizes that the Egyptian embassy there does not do much to help Egyptian workers. At the same time, there are no unions to protect workers' rights, and many do not think that they would find justice in the Saudi legal system. According to Ahmed, he and other workers try to keep their employers happy by avoiding any problems. So they usually prefer to keep silent or to find Saudi mediators to help in collecting at least part of the pay. Although "new legal regimes" are being created to mediate the interaction between transnational corporations and different nation-states (Sassen 1996: 213), migrants like Ahmed do not find legal protection either in the representatives of their governments or in the Saudi legal system.

Keeping Him Connected

In contrast to women's travel abroad, which is often depicted in negative terms (as discussed in chapter 3), men's travel is desired and encouraged.

It is seen as the source of financial and social prosperity. Many young men dream and, with the financial and moral support of their families, try hard to travel (often unsuccessfully) to an oil-producing country. The migration of a young man, however, is surrounded by uncertainty and raises many questions: Will he succeed in finding or maintaining a good job? Will he remember his family and commitment at home? Will he come back prosperous and safe? These fears and questions are justified since, unlike Magdy, several young men fail to make the expected income or do not send their families substantial amounts of money. In fact, one of Magdy's older brothers,[3] who worked in Iraq and Libya, exemplifies how young men may not only fail to save money but also acquire "bad" habits such as drinking and frequenting nightclubs. Thus, many parents try to ensure that their children do well in their work and save as much money as possible. In this regard, ensuring continuous communication with young men and encouraging them to buy housing units or remodel existing apartments are important techniques that secure the flow of currency and reinforce the attachment of labor migrants to their families and neighborhoods in Cairo.

TAPES: THE ART OF HEARING

Besides the flow of money and goods from Magdy, there is a continuous flow of ideas, news, and information that enables him to participate effectively in making decisions related to the daily life of his family and friends. Letters, phone calls, photos, and tapes are significant in bridging the physical distance that separates Magdy from his mother, siblings, and fiancée. One of his sisters, Nisma, who is very close to Magdy, is the main letter reader and writer. She is more educated than her other siblings and has better handwriting. While his other siblings can read his letters, they either do not know how to write or think that their handwriting is illegible. Sometimes, when Nisma was not available or when she refused to write to ask for more money, Magdy's mother asked me to write letters on her behalf. Writing to relatives abroad was not a task I had anticipated before starting my field research. It was nonetheless a task I welcomed, as it opened my eyes to several methodological and conceptual points and provided me with an unexpected chance to learn about the dynamics of interaction between migrants and their relatives. Writing letters also allowed me to follow the lives of some women and to grasp how changes in their lives shaped the interaction with male migrants.

Nadia, for example, has been married for five years. After the wedding, her husband, Karim, left her pregnant with their first child and traveled to Saudi Arabia to resume his work as a blacksmith. Although she has her own apartment in another neighborhood, Nadia returned to live with her parents in al-Zawiya al-Hamra. The idea of living alone appeals neither to her nor to her family. Nadia went to school for six years, and she knows how to read. Nevertheless, she cannot write. So she often asks other women, such as Nisma and me, to write to her husband. She usually asked me to read the most recent letter sent by her husband, and then we cooperated in writing the response. She would ask me to respond to all the issues he raised in his letters. Yes, she talked to his brother about hiring a worker to fix their balcony, but no, she could not buy a new stove because she was fifty pounds short of the requested price. Nadia usually insisted that I follow the format of her husband's letters. She would ask me to copy almost literally his greetings to her and then instruct me to send him greetings from all the people that he mentioned in his letter, following the same order that he used. After she gave birth to their first child, she would ask me to write news about the baby and sometimes instructed me to write as if the child himself were asking for money, clothes, and toys. She would also respond to her husband's requests for pictures of their son, whom he did not see until the child was three years old.

In addition to letters, phone calls and audiotapes facilitate the flow of information between migrants and their families. A phone call is a very fast way of communicating that allows direct discussion of pressing issues. Although the number of phones is limited in al-Zawiya al-Hamra, a migrant can always talk to his family by calling a neighbor who has a phone. Phone calls, however, are very expensive and are used infrequently. Audiotapes are another important alternative for effective communication. A tape represents an intermediate form of communication between the fast but expensive phone call and the cheap but slow letter. A tape, though, is more exposed to the control of the government. Unlike fax and e-mail, both of which are available for upper-class Egyptians and can escape the censorship of the government, tapes have to go through the state apparatus. When Magdy's sister takes a tape to the post office, she also needs her identity card. Her name and address have to be clearly printed on the envelope, and the employee in the post office keeps track of her identity card number. Nisma explains that tapes are monitored and approved before they are sent out: "They listen to parts of the tape. They want to make sure that the tape does not contain religious material or attacks against the government. I am sure that they only listen to part of it, and when they hear only greetings from us to Magdy, they stop listening." To avoid state censorship and the long mailing time, Magdy and his family try to keep track of travelers to carry tapes and other gifts to and from Kuwait.

Even though a tape sent via mail is more costly, is monitored by the state, and requires coordination between family members, it is usually preferred to letters for various reasons. First, a tape enables illiterate parents and relatives to communicate with their beloved ones without a mediator (i.e., writer/reader of the letter). Most parents in al-Zawiya al-Hamra are illiterate, and even some siblings who went to school for six years (and sometimes even for nine) cannot write. Thus, with the help of a tape, Magdy's illiterate mother can communicate with him directly. The sincerity and warmth of her prayers are almost impossible to express in writing. Her expressions of affection often turn into cold words when inscribed in a letter written by a daughter or a neighbor. But when she records for Magdy, her soft deep voice reflects her strong emotion, and her words express her longing for him. She also can communicate to him her pride in his achievements, retell her expectations, and repeat her advice. As a letter writer, Nisma is always selective. She sometimes dismisses her mother's requests for money or refuses to write about some problems in the family. No one, however, can stop his mother from saying what she wants when recording for Magdy. They may comment on what she tapes, but still she has the chance to express her ideas without the mediation of a third party. At the same time, a tape from Magdy allows her to hear his voice repeatedly, especially when she misses him. I often saw her happy face and big smile while she replayed one of Magdy's tapes, heard his tender words addressed directly to her, or listened to one of his jokes or funny stories.

In addition, a tape provides flexibility to discuss in detail various issues and to include the voices of several relatives and friends. A tape allows Magdy to address all of his family members and to discuss different topics such as the health of his mother, the future career of his younger brother, and the weight of his younger sister. Tapes also enable Magdy to transmit the latest songs from Kuwait to Cairo and allow his brothers and sisters to provide him with the latest Egyptian songs and jokes. Some sing for him to express how much they miss him, while others, less confident of the beauty of their voices, record a song from the radio. A tape also brings together all his siblings and Magdy's close friends. Taping often becomes a session for telling stories and jokes. Such tapes give Magdy a feeling for his neighborhood, remind him of the days when they used to be together, and provide him with assurances of his family's well-being.

At the same time, a tape is expected to provide more "spontaneous" communication than a letter, enabling the migrant to analyze the tone and quality of the voice on the tape and to conclude things that his relatives do not verbally mention. Nadia, for instance, asked me to write to her husband in detail about issues such as the relatives who visited her after she delivered her baby, the length of their visits, and how much money they gave as gifts to the baby. Despite this, her husband asked her to send him a tape that would inform him about all of this in even greater detail. Nadia's husband wanted not only to read her words, mediated by writers such as Nisma or me, but also to monitor the voice of his wife to figure out how she really felt about the visits of his family. Similarly, Magdy realizes when his mother is sick or in distress, even though she tries to cover that up while recording for him. When he feels that her "voice is different," as he stated in one of his letters, he writes or calls to ask for explanations and assurances from his siblings regarding his mother's health.

But above all, a tape can be and is often used as a "document" that is circulated between family members and close friends and that can be replayed several times for literate and illiterate members. While they cannot save a phone call and a letter is accessible only to those who can read, Magdy's family and future in-laws save the tapes that clearly express Magdy's preferences and reactions. These tapes are consulted when disagreements emerge regarding any proposed changes to his apartment.

These tapes, therefore, keep the migrant informed of what happens in his neighborhood and ensure his emotional and material connectedness with his family. They often aim to remind the young man of his obligations, encourage him to save more, and persuade him to invest his money in durable items. Investment in material objects, and particularly in an apartment, becomes a powerful tool that ensures the continuous flow of cash and information from the migrant and that includes him in the production of locality.

BUILDING MODERN DREAMS

As stated in earlier chapters, the apartment, the organization of its space, and the quality of its furniture are all central to the representation of the self in daily life in al-Zawiya al-Hamra. The housing unit is a material manifestation of the man's ability to earn money and the woman's skill in cleaning and beautifying their home. It is a visible and privileged site for expressing the identity and status of the family. This is clearly manifested in the various changes that people have introduced to the housing units. Many of these changes, as discussed in chapter 2, are signs of distinction and manifestations of the material and symbolic capital of the inhabitants. The role of the apartment gains considerable significance for young unmarried migrants, who are encouraged by their families to invest a major part of their income in restructuring, furnishing, and decorating their housing units. The apartment shows that the migrant "did something." It not only signifies his success and distinction but also symbolizes and reinforces his belonging and attachment to his neighborhood.

MAGDY'S APARTMENT

Young men like Magdy are desirable future husbands. Like many other young women, Magdy's sisters dream of marrying men who work in oil-producing countries. They explain that, in a relatively short time, a man who works in Kuwait or Saudi Arabia will have enough money to secure the apartment and its furniture, both of which are essential social requirements for marriage. So when Magdy proposed to Laila, a twenty-three-year-old woman who lives in *el-ahali* but works as a secretary in a middle-class neighborhood, she and her parents accepted immediately. Besides his good looks and pleasant manners, they knew that he had been working in Kuwait for years and that he could fulfill Laila's dreams. Although Magdy did not have the chance to know his fiancée well, he trusted the judgment of his mother, sisters, and neighbors. In their opinion, Laila is beautiful and comes from a good family. After meeting her a couple of times, he decided to ask for her hand in marriage. He bought her the customary golden jewelry (*shabka*) and had a big engagement party. Like many other engagement and wedding celebrations, their party was video-taped, and his family and fiancée replayed it for me several times.

Once Magdy was engaged, finding an apartment became even more important. Magdy, however, did not manage to find a suitable unit before going back to Kuwait. So he left the money in a bank account under his sister's name. He chose Nisma not only because she had a more flexible schedule than her working brothers but also because, as he knew, she would not spend any of his money without his instructions and permission. His older brothers had gone through repeated financial crises that had forced them to borrow part of the money that Magdy sent to his mother. Nisma kept her eyes open for vacant apartments. Within a few months, she heard that one neighbor in Hisham's building was going to move to a larger unit in another neighborhood. She thought that the neighbor's two-bedroom apartment was a good catch because it was very close to the apartments of both Magdy's family and Laila's family. After discussing the issue with the rest of the family and Magdy's fiancée and obtaining Magdy's approval, Nisma inquired about the price and bargained with the owner. At first, the owner asked for fifteen thousand pounds (at that time, an Egyptian pound equaled thirty-three American cents), but she managed to reduce it to fourteen thousand pounds. One of her brothers finalized the agreement with the owner, and Nisma paid ten thousand pounds up front. A few months later, Magdy sent the remaining amount.

Even before the search began, it was clear to everyone that Magdy's apartment would reflect his income and status. His younger brothers were forced to consider renting or buying units in satellite cities outside Cairo, an option that they did not like but that still might be the only one available given their incomes. From the beginning, his family took it for granted that Magdy could afford to buy an apartment near them in al-Zawiya al-Hamra. While his younger brothers were searching for one-bedroom apartments, it was assumed that Magdy could afford at least a two-bedroom unit. Compared with the apartments of his married siblings, the unit that Magdy bought is much larger. The original structure of Magdy's apartment consisted of two bedrooms, a living space, a bathroom, and a relatively spacious separate kitchen. This apartment was identical to his family's apartment, where, until recently, ten to twelve individuals lived (see Figure 11). Meanwhile, his older brother Fahmi, a driver in his mid-thirties, lives with his wife and an eight-year-old son in a one-bedroom apartment. Although Fahmi and his wife were lucky to find this unit ten years ago, given that it is close to both of their families, the apartment is considered very small for them. In addition to the bedroom, there is a small hallway, but there is no separate living space that can be used to receive guests. A couch, placed in the hallway next to the entrance, is used to seat visitors (see Figure 12). This area is so small that if two or three people visit simultaneously, the place becomes uncomfortably crowded. Fahmi's wife is especially unhappy with the fact that her "kitchen," which consists of a sink and a gas stove occupying the corner of the hallway, is exposed to visitors who are seated on the couch in the opposite side of the hallway. Since I met her in 1993, she has been dreaming of saving enough money to install a metal balcony, part of which she can use as a kitchen.

The changes that Magdy is introducing to his apartment increase the

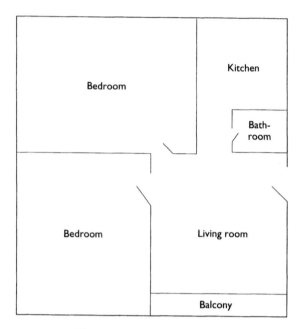

FIGURE 11: The apartment that Magdy bought was
originally identical to his family's apartment, where,
until recently, ten individuals lived.

differences even more between him and his siblings. These changes are
encouraged by his family and future in-laws, who often draw on modern
images and ideas to motivate Magdy to invest in expanding the apartment, organizing its space, and buying fancy furniture.[4] A few months
after buying his unit, Hisham and two other families in the building
decided to expand their apartments by building new structures attached
to the units allocated to them by the state. Although Magdy's new two-
bedroom apartment is considered spacious and few young men of his age
can afford to acquire such a unit, his family and fiancée thought that
expanding his apartment would be a good investment that could save him
money in the future. Building with the neighbors was not only important
because they would collectively share the high cost of the foundation of
the new additions. It was also crucial to avoid the state's attempts to
remove the new unlicensed structures. Neighbors cooperate to collect
money to pay off government employees to overlook such changes. At
the same time, conducting the additions as a group makes it harder for
government officials to demolish the new expansions.

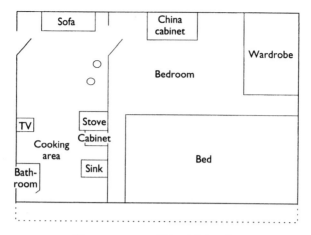

FIGURE 12: The apartment of Magdy's brother. A couch, placed in the hallway next to the entrance, is used to seat visitors. This area is so small that if two or three people visit simultaneously, the place becomes uncomfortably crowded.

Magdy's family and his future in-laws collectively produced a tape that in detail explained to him the plan and the money needed. Magdy approved of the proposal and sent the required money to his family. His siblings, his fiancée, her father, and some of Magdy's close friends supervised the implementation of the expansion. Currently, Magdy's apartment has two bedrooms, one living room, a dining room, a spacious kitchen, two bathrooms, and a large balcony (see Figure 13). Communication with Magdy has continued through tapes, letters, and phone calls to discuss minute developments related to the shape and structure of the additions and the furniture. Magdy, Laila, and their families discussed the choice of door for the kitchen (a beaded curtain or a swinging door) and the bathroom (metal, wood, or glass), the color of the ceramic tiles, and electrical and water installations, taking into consideration expected purchases of appliances such as a water heater and an automatic washing machine.

It is interesting to note that Magdy's migration has brought his family closer to his friends and future in-laws. His apartment in particular has become a link that brings his family closer to his fiancée and her parents. In his absence, his mother and siblings are expected to visit Laila during major religious holidays and to offer her gifts on special occasions. Still, the apartment created another need to communicate with her on regular basis. Currently, the unit represents a blending of Magdy's ideas, the expectations of his family and friends, and the opinions of his fiancée and

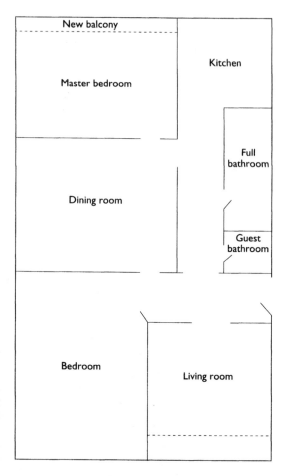

FIGURE 13: Magdy's apartment after the latest additions. Currently, the unit has two bedrooms, one living room, a dining room, a spacious kitchen, two bathrooms, and a large balcony.

her family. They all contributed in one way or another to the renovation of the apartment. Laila shopped with two of Magdy's sisters for the ceramic tiles to be installed in the kitchen and bathrooms. One of his close friends helped in transporting the tiles from the market to the apartment. Laila's father contacted the workers and supervised the installation of the tiles. One of Magdy's brothers found the technicians who installed the electrical and water connections needed to install the automatic washing machine that Magdy is expected to buy. During all of this, there is clear supervision of the money and how it is spent. Each time Laila goes to buy something, she takes one of Magdy's sisters with her to witness the transaction and the amount of money she spends. One of his sisters keeps a written account of the various expenses to report to Magdy on a regular basis. In short, the apartment becomes a project that unites all of them in their attempts to help Magdy in materializing his dreams.

Magdy's travel allows his fiancée more freedom in shaping their future home. Although women are active in organizing, cleaning, and decorating their apartments, they usually assume this role after marriage. The bride is rarely involved in preparing her future home until the final stage, when she and her sisters (or female friends) arrange the furniture that she buys (normally for the living room and the kitchen) and organize her belongings in the bedroom. In contrast to this general tendency, the role of Laila and her family has been central to the changes introduced to Magdy's apartment. Laila decided on various issues related to the unit, such as the color of the ceramic tiles, the kind of bathtub, and the paint of the unit. She is also taking initiatives in the organization of the unit. She helped in supervising the work and in removing, with the help of Magdy's sister, the debris left behind by the workers. She also went with her father to their village of origin, two hours by bus from Cairo, to see a carpenter whom he knew and recommended. She showed the carpenter her favorite design of kitchen cabinets and asked him to duplicate it. She and her father visited the carpenter several times to check on his progress and to make sure that he was the right person to hire to make the bedroom furniture. After these visits, she went to her future mother-in-law to inform her about the kitchen, the wood they are using, and the color they will select to paint the cabinets.

Unlike most brides, Laila is also participating in decisions related to her future bedroom. While a bride participates in the selection of the furniture of the living room and kitchen, the furniture of the bedroom, which is closely linked with sexuality, is the responsibility of the groom and his family. In Magdy and Laila's case, she is the one who is deciding on these issues. To be able to select the most fashionable and beautiful furniture, Laila watched TV, looked through magazines, and visited various newly married women to see their bedrooms. After deciding on a style, she sent a picture of the furniture she liked to Magdy to solicit his opinion. She said that Magdy liked the design of the room and suggested a white color. Laila, however, prefers black and wine-red colors. According to her, the white is very common and dated, while the black and the wine-red are newer and more fashionable. After discussing her preferences with Magdy over the phone, he told her to choose the color that she prefers.

In addition to the structure of the housing unit, people expect Magdy to display his wealth in the furnishings of the apartment. Compared with his siblings and other men of his generation, he will be buying furniture that is very expensive. He will have to furnish not only the bedroom but also the dining room. One of the purchases that Laila is currently planning, a dining room set, is a clear expression of Magdy's distinction. Even though, as she explains, the dining room will rarely be used, Laila is currently trying to select a dining set that would seat six to eight persons. When she finds a set that she likes, she will send a picture of it to Magdy to see if it is to his liking. She plans to have a small table in the kitchen where she and Magdy will eat and to buy another wooden low round table (*tabliyya*), which is usually used for serving food in al-Zawiya, to use when their families and neighbors visit. Meanwhile, they need the dining room as a visible sign of Magdy's success to be displayed to their visitors.

At the same time, the desired home of Magdy and Laila is constructed by images transmitted via television programs and visits to other neighborhoods. The manner and style in which Magdy has chosen to remodel and furnish his housing unit also reflect his experience outside his neighborhood. Items such as the water filter, the kitchen fan, and the vacuum cleaner, which he purchased in Kuwait, are not common in al-Zawiya al-Hamra. He also decided to invest money in building both a full bathroom and a separate guest restroom (with a toilet and a sink). Among the many apartments that I visited in the neighborhood, Magdy's unit is the only one that has two bathrooms and the only one that has a bathtub.

Making Urban Spaces

Unlike Magdy's spacious apartment, Hisham's unit consists of only a small bedroom, a tiny living space, and a small kitchen and bathroom. Despite differences in the size, shape, organization of space, and the expected furniture, both apartments are part of a large set of strategies that are transforming the housing project and the neighborhood. Along with religious identity, discussed in the previous chapter, these housing additions are techniques that facilitate the inclusion of the relocated group in the neighborhood and inscribe their presence on Cairo's "face." Unlike the state's discourse, which presented them as unproductive, pathological, isolated fragments of the nation, these changes present Hisham and his neighbors as active agents who creatively participate in the making of their neighborhood and Cairo at large. These additions join the many changes introduced to individual housing units and shared spaces, discussed in previous chapters, that are shaping *el-masaakin* and al-Zawiya. Although these additions aim to satisfy some direct needs for housing (in Hisham's case) and express distinction and social status (in Magdy's case), their cumulative effects go beyond these aims to shape the project and the neighborhood. For one thing, they demand cooperation and consolidation of relationships between neighbors. Simultaneously, they are producing new physical realities that convey to the group and to others the active role of Magdy and his neighbors in the making of the neighborhood and Cairo at large.

BUILDING HOUSES, BUILDING RELATIONSHIPS

Just as Magdy's unit brings his family, in-laws, and friends together, the changes he is introducing demand coordination and cooperation between neighbors. As previously said, neighbors cooperate to secure the money for the foundation and to collect money to pay off officials. They also gather information about new policies and laws and prepare to defend the additions if threatened by the local police. While the government's inter-ference in changes introduced to the interior of the housing unit has relaxed and almost disappeared over the years, external changes, especially large additions such as those introduced by Hisham and his neighbors, continue to be the targets of the state gaze and its disciplinary regulation. There is the strong possibility that additions will be demolished or that the owners will be fined and/or imprisoned. So people try to monitor government actions and regulations to determine which changes are tol-erated. Other housing projects in various areas provide models for changes as well as indicators about how the state is going to react to these changes. People in al-Zawiya have a good sense of which changes are tol-erated and know that the state can and did demolish some constructions, particularly roof additions and those introduced by individual families. Adding rooms to the top floor, which is seen as threatening to the struc-ture of the building, is expected to be severely punished, and people refer to cases when such additions were removed. Neighbors are unwilling to support or allow such changes, which may threaten the safety of the whole building.

People know that the critical time is during the construction process itself, which should be completed as quickly as possible because at that time it is easy for government officials to demolish the additions. In some cases, the workers may simply disappear when they notice the presence of government officials and act as if no construction is being conducted. Sometimes the additions are quickly painted with a color that is similar to the rest of the units to give the impression that they are part of the original block. Most often, however, money is collected from neighbors to pay the officials who see the construction and threaten to report it to higher authorities. In the case of easily noticeable additions, such as those conducted by Hisham and his neighbors, the same officials who pocket the money are expected to report the expansions after they are completed. The police station will then call upon the residents and issue a formal report (*muhdar*), which will be transferred to the court. The next step, which nobody I know has reached yet, is to see the judge who will determine the future of such additions. Neighbors prepare themselves for this moment and discuss the best ways to deal with the Egyptian bureaucracy.

Hisham and his neighbors are also careful not to antagonize any officials and police officers who tour the area. I heard of only one incident when additions were destroyed. The reason, as explained by one of my female informants, was that the young male "owner" reacted strongly when a police officer commented on the "illegal" status of his additions. They exchanged verbal insults, which made the officer very angry. He left the scene to come back shortly with a bulldozer, and the partially constructed addition was demolished on the spot. When pleading, bribery, and mediation do not work, women and children become the main agents in protecting the additions and changes introduced to the units. I was told about an incident when government officials tried to demolish a newly constructed balcony. The mother and her children stood in the balcony and challenged the workers to tear it down. The neighboring women also gathered and shouted at the workers, who had to leave without being able to touch the balcony.

Men and women also follow developments in legislation (such as the military decree issued by the prime minister in 1996 that aimed to prohibit any construction on public land) and changes in the governance of the city (such as the appointment of a new governor of Cairo) that may affect their constructions. A new governor, for example, "tries to act tough," one seller says. For some months after his initial appointment, people are extra careful in building on and using public space. Sahar, for instance, stopped using video games in her small shop for a while after the assignment of Cairo's new governor. She said that all merchants were afraid of the visible increase in the number of policemen touring the area, who might penalize the traders and confiscate their belongings. These additions, therefore, demand and produce a continuous flow of information between neighbors and between al-Zawiya and other neighborhoods. They also foster cooperation and strengthen a sense of solidarity (at least temporarily) between residents of the housing project.[5]

REMAKING 'EL-MASAAKIN'

> *One of the difficult visual problems of project salvage will be to*
> *make these places look lively and urban enough; they have so much*
> *grimness and visual repetition to overcome.*
>
> Jane Jacobs, *The Death and Life of Great American Cities*

In addition to their role in bringing neighbors and family members together, the cumulative impact of these changes goes beyond the individual units and the shared spaces and extends to reshape al-Zawiya and Cairo at large. To take one example that shows the larger effect of such changes, we need only to look at how they have been rupturing the visual homogeneity of *el-masaakin*. As previously mentioned, the buildings were identical in shape, color, number of floors, external design, and internal arrangement of space. The uniformity of blocks and standardization of individual units, which have long been associated by planners and policy makers with order and beauty, clearly define *el-masaakin* and separate them physically from *el-ahali*. The monotony and repetition of the same blocks and *murabba'at* not only was aesthetically dull but also caused many "to lose their way" when they first moved to the area. As in projects in other parts of the world, "what seems like rationality and legibility" to policy makers and planners "seems like mystifying disorder for the ordinary residents who must navigate the city" (Scott 1998: 127). One young woman described how shocked she was when she came out from the bedroom to find their living room filled with strange men who thought they were in the apartment of one of their relatives. While officials and planners often consider the new changes to be disorderly and chaotic, at the community level, they are important "visual interruptions" (Jacobs 1961: 380) that introduce vitality and diversity to the housing project. Hisham's new apartment, the metal and cement balconies of other neighbors, carts and glass-fronted cabinets, shacks on rooftops or in front of blocks, housing units turned into clinics, stores, and workshops, and gardens in public spaces are all transforming the homogenous project, crossing the boundaries between private and public and between residency and work, as discussed in chapters 2 and 4. The visual effects of these alterations go beyond the individual unit and the satisfaction of important daily needs.

Like many other modernist plans, the housing project was designed as a bounded entity separated physically from the rest of the neighborhood (for a similar case from Brazil, see Holston 1989). As we have seen in the previous chapters, however, people's activities are not bounded by the walls of the housing unit, the confines of the *murabba'*, the borders of the project, or the boundaries of the neighborhood. While neither the physical separation of *el-masaakin* nor the state discourse (discussed in previous chapters) has facilitated the relocated residents' interaction with other groups in al-Zawiya, the new modifications are slowly integrating the project with the rest of the neighborhood. As in *el-ahali*, many of the new constructions are built from mud brick and tend to physically and visually integrate (though very slowly) *el-masaakin* within al-Zawiya. Although these attempts are obstructed by the restrictions imposed on vertical changes, which keep the number of floors unchanged, the diversity and vitality introduced to individual units and shared spaces are slowly disrupting the material markers that separate and physically segregate the project from the rest of the neighborhood.

THE MAKING OF AL-ZAWIYA

Such changes also play a central role in expressing how Hisham and his neighbors belong to al-Zawiya and in legitimizing their presence in Cairo. This is clearly manifested in the way people construct the history of the neighborhood. The presence of multiple groups who came from different parts of Egypt and Cairo and at different times, and who live in different parts of the area, makes it hard to talk about a single history of al-Zawiya. Various histories are told: a man tells the history of his migration from his village to Cairo, a woman narrates her movement from Bab al-Sha'riya to al-Zawiya when she was a teenager, and her neighbor tells how she moved from the center of Cairo to the old public housing project and then to *el-ahali* after she got married. Despite these differences, both the old and the new residents emphasize the way their presence altered the area and was central to the construction of the neighborhood.

Al-Zawiya al-Hamra literally means "the Red Corner." In the old days, many explain, there was a small red mosque, usually referred to as *Zawiya*.[6] Even though the mosque does not exist any more, al-Zawiya al-Hamra still bears that name. Others link the red color with the red brick houses that dominated the neighborhood until recently. Generally, people use *al-Zawiya* only to refer to the area and rarely use *al-Hamra*. This usage of the word *al-Zawiya* (the corner or the small mosque) is not accidental. Rather it signifies a general feeling among people, especially the youth, that their neighborhood is marginal in the city or, as one young man said, "is not on the map." They feel that the state neglects their neighborhood and point to the deteriorating infrastructure (such as roads and sewage system) as proof. At the same time, the word *al-Zawiya,* with its religious connotations, indicates the importance of religion in people's life, a topic that was examined in the previous chapter.

Although neither the old nor the new inhabitants can claim to have given al-Zawiya its name, they compete to claim a more central role in its formation. They all refer to a "moment of colonization" that is common to the production of localities in various contexts (Appadurai 1996: 183). Residents of *el-ahali* who came in the 1940s, residents who moved to the old housing in the 1960s, and those who moved to the new housing project during the late 1970s and early 1980s all have similar narratives. "When we came to al-Zawiya, it was agricultural fields and the water of a nearby *tir'a* [irrigation or discharge canal] covered most of what you currently see as streets, houses, and shops. People used to fear leaving their homes after dark because wild animals and criminals threatened their safety." Such statements are very common among the relocated and the old residents in describing their contribution to the development of the neighborhood. In addition to wild and dangerous animals, usually signified by the wolf (*diib*), people emphasize the fear that was cultivated by robbers (*qutta'a turuq*) and fugitives (*matarid*) who used to hide in the thick plantation that covered the area and who used to steal the belongings of the residents. Not only did the residents inhabit a risky area, but they also cleaned and constructed it. Houses, shops, and mosques are all signs of their positive contribution to the making of al-Zawiya.

To underline the sacrifices and the role they played, the relocated people describe how house owners in Bulaq tried to discourage their tenants from moving by emphasizing the importance of the central location of Bulaq and describing the isolation and the horrible conditions in al-Zawiya. "They used to tell us that there were huge mosquitoes and dangerous animals in al-Zawiya," one woman explains. "They told us that we would not be able to go outside to buy even our daily foods. When we moved, we brought lots of food with us. We brought rice, macaroni, sugar, tea, and many other foods because we believed that we would not be able to leave our apartments after dark." These sacrifices are drawn upon to emphasize the role of the relocated population in constructing al-Zawiya. Commenting on the relationships between *el-ahali* and *el-masaakin* residents, a fifty-five-year-old woman said: "It is like Ahli and Zamalek [the two teams who usually compete over the annual soccer championship in Egypt]. They are both Egyptians but do not want to be defeated by the other team. When we first arrived, the people in *el-ahali* did not want us and tried to show that they were in control of the area. The 'good' old inhabitants know that when we came we brought life and prosperity to the area. Their businesses and work improved after we came. We helped in developing the area from being agriculture fields [*ghitan*] to what you see now." Another young man explains that "the people of Bulaq are known for their important roles in improving different areas. No matter where we go, the area we inhabit becomes very popular and attracts others. Take Madinat al-Salaam [a flourishing new community in northeastern Cairo], for example. It started to blossom only when part of us moved there." Such accounts celebrate the products of the labor and practices of the people. Both the old inhabitants and the relocated group selectively draw on a past that not only legitimizes their presence in the area but makes it crucial for al-Zawiya's existence as part of the urban scene. These views frame people's spatial expansions and constructions, which became important contributions to the development of the area and its integration into Cairo. They symbolize to the group and others their active role in the making of the neighborhood.

New Logics and Global Dreams

The practices of Hisham and his neighbors are producing their own social and economic logic. When I went back to Cairo in March of 1996 after an absence of fourteen months, I was struck by the boom in large-scale construction such as that erected by Hisham in *el-masaakin*. This recent boom comes at the end of the fifteen-year period that, according to the contracts given to the people when they were relocated, marks the shift of ownership from the state to the dwellers. I was also amazed by how quickly these expansions led to new criteria for evaluating housing units. The changes introduced to an apartment are largely determined by its location. One can easily introduce rooms and shacks to units on the ground floor, but additions to other floors demand cooperation between residents in the floors below and possibly those who are above. Similarly, the distance between the different *murabba'at* is now being included as part of the value of the unit. When two or more buildings are very close to each other, the vacant area may be limited, and expansions on either side may not allow enough visual privacy for the residents. Such limitations reduce the price of the unit.

The situation changed even more in 1997 and 1998. Construction increased, some people were taken to court by the government, and the market for buying and selling apartments flourished. Transactions in expanded apartments are providing new possibilities. One of my close informants, Salah, rented an apartment for one year to consummate his marriage and was hoping to find another apartment before the end of the year. His attempts failed because he lost his job as a driver in a private company and because his family's expenses increased after the birth of their first son. Salah and his parents decided to add two rooms next to their two-bedroom apartment. Together with his wife and son, he moved to one of the bedrooms; his parents continue to occupy one bedroom, and his two younger single brothers sleep in the third room. They all share the same bathroom and kitchen. Salah had been planning to turn the fourth room into a grocery store. His plans, however, changed when he realized that the value of their apartment had increased greatly. Like other apartments that overlook the main street and are on the ground floor, the apartment can be easily transformed into a shop.[7] While a two-bedroom apartment in other parts of the block costs around thirty thousand pounds, Salah and his family expect to get up to ninety thousand pounds for their unit. Salah is now planning to buy three one-bedroom apartments, one for his parents, another for his brothers, and a third for his own family.

The aesthetics of these changes are also becoming more elaborate, and different models are emerging. People visit and evaluate these new additions to select what suits their families and aspirations. This can be clearly seen in people's reactions to Magdy's apartment. Through his apartment, Magdy is not only participating in the material production of his neighborhood but also presenting new forms and ideas to the people around him. For many people, his unit has become a signifier of the modern, the new, the beautiful, and the desired. His sisters, for example, like the spacious kitchen of Magdy's apartment. They say that a woman spends most of her time in the kitchen and that having a big kitchen is very pleasant. Magdy's apartment also has become a model that attracts the attention of his neighbors and inspires them as they plan and organize their units. One neighbor, Um Hussam, came to see the unit because her only son is getting married and she would like him to live with her. Um Hussam was very impressed with Magdy's apartment and especially liked the idea of having two separate bathrooms in the same apartment. She thought that such an arrangement would allow her future daughter-in-law some privacy and make her more comfortable in sharing a home with her husband's family, especially in the early days of marriage. Thus, through his ongoing involvement and attachment to his neighborhood,

Magdy is introducing new forms to the surrounding urban space. His ideas and housing unit join the global flow of images and discourses (mainly through the media) in stimulating new desires and in presenting new physical realities that are evaluated and admired by his family and neighbors.

Through their spatial practices, Hisham, Magdy, and their neighbors situate themselves emotionally and materially in al-Zawiya. Although relocation excluded them from its center, they reinforce their belonging to Cairo through the products of their labor, which is placing al-Zawiya "on the map." What counts for them is not only the history of the center, which is accessible to visitors and upper-class Egyptians. They are making a history of Cairo from their particular location in the social space. But how are these changes viewed by government officials? Like many other states (for more on this, see Scott 1998), the Egyptian government still views its capital as a single entity that should be controlled through policing, rational planning, and central management. But is the city an entity, a whole that can be managed, controlled, and disciplined centrally? Is this a productive way to view the city and the practices of its dwellers? In the coming conclusion, I examine the implications of the practices of Hisham and his neighbors for the conceptualization of the city, agency, globalization, and religious identity.

Homes, Mosques, and the Making of a Global Cairo

Whoever built a mosque, Allah would build for him a similar place in paradise.

Prophet Muhammad, *Sahih Bukhari*

Beneath the discourses that ideologize the city, the ruses and combinations of powers that have no readable identity proliferate.

Michel de Certeau, *The Practice of Everyday Life*

"Conquering the Beast" was the title of a recent article about Cairo in the Egyptian newspaper *Al-Ahram Weekly* (December 2–8, 1999: 6), an interview with the governor of Cairo, Abdel-Rehim Shehata. In the interview, Shehata states, "Cairo is the city of problems," although he is also quick to declare that "our strategy is an all-out attack on those problems." The governor describes the comprehensive plan formulated by the governorate to deal with Cairo's infrastructure, cleanliness, traffic, water and air pollution, and cultural and human development, and he emphasizes that "the most dangerous obstacle we are up against is people's behavior. No matter how much we do, without deep-rooted changes in society's attitude, all our efforts will be short-changed, and we will have little to show for them" (7). He adds, "People do not like to listen to the government. . . . I don't know why. Old habits, I guess. They seem to doubt that the government is here to serve their needs" (6). According to the governor, this is why traffic congestion, crowded streets, dirty neighborhoods, and polluted air still exist. "The problem" he continues, "is that many of Cairo's inhabitants lack a feeling of belonging. Many do not come originally from the city; they are either recently arrived migrants or in transit. This is a big problem. You have to try and develop people's sense of belonging" (6). He emphasizes that if his strategy is fully implemented and "if people can change their behavior, then we will be one of the most beautiful capitals in the world" (7).

One often encounters remarks like the governor's about Cairo residents in the Egyptian public discourse. They convey a general feeling about people's practices and roles in the making of Cairo. These are usually invoked to rationalize the persistence of Cairo's problems but are rarely viewed as the source of the city's energy, liveliness, or vitality. This interview also illustrates that government officials still think of city management as a top-down endeavor. The government, its planners, and officials do the planning, and the people should follow their regulations. There is little room in the governor's view for dialogue between the government and the people or for people's participation. This interview recalls the fantasy of many planners and policy makers who have dreamed since the last century of controlling the city, its processes, and growth. From Haussmann, Le Corbusier, and Robert Moses to the current governor of Cairo, the vision of the city continues to be largely linked to rational planning, technological progress, and a "sweeping, rational engineering of all aspects of social life" (Scott 1998: 88). Despite strong criticisms by sociologists (Jacobs 1961; de Certeau 1988), anthropologists (Holston 1989), and political scientists (Scott 1998), the dream is still alive and well: if only we could implement our well-designed comprehensive strategies, and if only people would follow what we tell them, then all the city's problems would be solved and everyone would live happily ever after. Policy makers and planners still view laws formulated and enforced by government officials as the main ingredient for a vital and beautiful city. As Cairo's governor declared confidently, "There is no street in Cairo, even in the desert areas, which is not an open book to us. . . . Our only life buoy is law and order" (*Al-Ahram Weekly*, December 2–8, 1999: 7). How does this view relate to the practices of the ordinary dwellers of the city? Is it possible for government planners and policy makers to control how the city is made and practiced?

Living with the Beast

Since Sadat started his policies in the mid-1970s, Cairo has experienced many transformations. President Hosni Mubarak, who has been ruling since Sadat's assassination in 1981, continues to pursue a rigorous economic reform program.[1] As described in Rodenbeck's recent study, life in

Cairo improved in many ways under Mubarak. Unlike his predecessors, Mubarak is "a stolid manager, not a visionary. . . . He shunned grandiose projects and focused instead on fixing Cairo's shoddy infrastructure" (Rodenbeck 1998: 243). Cairo's metro, which started operating in 1989, regularly and efficiently connects various parts of the Egyptian capital. New satellite cities are being created, a new ring road and several bridges are being constructed, and housing projects in and around Cairo are proliferating rapidly. Various projects are implemented to beautify, discipline, and globalize the city. Families, markets, factories, and vendors are relocated to new communities outside Cairo. Since the mid-1990s, the Ministry of Foreign Affairs has been trying (with little success) to relocate more residents of Bulaq to beautify the area around its grand new building overlooking the Nile. The new governor of Cairo revived the idea of investing the vacant (since 1981) plot in Bulaq. He suggested utilizing the land for multistory parking and public gardens. Most recently, Mubarak has been emphasizing the value of information technology and the need for "a comprehensive technological renaissance" (*al-Ahram Weekly*, October 7–13, 1999: 2). In his 1999 presidential speech, he promised that "a national campaign will be launched to wipe out technological illiteracy, expand the use of computers in schools, universities, institutions, government agencies and NGOs and upgrade technical skills of Egyptian labour" (2). A media satellite, the first in the Arab world, was put into orbit in 1998, Internet cafes and new communication centers are growing very quickly in upper-class areas, and mobile phones are clear visible signs of distinction, acquired by the rich and desired by many others.

Al-Zawiya has been experiencing some of these rapid transformations. While until the early 1990s, people had to wait ten to twenty years for a new phone line, currently the waiting time is much shorter (only one to two years if one has the needed fees). Telephones are proliferating in homes, coffee shops, bookstores, and grocery shops. If a family does not have a phone at home, there are also public phone booths, which emerged in al-Zawiya only in 1998, that can be used with a calling card. Many young men and women strongly desire mobile phones, but none of my informants could afford one. Recently, natural gas pipes started supplying the homes of Magdy's family and their neighbors with cheap means for cooking and heating water. A new bridge is being constructed to facilitate the traffic movement from the neighborhood to the rest of Cairo. Despite these changes, al-Zawiya, like many other areas in Cairo, still suffers from serious problems. Sewage leaks are daily occurrences, and garbage collection is still a serious problem. There is often a shortage of water, especially in the summer. The water pressure is often insufficient to provide families on the fourth and fifth floors with uninterrupted supplies. The color and smell of the water dispensed sometimes indicate that it is not fit for human consumption. The buses that connect the area with other parts of the city center are old, shoddy, and very crowded, and al-Zawiya's roads are dotted with holes and garbage. Housing is an especially pressing problem for young men and women. Just like Hisham, many wait between five and ten years to be able to find an apartment to start their lives as married couples. Even the new communities around Cairo, which are relatively close to the capital, are beyond the reach of most young men in al-Zawiya.

Confronted by these hardships, people continue to build homes and mosques. In addition to the recent boom in the construction of apartment extensions similar to those described in the previous chapter, men and women in al-Zawiya are active in constructing and expanding mosques in different parts of the area. Pointing to one mosque in *el-ahali*, Um Hosni explained to me with pride that the mosque was constructed by the efforts and money of the residents. The youth, in particular, have been collecting donations from the people to finish the mosque, which started as one room with a reed mat for men only. The room was turned into a mosque with minarets, and a section is currently designated for women.[2] Another mosque on the border between *el-masaakin* and *el-ahali* that Um Ahmed frequents for her evening prayers expanded and had a wall added that replaced the curtain used before to separate the two genders. Until recently, its identity as a mosque was recognized only through the inscription of God's name above its entrance. The simple room, inserted between the housing blocks, has been turned into an elaborate structure, and its identity has been physically marked by a tall minaret. This mosque is part of the many expansions that are taking place in adjacent blocks.[3] Despite many differences between them, both these mosques (or Houses of God) and the additions of Magdy and his neighbors (houses of the people) display in visible forms the active role of the local population in the making of their neighborhood and Cairo at large.

Quiet Sounds, Visible Signs, and Moral Economies

The state is an ambiguous reality.
Pierre Bourdieu, *Acts of Resistance*

The previous chapters showed how, as active users, men and women in al-Zawiya have employed different strategies and tactics to transform the housing project and the neighborhood at large. Hisham and his neighbors are creatively finding new ways to articulate their daily practices and cultural dispositions with the state constructions of space. These practices are part of an "art of manipulating and enjoying" private and public spaces "by reintroducing into them the plural mobility of goals and desires" (de Certeau 1988: xxii). As shown in this book, living in an apartment, cooking in a kitchen, or walking in a street is different from planning roads and constructing buildings. Just as the individual apartment did not respect the fluidity of daily practices, the changing size of the family, or the interaction between neighbors, the project at large did not address the need for diversification, flexible social interactions, or mixing of activities. Through their practices (which range from shifting uses of various spaces to formalized strategies that localize change in visible forms), men and women have been reintroducing vitality, plurality, and diversity to the spaces allocated to them by the state.

It is tempting to label many of the practices described in this book as "resistance." In many ways, these practices challenge the socioeconomic and political inequalities that place Hisham and his neighbors in a particular social space. They are part of their continuous struggle to secure a space for themselves in Cairo and to inscribe their presence on the "face" of a city, which, through state policies, pushed them out from its center. They integrate the group within the neighborhood and display its active role in the neighborhood's formation. They defy the fantasies of rational planning that divide housing units into enclosed entities and assign functions to specific spaces.

The thick contextualization of these practices, however, makes it hard to "fit them into a fixed box called resistance," to use the words of Sherry Ortner (1995: 175).[4] This concept becomes slippery,[5] denoting many different, and at times contradictory, modes of action under its rubric (Maddox 1997; Bayat 1997a, 1997b). The concept of resistance also poses the thorny question of intentionality. Is resistance necessarily a conscious act, as some argue (Fegan 1986)? If so, how are we to account for the intentions of social agents? Are these intentions "inscribed in the acts themselves" (Scott: 1986: 29)? If not necessarily a conscious act, is resistance any "experience that constructs and reconstructs the identity of subjects" (Gupta and Ferguson 1997: 19)? In its traditional sense, the label *resistance* does not account for the multiple meanings and consequences of the practices described in this book; neither does it do justice to the wide range of daily tactics and strategies that I have been analyzing. Who is Hisham resisting when he builds his apartment? Is Magdy resisting when he invests most of his life savings in building his modern dreams and desires? Who is Um Hassan resisting by keeping a sheep or some chickens in her kitchen?

More important, the label *resistance* does not capture the ambiguous and shifting relationships between these practices and the state plans and discourses. The spatial practices of Hisham and his neighbors are neither foreign to the state's organization of the city nor in conformity with it. On the one hand, the new expansions are attached to the old structures and are believed to strengthen the buildings that were erected by state planners. They are "planned" in that they are attached to the buildings erected by the state. They also require planning and coordination between neighbors. In addition, they are manifestations of people's aspiration to improve their housing conditions and their desire for modern housing. They are often justified by notions of beauty, modernity, and privacy that have been common in the state public discourse since Sadat started his open-door policy. On the other hand, these additions are not subject to "rational planning." They are "unplanned" in that no official permits are obtained beforehand and no architects or planners are consulted. People dismissed my question as irrelevant when I asked about having an architect who might help in designing the new additions. "What for?" was the answer. "The contractor and the builder (*usta*) know what should be done." It is this continuity and rupture between the plans of the state and the practices of the people that I have been trying to emphasize in this book.

At the same time, these enactments emerge from a specific sense of meaning, justice, and order. People recognize that these acts are "illegal," and some excuse the government's attempts to restrict construction on state-owned land and the use of public spaces for unintended and unauthorized actions such as selling vegetables and goods on the sidewalk. One man, who himself has built two rooms next to his apartment, explained that the government should regulate the construction and usage of urban space. If the government did not effectively control who is building and where, the man argues, people would take over every inch of the city, and there would be no places for people even to walk. But such views, which are shared by others, are often followed by the argument "What else can we do? Shall we live in the street? Does the government want people to starve?" In many ways, these practices are "seen as natural and moral responses to the urgency of survival and desire for dignified life" (Bayat 1997b: 61).

While Magdy and his neighbors view the changes introduced to their housing project as positive contributions to the development and prosperity of the neighborhood and Cairo at large (as described in the previous chapter), government officials (including the governor) view these changes as major problems that prevent the development and beautification of Cairo. Additions such as those introduced by Hisham are labeled as part of unplanned areas or *'ashwai'at*. These areas are largely depicted in the state public discourse as the source of disorder, ugly deformities, cancer cells, and factories for the production of terrorism[6] (Hanna 1996; *al-Alam al-Yaum*, March–April 1993; *al-Ahram*, August 1993). In many ways, this is similar to how officials used negative constructions to justify moving the people of Bulaq twenty years ago. The implications of this strategy were discussed at length in chapter 3, where I illustrated how the language used in the state public discourse has been internalized by the old residents, who use it to stigmatize and segregate the relocated group.

People also have a good sense of the "spaces of tolerance" (Foucault 1979: 82) allowed in the system of power. They, for example, know which additions are considered "nice" (usually those changes that leave positive impressions on others, especially government officials) and which additions are seen as ugly and therefore are most likely to be penalized. As a woman explained, she was very scared when she saw government employees checking changes introduced to apartments around hers and expressing their intention to destroy some of these alterations. She was worried because her family had just added a room to expand their one-bedroom apartment (on the ground floor). The large amount of money and effort they had invested in this room made her "heart jump to her throat" out of fear that the officials would order the removal of their room or fine them. She relaxed quickly, as she explained, when she remembered that only people who implement shacklike additions (*'ishash*) are penalized (through fine or removal of the additions), while others, like her family, who invest a lot of money in making clean, well-painted, and "nice-looking" changes, do not have these changes removed. In most of these cases, additions are saved by paying some money to government employees.

These tactics and strategies are also linked to people's views of the state and its roles. Men and women know the state through its public discourses (mainly circulated in the media) and through their direct interaction with its officials, institutions, and agents. As shown in chapter 1, the state has a remarkable ability to present a unified image of itself. Government officials used the same set of negative constructions to describe the group and expressed similar views about progress, the public good, and modern housing to justify relocation. People also often view the government as a unified entity, especially when they discuss the government's role in providing and limiting their access to services and resources: "The government (*el-hukuma*) does not care for us because we are poor," or "The government targets us just because we are young men and walk in the city center," or "The government sends its parrots (religious men hired by the government) to preach to us." But they individualize its actors when they interact with its officials on a daily basis. They try to find different tactics (such as praising, begging, and pleading) and strategies (such as bribing and using mediators) to secure access to resources or avoid punishment.[7]

Similarly, government officials in Cairo are differentiated actors with their own interests and visions of order and the modern city. They differ in their priorities and expectations. In fact, there is a system (referred to in the literature as "informal") that allows government officials to use their positions and connections to increase their income and boost their symbolic power beyond the boundaries of their schools, offices, and police stations. Teachers in public schools, who are grossly underpaid, for example, "force" students to take private lessons — if they do not, they will not pass their exams. It is the money that teachers acquire from lessons, and not their government salary, that supports them and their families. A state bureaucrat may prefer to take some money rather than to charge a family for the unauthorized use of government electric connections. Many officials who interact with people seem to place less emphasis than planners and policy makers on ideas about order and beauty and choose to accept money to overlook various changes. A policeman is often more willing to supplement his little salary with some extra cash than to report or destroy new constructions. An officer may be more willing to get some fancy foods such as shrimp and fruits than to confiscate products or equipment that is used on the side of the street without a license from the authorities.

While this system allows some people to broaden their bargaining space and to negotiate many issues (from violation of land codes to traffic tickets), it also indicates to others, such as Hisham and his neighbors, that the government's apparatus is unjust and is not geared toward protecting their rights. Rather, it all depends on connections and money. People strongly believe that the rich, who have more money and better connections, enjoy more protection and secure access to various urban resources. In this context, the ability to manipulate state officials is highly regarded.

"Fooling" government officials, for instance, is viewed positively. It is part of a larger moral economy that legitimizes and highly regards the ability to trick the powerful, outsmart them, and get what one views as his or her right. It is a mixture of improvisation and utilization of available cultural elements to subvert and turn a challenging situation to one's advantage. Samih explained how the family is planning to protect the additions of his younger brother, Magdy: "When one goes to see the judge, it is important to cry in front of him and to explain that the additions are necessary for the survival of the family.[8] One should not say that 'I just felt like expanding (*awassi*) my apartment.' Weeping in front of the judge is crucial to make sure that he will not order the removal of the construction." This appeal, just like the suggestion made by Abu Hosni in the introduction, softens the heart of the judge and makes him rule in favor of Samih's brother. By playing on the judge's emotions and drawing on the support of others who also have made similar additions, people feel assured about the future of new constructions. They hope that even if they are not totally pardoned, the judge will only fine them, as has happened in other housing projects. They will then split the fine, and, as they calculate, it is much cheaper to pay the fine than to find an affordable apartment in Cairo. Some, especially those who have consulted lawyers, count on the inefficiency of the Egyptian bureaucracy and believe that their cases will "sleep" in the court and simply be forgotten.

In his study of squatter settlements in Iran, Asef Bayat (1997a, 1997b) coined the phrase "the quiet encroachment of the ordinary" to refer to "a silent, patient, protracted and pervasive advancement of ordinary people on the propertied and powerful in order to survive hardships and better their lives" (Bayat 1997b: 57). Bayat's important phrase "quiet encroachment" captures several features of the practices that I have been describing. For one thing, Hisham and his neighbors are "calmly and quietly" moving forward to improve their lives (56). They are motivated by "the force of necessity — the necessity to survive and live a dignified life" (58). Similar to the actions of urban squatters in Tehran, these changes are also "significant in themselves without intending necessarily to undermine political authority" (58). The aim of people in al-Zawiya, for example, is not to mobilize to change the laws that regulate the use of space but rather to create realities that deactivate current laws. My analysis, however, departs from Bayat's in at least two important ways. First, although the additions I examined in al-Zawiya are implemented quietly and quickly so that they will not be seen or heard by government officials, as soon as they are finished, they become important visible signs that have the power to transform the project and Cairo at large. The word *quiet* downplays the ability of Magdy's new apartment, his brother's shop, and the balconies of many of his neighbors to disrupt the state's attempts to homogenize their housing project and Cairo's image. Second, Bayat emphasized that these acts become "political"[9] only when they are threatened by the state. It is then that people mobilize collectively to protect and defend their gains. However, I have aimed to shift attention to the broader political implications of these acts and to the ways that their intended and unintended consequences challenge the government's attempts to control Cairo and its spaces. As discussed in chapter 1, the state discourse emphasized the importance of the face of Cairo, which was to be "surgically beautified," in presenting a modern image of the Egyptian nation. This discourse placed great emphasis on objectifying modernity in visible forms that could be gazed at by tourists and upper-class Egyptians. By objectifying their socioeconomic needs and status into visible forms, the residents of al-Zawiya also transform this modern image and remake it from their particular location in the social space. These changes therefore become visible signs that convey to others (including government officials) the active role of Hisham and other residents of al-Zawiya in shaping the city.

What interested me in this book was not to classify these practices as resistance and/or confirmative. In fact, I find this dichotomy to be unproductive in that it reduces the complexity of people's practices into rigid categories and ignores the multiple meanings and consequences of these practices. It also puts the researchers in the position of a judge who is evaluating and attaching positive (i.e., resistance) or negative (i.e, confirmative) meanings to these practices. One of the most interesting things about the practices I have been describing in this book is their effects and ability to transform plans, projects, spaces, and images. It is this power, I believe, that is significant in understanding the role of the ordinary practitioners in the making and remaking of the city. Focusing on this power allows us to go beyond viewing the city as a ready-made whole that is beyond the practices of Hisham and his neighbors. It is not sufficient to recognize these practices as adaptive or survival strategies and examine them *in* the city. Rather, they should be placed at the center of any theorization *of* the city and urban life. Vendors running with merchandise when they see the police, merchants struggling to use the street corner rather than limiting their activities to the bounded formal markets, young men visiting local coffee shops, women taking daily trips to the vegetable market, Muslim activists preaching in the city bus and reciting the Quran in the tramway, and the numerous mosques that are proliferating around and within the project are all shaping not only the housing project and al-Zawiya but also Cairo at large. In short, although history tends to privilege grand plans of the state and its designers, cities are not made only by the powerful, the planners, and policy makers. They are also made and remade through the practices of the city dwellers.

Therefore, it is not enough to examine state policies and how they are translated into housing projects, schools, markets, streets, and green areas. The study of urban space must also include a close analysis of the global forces and discourses that inform national policies and plans. Above all, it has to conceptualize the central role of the spatial practices of the urban dwellers who continually remake the city through their daily activities and movement. These practices are central to an adequate view of urban space as always being in the process of formation and to the conceptualization of change not as an interruption in a steady flow of continuity but as a central feature of daily life and the production of urban spaces. The role of the ordinary practitioners of the city is especially important for a productive understanding of how local, national, and global forces are articulated in the formation of urban spaces and cultural identities.

Competing Discourses

> *The modern metropolis has always evoked feelings of alienation and disorientation, but it has equally been associated with new possibilities for encounter and solidarity.*
> Kevin Robins, "Prisoners of the City"

Ali, the shoe factory worker mentioned in chapter 5, has many dreams and desires that are largely informed by the movies he watches, the stories he hears from friends (who work or have relatives in other Arab countries), and the strolls he takes with his peers in upper-class areas. One of his dreams is to buy a villa in Switzerland for skiing during the winter, another villa in India where he would hire singers and dancers to perform for him as he has seen on videotapes, and a palace in Saudi Arabia to facilitate his performing the pilgrimage (*hajj*) every year. To travel in comfort to all these places, Ali dreams of buying a yacht that will enable him to get around far removed from the hassles of public transportation that he experiences daily. Meanwhile, Ali's mother went to Saudi Arabia to perform the *omra* (an abbreviated form of the *hajj* that may be performed at any time of the year). Although she had wanted to perform *hajj* for years, she had not been able to secure the money needed for the journey. Like some other "lucky" low-income people in Cairo, she decided to go to do the *omra*, which is considerably cheaper than the *hajj*. She planned to wait in Saudi Arabia for five months until the season of the pilgrimage. Her trip was arranged by an Egyptian travel agent who has several houses in Saudi Arabia. He charged her much less than she would have paid during the *hajj* season. However, to avoid deportation for "illegal *hajj*," she had to hide for most of the five months in a room, which she shared with several other Egyptian women, in one of the agent's houses in Mecca.

I grounded my discussion of globalization in concrete examples and precise enactments to illustrate how global images, goods, and discourses are appropriated in the formation of spaces and identities. The framework that I presented in this book connects sites, practices, and feelings and shows how these connections are central to the continuous production of urban locality. Tracing the logic of flows through precise enactments allows us to follow individual and collective trajectories (which may take us to India, Saudi Arabia, or Switzerland) and to analyze how global flows are articulated, transformed, and resisted in different contexts and by various social groups. It therefore allows us to avoid limiting globalization to a geographically based concept that focuses only (or even primarily) on flows between the West and the Rest. Ali's dreams take him not only to Switzerland but also to India and Saudi Arabia. His mother's desires and religious devotion take her to Saudi Arabia. As I tried to demonstrate throughout this book, class and gender structure people's access to jobs and travel destinations as well as their appropriation of various global discourses and images. Magdy's aspirations take him to Kuwait, and his brother travels to Libya to acquire the money and goods he desires. While upper-class Egyptians travel with ease to and from the United States and Europe (for education, vacation, and treatment), cities such as Paris, London, and New York are largely off limits to young men like Magdy. The West as a travel destination is so far removed from their reality that it is not even a dream. While there are "lucky" men like Magdy, who have managed to travel to the Gulf or Libya and to acquire the money needed to secure spacious and well-furnished homes, this market is getting tighter every day. Many young men, including Magdy's other three brothers, cannot find the jobs and the income they aspire for at home or abroad. Sadat's promise that young men would be able to own villas, drive cars, and acquire more consumer goods has not materialized for most Egyptians. Young men and women experience the frustration of dreaming of fancy cars, beautiful homes, and mobile phones. While I agree with Appadurai (1996) that there is pleasure where there is consumption, my ethnography also shows that there is pain and frustration. I have repeatedly emphasized the powerful desires stimulated by modern discourses and provided various examples of the dreams (of children and young men and women) informed by global images circulated in the media. The unfulfilled dreams of Ali and Amal (the young girl whose story was included in chapter 2) are representatives of a more general frustrating gap between what is desired and what is possible. Globalization excites the imagination, stimulates new desires, and introduces new expectations. But it also introduces the frustration of the failure to satisfy these desires and aspirations. These dreams and frustrations simultaneously privilege and challenge the appeal to religion as the basis for a unifying identity and for the moral power needed to appropriate positive aspects of modernity while relinquishing what is viewed as negative.

As I argued earlier, while the state public discourse has stigmatized the relocated group and the project has physically separated them from the rest of the neighborhood, religion in general and the mosque in particular have facilitated their interaction with other residents. Religion is also important in people's selective appropriation of modern discourses and images. In light of the tendency in sociological literature and popular media to equate Islam with fundamentalism, it is worth repeating here that the religious identity I have been discussing is situated between two extremes: the government, which since the early 1970s has been showing a strong orientation to Western modernity, and Muslim extremists, who try to reject various modern objects and discourses. Just as the practices of Hisham and his neighbors transform and redefine notions of modernity embedded in the housing units allocated to them by the state, people's attraction to religion is part of their critique of the state's strong identification with Western modernity. At the same time, the religious identity of Nuha and her neighbors is constructed through their struggle against the extreme position of some Muslim activists who try to restrict people's appropriation of various aspects of modernity in their efforts to replicate the practices of the Prophet in the modern time. As discussed in chapter 5, religious identity is not defined in isolation from modern discourses and objects. The growing number of modern educational and health services that are being offered in mosques,[10] the active use of the city bus by Islamic groups to communicate with people and "let them know," and the increasing display of religious signs in homes, shops, and vehicles are indicators of both increasing modernization and increasing

Islamization of Cairo and its people. Modernity cannot be seen as a master narrative that entails similar changes, in particular the shrinking of religiosity, in different societies, as modernization theorists have argued. Nor can it be seen as a totality that is either taken or rejected. Modern discourses and projects stimulate desires. They motivate dreams, bring joy, cause disruption, pain, and suffering. Rather than simply assuming that there are multiple modernities, I have aimed to draw attention to how certain aspects of modernity are appropriated in the daily life of actors like Nuha and Abu Hosni. This possibility of selectively appropriating modern discourses and images and using them to control and/or empower certain social groups is what really is unique and perhaps exciting about the current globalization of cultural signs and products.

Ali's dreams and his mother's trip highlight part of the structured globalization of Cairo. The huge gap between Ali's dreams and his family's realities is manifested in his mother's first and only trip outside Egypt. Unlike upper-class Egyptians, who can tour the world in jumbo jets, Ali's mother had to take a bus and a ferry boat to reach Saudi Arabia. While the trip by plane hardly takes two hours, Um Ali spent two whole days on the way in each direction. Her desire to perform the *hajj* forced her to stay away from her family and to live in hiding for almost five months. Just as trips to the mosque are linked with extra rewards that could contribute to the path toward paradise, the hardships confronted in performing the *hajj* are also invested with religious meanings and values. Ali's mother and others who take similar trips emphasize the rewards that they acquire by taking the long and arduous journey. While Islam structures Um Ali's daily life and interactions and helps her make some sense out of various hardships and inequalities, for her son and other young men, religion plays a more ambiguous role. Ali's desires and aspirations take him in different directions. He follows the struggles of Muslims in different parts of the world (from Bosnia to Chechnya) and talks about them as part of the same community. He also uses religion in his critique of government policies and actions and in his discussions of gender inequalities (especially when asserting the rights of men). Religion, however, is far from structuring his dreams and desires. Unlike his mother, who performs prayer on a regular basis, Ali rarely prays or goes to the mosque. He often refuses invitations to go to the mosque in favor of watching movies starring Arnold Schwarzenegger, attending local coffee shops, and smoking hashish with his friends. What will be the future role of religion for a young man like Ali, with his grand dreams and frustrated expectations?

Throughout this book, I have highlighted the uncertainty of the long-term role of religion, which has to compete with many other discourses and images, in shaping practices and identities. It is true that Islam is facilitating the creation of a sense of belonging between Muslims in the area. But the appeal to religion is also increasing the opposition between Muslims and Christians. It is true that Islam is used to criticize government policies and plans, but it is also true that religion is used to justify and legitimize various social (including gender) inequalities. While religion plays a powerful role in the life of Ali and his neighbors, it has to compete with other global forces and national policies that shape people's daily practices, expectations, and desires. Walls of buildings in al-Zawiya display symbols and signs related to people's identities and daily struggles. Inscriptions on walls encourage people to embrace some Islamic practices (e.g., calling upon women to veil themselves); verses from the Quran frame advertisements for schools and bookstores as well as slogans that support the president and the National Democratic Party; announcements invite women to join clinics in local mosques to lose weight; huge signs with images of bottles of Coca-Cola and Pepsi stimulate people to drink cold soft drinks; and advertisements call upon men to visit the "gym of Hercules"[11] to build their bodies. Announcements for local elections are posted with signs of the pyramids, fans, candles, phones, and guns, which are included to remind illiterate voters of the names of the candidates. All these symbols manifest competing desires and shape people's experiences and senses of belonging.

Religion, however, is an option that derives its power from its promise to address and resolve current daily problems associated with modernity and urban life. In one speech I attended in a mosque in al-Zawiya, the sheikh recited the following tradition (*hadith*): "There are four things that are the source of a man's happiness. These are a virtuous wife [*mar'a saaliha*], a righteous neighbor [*gaar baarr*], a spacious house [*daar fasiha*], and a comfortable vehicle [*markib hani*]. And there are four things that are the source of a man's misery. These are a bad wife [*mar'a taliha*], an undutiful neighbor [*gaar 'aqq*], a narrow house [*daar dayyiqa*], and a bad vehicle [*markib sayyi'a*]." The sheikh provided a detailed interpretation of this tradition, linking it directly to pressing issues in the daily life of al-Zawiya's inhabitants: housing, transportation, and relationships between spouses and neighbors. For example, he interpreted the *markib sayyi'a* as the current transportation system in Cairo and described riding the city bus or the *otobis* as the utmost insult (*akhir bahdala*). His interpretation also touched upon the many changes that continuously transform people's lives. A bad woman, he explained, is the wife who does not encourage her husband to worship God, while the virtuous woman is the one who does not ask her husband to turn off the television when the Quran is being broadcast.

The linkage between happiness and space did not need elaboration. I was cramped with hundreds of other women and children in the section designated for us in the mosque. Many of these women are struggling to secure better housing options for their families. I was sitting next to Um Amal (the mother of the child whose story I included in chapter 2) and three of her young daughters who had insisted on joining us for Friday prayer. Compared to Hisham and Salah, Amal's family is unlucky. They live on the fifth floor and need the cooperation of all the neighbors who live in their block. Their one-bedroom unit is also close to the police station, which makes any expansion directly exposed to the gaze of the state. These two factors prevent them from expanding their apartment. After that sermon, Um Amal started trying to convince her husband to sell their current unit, hoping to secure enough money to buy a larger one even in the remote neighborhood of Hilwan, an option that is not preferred by her but seems to be the only one left. As far as I know, they are still searching.

Notes

Introduction: Researching "Modern" Cairo

1. The name of the neighborhood is pronounced "iz-Zawiya el-Hamra." It is written in different ways in the literature. To avoid confusion, I use the classical transliteration throughout this book. People usually drop "el-Hamra" and refer to the area as iz-Zawiya.

2. See Singerman (1995) for a detailed analysis of informal networks in Cairo's old quarters and the political significance of these networks.

3. The literature also often refers to al-Zawiya only in the context of these clashes (Ansari 1984; Kepel 1993; Hanna 1997).

4. See, for example, Cairo's map in Seton-Williams and Stocks (1988).

5. *Baladi,* which is discussed further in chapter 3, is a complex concept that signifies a sense of authenticity and originality. It is derived from the word *balad,* which refers to different units such as a village, a city, or a country. *Baladi* in this context refers to the areas and residents of old popular quarters in Cairo.

6. These neighborhoods have also attracted the attention of writers such as Naguib Mahfouz, whose wonderful novels document various aspects of life in old Cairo.

7. At that time, an Egyptian pound was equivalent to around thirty-four American cents.

8. The published data from the 1996 census do not disaggregate the population by religion.

9. Relationships became familylike with some informants. So when members of my family visited from Jordan, it was necessary to exchange visits with close informants.

10. Huda and Ahmed have enacted the marriage contract, which means that legally they are married. Socially, however, they are not married (i.e., they are not

supposed to have sexual relations) until Ahmed secures an apartment and they have a wedding party.

11. For a critique of these studies, see Lapidus (1979), Abu-Lughod (1987), and Eickelman (1989).

12. Because Zidane was Algerian and Muslim, people assumed that he was also Arab. No one in the neighborhood mentioned his Berber origin.

13. Until recently, social theories tended to treat space as "the dead, the fixed, the undialectical, the immobile," while time was seen "richness, fecundity, life, dialectic" (Foucault 1980b: 70). This approach has been criticized by several authors who emphasize that space is not a mere container for social activities: "space is socially constructed" and "the social is spatially constructed" (Massey 1994: 70).

14. In this work, Foucault shows how prisoners who are distributed in space so that they can be observed without being able to see their observers internalize the feeling that they are under the gaze of power and become reproducers of their own subjugation.

Chapter 1. Relocation and the Creation of a Global City

1. For more on Cairo's history, see Stewart (1968), Abu-Lughod (1971), Mitchell (1988), Raymond (1993), Rodenbeck (1998), and Myntti (1999).

2. As will become clear from this brief background, history privileges the role of political leaders in the making of cities. There is very little information on the role of ordinary dwellers in the building of Cairo — or other cities, for that matter.

3. Although it was not mentioned in national newspapers, people also stated that part of the group was relocated to Madinet el-Saalam, in northeastern Cairo.

4. Relocation to construct facilities for tourists is also common in other parts of Egypt. In one village near Luxor, clashes erupted between the police and the villagers over the demolition of houses built on "land claimed by the state as archaeological sites" (*Economist*, January 31, 1998: 8). The villagers were to be removed "to make way for tourists. Villagers note with bitter irony that while their houses are being torn down, other buildings are going up — including, recently, a police station" (8). The confrontation led to the death of four people, and twenty-nine were injured.

5. It is worth noting that "investment companies, banks, and tourism" were the main areas of the economy that flourished during *infitah* (Waterbury 1983: 145).

6. For a discussion of modernity and how it privileges the visual, see Massey (1994), Lefebvre (1991), and Scott (1998).

7. The image of Egypt and how the country is viewed by others is of great importance for most Egyptians. See Diase (1996) for a discussion of the "anger" of the educated about "media programs that were allegedly giving audiences a very negative picture of Egypt" (95).

8. See Wright (1983) for a rich description of similar projects in the United States during the 1930s.

9. Negative constructions of the urban poor have been produced historically and used to justify different policies implemented by various governments. See Mitchell (1988) for an analysis of such constructions under the British colonization of Egypt. See also Wright (1983) for an interesting discussion of the poor in the United States and how they have been blamed for problems in big cities since the last century. See Mele (2000) for a discussion of the various stereotypes and negative representations of New York's poor used to legitimize the planning and restructuring of parts of the city's spaces.

10. The term used by the minister was *ghawazi,* which refers to female dancers but indicates that they are also willing to perform sexual services.

11. The language is similar to that used around the middle of the twentieth century in the United States that emphasized "sanitation, ventilation, privacy, and order" in the construction of public housing (Wright 1983: 232; see also Mele 2000).

12. Projects with similar objectives are well known in other countries such as Brazil, where officials assumed that "human 'recuperation' would follow physical rehabilitation" (Perlman 1982: 229).

13. National newspapers emphasized that the relocated population consisted mainly of working-class Egyptians. Each person who was interviewed was questioned by the president and the journalists about his work and about job opportunities that were available in al-Zawiya al-Hamra.

14. A title that Sadat acquired among others, such as the Hero of Victory, the Hero of Crossing (in reference to the crossing of the Suez Canal in the 1973 war), the Hero of Peace, and the Hero of Democracy.

15. It is worth noting that after a few months, both newspapers stopped publishing anything against the project. They both stressed its positive impact on people's life and reported on Sadat's visits to the area. In mid-1981, however, *al-Sha'b* started attacking the project and used it to argue against the government's attempts to remove other parts of Bulaq.

16. Although part of the relocated population used to occupy the state land (*hikr*), the ownership rights were blurred over many years of residency in the area, and house "owners" got compensation regardless of their ownership status. A law was issued to strip ownership from the people and give the Governorate of Cairo the right to decide on the compensation offered to people.

17. The chants of the demonstrators are documented in Abdel Razaq (1979: 81–82). I translate some of them here:

1. He [Sadat] wears the latest fashions while ten of us live in one room.
2. Thieves of the *infitah,* the people are hungry, not comfortable.
3. It is not enough that we wear sackcloth, they also want to take away our bread.

18. The emphasis on wide streets as signs of modernity in the new location cannot be missed here.

19. Recently, the new governor of Cairo revived the idea of investing in the

vacant area. He suggested that a park and multistory underground parking facility be constructed (see *al-Gomhuria,* November 18, 1997).

20. In 1997, a conflict erupted between the Ministry of Foreign Affairs and the residents of Bulaq who lived near the ministry, which relocated its building to Maspiro in 1992. The ministry was trying to "beautify" the area by removing some of the houses that surrounded its building. It was offering compensations and/or housing options in other parts of the city, but residents of Maspiro refused these offers and decided to go court to cancel an administrative decision that confiscated their land for "the public good" (*al-Hayat,* August 7, 1979: 1).

Chapter 2. Relocation and the Daily Use of "Modern" Spaces

1. An Egyptian pound is worth around thirty-four American cents. There are one hundred piasters in one pound.

2. The number of apartments in the block varies depending on the number of bedrooms in the individual unit. For example, blocks with one-bedroom apartments have twenty units (four on each floor), while blocks with two-bedroom apartments have ten units (two on each floor).

3. There are many who believe that Sadat did not know about these small and disliked units. He thought, as people emphasize, that all the units were two or three rooms.

4. If the deceased is a relative, a friend, or a neighbor, it is customary to wait for at least forty days before the wedding (often with little or no festivity) takes place.

5. Some families tried to get larger housing units by bringing relatives from the countryside and presenting them as residents of the housing unit. People also claim that some of those who had connections with the Egyptian bureaucracy managed to get a larger apartment when the family size was considered large.

6. Throughout this book, I avoid using the word *adaptation,* a common word in studies of relocation. This is motivated by my desire to avoid the passivity, conformity, and unidimensional connotations of this word. *Adaptation* is defined in *Merriam-Webster's New Collegiate Dictionary* as "the act or process of adapting: the state of being adapted" and as "adjustment to environmental conditions: as a: adjustment of a sense organ to the intensity or quality of stimulation b: modification of an organism or its parts that makes it more fit for existence under the conditions of its environment." Rather than simply viewing these spatial practices as adaptation, I aim to show their complexity and how they transform and shape individual housing units and the project at large.

7. A monolithic definition of modernity also tends to be assumed in studies of urban housing in Egypt (see, for example, Steinberg 1991; as-Safty 1987; Hassan 1985).

8. In this regard, I disagree with some writers who have seen in this distinction a dichotomy that corresponds to a rigid differentiation between a powerful

dominant group and powerless dominated masses (see, for instance, Frow 1995; Turino 1990). Instead, I read de Certeau as saying that the same social agent is an "active user" who is simultaneously a strategist and a tactician. This "active user" finds various ways to achieve his or her shifting goals and to challenge objective realities. This agent is more active than Bourdieu's "actor," who is constrained by the limited strategies that are structured by the habitus.

9. Officials promised, as reported in daily newspapers, that families who arranged their apartments "quickly and nicely" would be given E£ 10. Sadat also donated some furniture to two needy families who were not able to furnish their apartments.

10. Women also felt sorry for me because I was living away from my family, a role they all volunteered to fill. They also thought that my apartment, which was owned by the American University in Cairo, was not a good deal. Since the apartment was furnished, we tenants did not have any claims on the apartment in the long run; the owner legally had the right to evict us whenever he or she wanted. The fact that the place was furnished also limited my choices in displaying my social distinction.

11. In some cases, residents on the ground floor created new entrances for their apartments, turned the area in front of them into a small garden, and formed a unit that was totally separate from the rest of the block.

12. My discussion here should not be understood as denying any interest from male family members in the housing unit. In fact, men also inspect their housing units, and a husband may start a fight with his wife if he feels that she is not taking good care of their apartment. He is socially supported in this case, and the woman's duty in taking care of the housing unit is reinforced through direct interference from her family and in-laws.

13. Only a few openings were made by the original designers to allow people access to the roof. To drill a hole in the blocks with no access to the roof, people have to negotiate with the residents of the fifth floor, and if the latter refuse, as is the case with Um Hassan, no one can use the roof. In other cases, people have agreed on drilling the hole and have cooperated to raise poultry on the rooftop.

Chapter 3. Old Places, New Identities

1. *Sha'bi,* as will be discussed later in this chapter, is derived from the word *sha'b,* which means "people" or "folk." It indicates authenticity and rootedness and is linked with many positive qualities, such as cooperation between neighbors, respect for traditions, and willingness to help those in need.

2. It should be noticed that while most of the neighbors of this young woman are from Upper Egypt, the group in Bulaq includes many families who immigrated from Lower Egypt and who consider themselves *Fallahin* as well as others who consider themselves urbanites.

3. Eshash al-Turguman is viewed by its people as part of Bulaq, and they define themselves as Bulaqis. Other Egyptians tend to separate it from Bulaq and

emphasize its character as a slum area that had to be removed. They also tend to think that only residents of Eshash al-Turguman were relocated. It is important to note that this is not a correct assumption: others were relocated from other parts of Bulaq.

4. People still refer to their own *hara* when they want to distinguish themselves from others or when they try to show their closeness to those who used to live in the same *hara*.

5. As a woman from New York who was visiting her son in Texas explained to me in Austin's airport, "It is the smell of bread and other foods that give a place a 'homey feeling.'" Even though all her children are grown up and live outside New York, she still finds herself compelled to cook and bake pastry on a regular basis. She often gives what she bakes to her neighbors. What is important for her is the smell that cooking gives to the house.

6. My usage of the term *capital* draws on the work of Pierre Bourdieu (1984, 1990), who differentiated between economic (or material), social (connections within the group and relationships with others), cultural (information and education), and symbolic (accumulated distinction and prestige) capital.

7. Women also used to shop in government cooperatives in other upper-class neighborhoods around their area such as Garden City (Early 1993).

8. *Al-balad* refers to different localities that range from the whole country to a city, a town, or a village.

9. What is considered by government officials and some writers as "lack of privacy" (Rugh 1979: 20) is seen by the people as closeness that facilitates cooperation and creates solidarity. See chapter 4 for more on the theme of privacy.

10. For more on *gam'iyyat*, see Hoodfar (1997) and Singerman (1995).

11. This is also one of the main reasons for people's unwillingness to live in the new communities and cities that are constructed around Cairo.

12. I find people's attitudes toward mountains very interesting. Mountains are feared and associated with danger. People could not believe it when they saw pictures of Lebanon and Jordan that show houses constructed on the top of mountains. I believe that this attitude is largely related to the fact that their experience of mountains is limited to the Egyptian media, which tend to present them as shelters for wild animals, thieves, and fugitives.

13. In a few cases, when the family could not get rid of an *'afriit* that inhibited their apartments, they sold these apartments with a big loss to move into another unit. Such an *'afriit* emerges usually in the bathroom and can be pacified through thinking of God (but without verbally pronouncing his name) and reciting a special prayer to protect the self against being possessed by it.

14. Many parents do not allow their daughters to enter *el-masaakin* without being chaperoned by a family member.

15. One way in which women contest these ideas is through songs that describe how capable and experienced they are. Even the phrase *tarbiyyat masaakin* is subversively used in daily conversations to indicate how skillful and strong they are.

Chapter 4. Gender and the Struggle over Public Spaces

1. After beating a female relative (usually a sister or a wife), especially if that happens for what is considered a "trivial" reason, the male relative apologizes to her, offers her tea or a cold drink, and often gives her some money to compensate for the pain he caused her.

2. The notion of privacy has not been sufficiently addressed in the literature on the Middle East. Aside from the dichotomy between outside (public) and inside (private) and its relation to Islam, little attention has been devoted to the meaning of privacy and how family members, and not only women, construct and negotiate notions of privacy.

3. The word *khas* means among other things "private" or "personal," while *'aam* means "general" or "public." These two words, however, do not have the same connotations implied in the Greek distinction between the *polis* or the public domain and the private domain of the family. Among certain social groups, the Arabic word *khususia* is increasingly acquiring a meaning that is similar to the English word *privacy*. But this meaning is still far from being universal and is absent in al-Zawiya al-Hamra.

4. As mentioned in chapter 2, the distribution of the housing units proceeded on the basis of the number of rooms that the family used to occupy in Bulaq. It was only when more than one nuclear family shared the same unit that each was given a separate apartment. Some families managed to acquire more than one unit by bringing a relative from the countryside. Abu 'Abdo, for example, brought his mother-in-law from Upper Egypt when he heard about the plan to relocate them. He then appealed to the local authorities and managed to get an extra one-room apartment because his family was large and his mother-in-law was staying with them.

5. Various studies suggest that segregation is class based. While rich families can afford, as Tucker (1993) argued, to keep women at home, economic needs frustrate the attempts of the poor to keep women secluded.

6. This has been reported in projects in other countries. See, for example, Shami (1996) for a discussion of an upgrading project in Jordan.

7. In some cases, young women secretly go out with a boyfriend or a fiancé to some of these local attractions, especially the zoo and el-Qanatir.

8. *Khimar* is a garment that is considered the "true Islamic dress." It covers the upper part of the body, including the hair, the neck, the shoulders, the breasts, and the back.

9. Similarly, Halla's male siblings immediately blame her work when she refuses to serve them food late at night or to iron their clothes.

10. The same tendency was reported in other public housing projects in the United States and England (see Jacobs 1961).

11. It is important to note that these hopes remain more an ideal than a reality. Not many mothers have the time and power to keep track of their children's movements, especially those who have only male children.

12. Due to this fact, my data on the coffeehouse are based mainly on accounts of young men and their parents.

13. These coffee shops (*qahawi*) are better called tea shops because few drink coffee while most drink tea.

14. Few married men can afford to go to the coffee shop because they work most of the day, often in two jobs.

15. A notable recent exception is Deborah Kapchan's wonderful study (1996) of women and the market in Morocco.

16. This is one of the main reasons why women avoid wearing golden necklaces, which are easy to snatch, and choose bracelets instead.

Chapter 5. Religion in a Global Era

1. Muslims represent about 88 percent of al-Zawiya's inhabitants, as was mentioned in the introduction.

2. I use the word *promise* to highlight the fact that although religion is very important in forming a collective identity, it has to compete, as will become clear later, with other forces that shape people's daily life and struggles.

3. This is not only true of this particular group. The state discourse continues to use similar negative constructions when officials and planners discuss *'ashawi'at* (unplanned or random areas). These areas are depicted as cancer cells, devilish expansions, and "factories for breeding terrorism" that should be surgically removed (see *al-Ahram*, August 1993; *al-Hayat*, April 17, 1993; *al-Gumhuriyya*, April 22, 1993; Hanna 1993).

4. This was confirmed by the Minister of the Interior, who explained that the land was owned by the Governorate of Cairo and was designated to be used to build the Animal Feed Factory and a mosque for its workers. The Christian man bought it from another Muslim person in the area and acquired legal documents that proved his ownership of the land (*Al-Akhbar*, June 21, 1981: 3).

5. Christian informants emphasize that the land was legally owned by 'Aziz. Similarly, Milad Hanna (1997) wrote that the Christian man acquired documents from the court that proved his legal ownership. According to him, the Animal Feed Factory, with the support of the ruling party, managed to get an administrative order from the Governorate of Cairo to use the land to build a mosque.

6. In January 1998, president Hosni Mubarak issued a decree that granted governors the authority to make decisions related to the repair and maintenance of churches. The power to license the building of new churches, however, is still retained by the president (see *al-Ahram Weekly*, January 29–February 4, 1998).

7. According to the transcripts of the public prosecutor, Jama'at al-Jihad was the active group in al-Zawiya during these clashes (Ansari 1984). People, however, refer to these activists as *al-Sunniyin*.

8. One Christian informant emphasized that the police were supportive of Muslims and that Sadat was to be blamed for these clashes. He told me that his family and relatives always say, "May God send Sadat to hell" (*Allah yighimu*).

9. The Minister of the Interior stated that 10 people were killed (4 Muslims,

5 Christians, and 1 unidentified), 54 injured, and 113 arrested (*al-Akhbar*, June 21, 1981: 3).

10. As usual, he blamed the communists for escalating the conflict, which started as "a simple fight" between two female neighbors, one of whom happened to be a Muslim and the other a Christian.

11. One woman suggested that Sadat had to "say something" to explain the clashes when he was confronted by journalists and politicians in the United States. She emphasized that after coming back to Egypt, he retracted his statements.

12. Boycotting Christian merchants has been publicized by Islamic groups as necessary to prevent Copts from gathering money that they supposedly invest in buying weapons (Ansari 1984).

13. Personally, I never managed to see physical differences between Muslims and Christians. The cross on the inner wrist and clothes, however, are strong visible indications of religious identity.

14. People are very sensitive to names, which are often used as clear indicators of the religious identity of the person.

15. While my discussion here is limited to the mosque, studies suggest that the church plays a similar role in the Christian community (Abdel Fattah 1997).

16. This is to prevent confusion among those who do not know the rules of the performance and who could make mistakes by standing when they should be sitting or vice versa.

17. In the women's section, which I had access to, the Friday prayer was coordinated by a woman who made sure that we were standing correctly and secured room to squeeze in newcomers.

18. It is important to notice that my discussion of the mosque and religious identity is not a negation of their importance in the old location (see Early 1993 for a discussion of what she calls "popular Islam" and "religious conservatism" or "new orthodoxy" in Bulaq). I argue, though, that they gained more significance in articulating the presence of the people in al-Zawiya al-Hamra.

19. The mosque also attracts many people who seek some basic modern services. Through charitable organizations, the mosque provides socially required services such as affordable education, health care, vocational training, day care services, and financial support to the poor.

20. Young women who choose to pray in mosques outside their neighborhoods are also provided with a morally unquestionable chance for a social outing. Detailed narratives are constructed after each trip, describing such things as the long time they waited for the city bus, the impressive *khutba,* and the large crowd gathered to pray inside and outside the mosque.

21. The most needy (such as widows) are offered small amounts of money to encourage them to attend these lessons together with their children.

22. Other factors (such as passengers' temporary captivity in the bus, the relative diversity of passengers, and the protection that the mobility of the bus offers to the activist) also make the bus a strategic site for *al-Sunniyin.*

23. It is ironic that al-Zawiya is viewed as *'ashwai'* by many Egyptians and is often depicted as such in the state public discourse.

24. Unlike Western modernity, this modernity includes a desire to maintain some form of continuity with the past. See Armbrust's (1996) study of Egyptian mass culture for a sophisticated analysis of this aspect of "Egyptian modernity."

25. A clear example of this is the widely publicized case of the "devil's worshipers." The "transgression" of the accused was directly linked in the public discourse and daily conversation with money, traveling abroad, dressing in black, and listening to foreign music.

26. For example, Sadat managed to get a religious decree (*fatwa*) to support his peace treaty and used part of the American aid in 1978 to strengthen the Koran Program Services (Diase 1996).

27. See Eickelman and Piscatori (1996) for a critique of modernization theory and its assumptions regarding religion.

Chapter 6. Roads to Prosperity

1. The key money is an advance that is paid to the owner before moving into the apartment.

2. Appadurai (1996) made a distinction between locality and neighborhood. The latter is "the actually existing social forms in which locality, as a dimension or value, is variably realized" (179).

3. Magdy has three sisters and four brothers. Only one of the four brothers managed to travel to Libya and Iraq. The other three have been dreaming of and planning on traveling (without success) to a neighboring Arab country.

4. Paradoxically, to realize his dreams and meet the expectations of others, Magdy has been forced to work abroad for much longer than anticipated. Though his future in-laws expected him to return permanently by the end of the first year after the engagement, Magdy will not be back until the end of the fourth year. He also borrows money from his co-workers and participates in savings associations to secure large sums of money to send back home. When his fiancée expresses her frustration with his long absence, he reminds her that he needs to furnish the apartment and save some money to start a business in Cairo because he does not want to travel after getting married.

5. I say "temporarily" because there are indications that the government tries to break down such collective cooperation by prosecuting individual families separately. So this collectivity may not last for long.

6. A *zawiya* is usually a place for Sufi Brotherhood meetings. This association, however, was not made in people's interpretation of the name.

7. Many similar apartments in the old and the new housing projects have been turned into shops, workshops, and clinics.

Conclusion. Homes, Mosques, and the Making of a Global Cairo

1. For more on Mubarak's policies, see Springborg (1989) and Rodenbeck (1998).

2. Whenever I went to local mosques for Friday prayer, a young woman carrying a box asked us to donate some money to build or expand mosques. We were usually prepared with bills of twenty-five or fifty piasters to deposit in the box.

3. Just like these expansions on the side of the main street, many mosques extend to the sidewalk on Friday. Plastic mats are placed in front of various mosques to accommodate the growing number of worshipers.

4. A major part of the problem in conceptualizing resistance is that, as Sherry Ortner (1999) argued, most discussions of resistance tend to be "culturally 'thin,'" insufficiently grounded in local views of the meaning of morality, justice, subjecthood, and agency" (146).

5. A good example of this tendency is reflected in two articles (Ortner 1995; Abu-Lughod 1990) that are often cited in anthropological discussions of resistance. Although both Sherry Ortner and Lila Abu-Lughod presented insightful critiques of studies of resistance, neither of them tried to crystallize a specific meaning of "resistance," which comes out everywhere and nowhere simultaneously.

6. Similarly, mosques that are outside the grip of the state are viewed as sites where extremists brainwash the youth and recruit their followers (Abdel Fattah 1995). These mosques and Hisham's additions are seen as threatening to the country and national unity. The Egyptian state has been struggling for the past twenty years to extend its control over private mosques. A 1996 law, for example, does not allow preaching in mosques (private and public) without a permit from the Ministry of Endowment (al-Wasat, April, 10, 2000: 7).

7. Although it is rarely reported in the media, one often hears rumors about conflicts between ministers and officials over plans to upgrade and beautify Cairo. The Egyptian capital is run by officials (such as the governor) appointed by the president, while elected representatives merely play a consultative role (Denis 1997). The presence of all ministries in Cairo, however, often creates conflicts and contradictions over providing services and managing different aspects of life in the city.

8. Because this boom in construction is recent, no one that I know has been to see the judge yet. However, people discuss and prepare themselves for this possibility. They base their expectations and strategies on the experience of people in housing projects in other parts of Cairo.

9. The notion of the "political" remains vague in Bayat's analysis (see also Bayat 2000). There is little discussion of what makes an act political aside from its being linked to collective action. At the same time, the additions of Magdy and his neighbors demand more cooperation, coordination, and sharing of information than indicated by Bayat (2000: 548).

10. Some mosques also host classes for sewing and needlework and adult education and offer spaces for funerals and weddings.

11. *Hercules,* the American TV serial, became very popular in al-Zawiya during 1996–1997. The name Hercules started appearing on many items, especially those geared toward children and young men, such as caps, school bags, and packets of chips. It is also used to name gyms and sports facilities.

Bibliography

Newspapers and Magazines

Al-Ahram, daily (in Arabic)
Al-Ahram Weekly
Al-Akhbar, daily (in Arabic)
Al-Alam al-Yaum (in Arabic)
Al-Gomhuria, daily (in Arabic)
Al-Hayat, daily (in Arabic)
Al-Sha'b, daily (in Arabic)
Al-Wasat, weekly (in Arabic)
The Economist, weekly
The Egyptian Gazette, weekly
Mayo, weekly (in Arabic)

Dictionaries

Al-Mawrid English-Arabic Dictionary, 20th ed. 1986. Beirut: Dar El-Ilm Lil-Malayen.

Merriam-Webster's Collegiate Dictionary, 10th ed. 1996. Springfield, Mass.: Merriam-Webster.

Oxford English-Arabic Dictionary of Current Usage. 1972. Oxford, England: Clarendon.

Books and Articles

Abdel Fattah, Nabil, ed. 1995. *The Religious Condition in Egypt* (in Arabic). Cairo: Al-Ahram Center for Strategic and Political Studies.

———. 1997. *Text and Bullets: Political Islam, the Copts, and the Crisis of the Modern State in Egypt* (in Arabic). Beirut: Dar al-Nahar.

Abdel Razaq, Hussain. 1979. *Egypt during the 18th and 19th of January: A Political Documentary Study* (in Arabic). Beirut: Dar al-Kalima.

Abu-Lughod, Janet L. 1971. *Cairo: 1001 Years of the City Victorious.* Princeton, N.J.: Princeton University Press.

———. 1987. "The Islamic City: Historic Myth, Islamic Essence, and Contemporary Relevance." *International Journal of Middle East Studies* 19, no. 1:155–76.

———. 1990. "New York and Cairo: A View from Street Level." *International Social Science Journal* 125:307–18.

Abu-Lughod, Lila. 1986. *Veiled Sentiments: Honor and Poetry in a Bedouin Society.* Berkeley: University of California Press.

———. 1988. "Fieldwork of a Dutiful Daughter." In *Arab Women in the Field,* edited by Soraya Altorki and Camillia Fawzi El-Solh. Cairo: American University in Cairo Press, pp. 139–62.

Ahmed, Leila. 1992. *Women and Gender in Islam.* Cairo: American University in Cairo Press.

Al-Akyabi, Mahmmod Abed el-Hadi. 1991. *Cairo, the City and Its People: The Problem and the Solution* (in Arabic). Cairo: Hilwan University.

Altorki, Soraya. 1986. *Women in Saudi Arabia: Ideology and Behavior among the Elite.* New York: Columbia University Press.

———. 1988. "At Home in the Field." In *Arab Women in the Field,* edited by Soraya Altorki and Camillia Fawzi El-Solh. Cairo: American University in Cairo Press, pp. 49–68.

Anderson, Benedict. 1991. *Imagined Communities: Reflections on the Origin and Spread of Nationalism.* London: Verso.

Ansari, Hamied N. 1984. "Sectarian Conflict in Egypt and the Political Expediency of Religion." *Middle East Journal* 38:397–418.

———. 1986. *Egypt: The Stalled Society.* Albany: State University of New York Press.

Appadurai, Arjun. 1996. *Modernity at Large: Cultural Dimensions of Globalization.* Minneapolis: University of Minnesota Press.

Armbrust, Walter. 1996. *Mass Culture and Modernism in Egypt.* Cambridge: Cambridge University Press.

Asad, Talal. 1986. *The Idea of an Anthropology of Islam.* Washington, D.C.: Center for Contemporary Arab Studies, Georgetown University.

Baha' al-Din, Ahmed. 1987. *My Debates with Sadat* (in Arabic). Cairo: Dar al-Hilal.

Barakat, Halim. 1993. *The Arab World: Society, Culture, and State.* Berkeley: University of California Press.

Barber, Benjamin. 1995. *Jihad vs. McWorld.* New York: Random House.

Basham, Richard. 1978. *Urban Anthropology: The Cross-Cultural Study of Complex Societies.* Palo Alto, Calif.: Mayfield.

Bates, Daniel, and Amal Rassam. 1983. *Peoples and Cultures of the Middle East.* Engelwood Cliffs, N.J.: Prentice Hall.

Bayat, Asef. 1997a. "Cairo's Poor: Dilemmas of Survival and Solidarity." *Middle East Report* 27, no. 1:2–6.

———. 1997b. "Un-Civil Society: The Politics of the 'Informal People.'" *Third World Quarterly* 18, no. 1:53–72.

———. 2000. "From 'Dangerous Classes' to 'Quiet Rebels': Politics of Urban Subaltern in the Global South." *International Sociology* 15:533–55.

Benhabib, Seyla. 1992. "Models of Public Space: Hannah Arendt, the Liberal Tradition, and Jurgen Habermas." In *Habermas and the Public Sphere,* edited by Craig Calhoun. Cambridge, Mass.: MIT Press, pp. 73–98.

Berman, Marshall. 1988. *All That Is Solid Melts into Air: The Experience of Modernity.* New York: Penguin.

Beyer, Peter. 1994. *Religion and Globalization.* Thousand Oaks, Calif.: Sage.

Bourdieu, Pierre. 1966. "The Sentiment of Honour in Kabyle Society." In *Honour and Shame,* edited by J. G. Peristiany. Chicago: University of Chicago Press, pp. 191–241.

———. 1977. *Outline of a Theory of Practice.* Cambridge: Cambridge University Press.

———. 1979. *Algeria 1960.* Translated by Richard Nice. Cambridge: Cambridge University Press.

———. 1984. *Distinction: A Social Critique of the Judgement of Taste.* Translated by Richard Nice. Cambridge, Mass.: Harvard University Press.

———. 1990. *The Logic of Practice.* Stanford, Calif.: Stanford University Press.

———. 1998. *Acts of Resistance: Against the Tyranny of the Market.* New York: New Press.

Brink, Judy. 1991. "The Effect of Emigration of Husbands on the Status of Their Wives: An Egyptian Case." *International Journal of Middle East Studies* 23:201–11.

Brow, James. 1990. "Notes on Community, Hegemony and the Uses of the Past." *Anthropological Quarterly* 63, no. 1:1–6.

Calhoun, Craig. 1992. "Introduction: Habermas and the Public Sphere." In *Habermas and the Public Sphere,* edited by Craig Calhoun. Cambridge, Mass.: MIT Press, pp. 1–50.

Campo, Juan Eduardo. 1991. *The Other Sides of Paradise: Explorations into the Religious Meanings of Domestic Space in Islam.* Columbia: University of South Carolina Press.

Castells, Manuel. 1997. *The Power of Identity.* Oxford, England: Blackwell.

Central Agency for Public Mobilization and Statistics. 1986. *Population Census of 1986: The Final Results of the Governorate of Cairo.* Cairo: CAPMAS.

Cernea, Michael M., and Scott E. Guggenheim, eds. 1993. *Anthropological Approaches to Resettlement: Policy, Practice, and Theory.* Boulder, Colo.: Westview.

Clifford, James. 1988. *The Predicament of Culture.* Cambridge, Mass.: Harvard University Press.

———. 1997. "Spatial Practices: Fieldwork, Travel, and the Disciplining of Anthropology." In *Anthropological Locations: Boundaries and Grounds of a Field Science*, edited by Akhil Gupta and James Ferguson. Berkeley: University of California Press, pp. 185–222.

Comaroff, Jane. 1985. *Body of Power, Spirit of Resistance: The Culture and History of a South African People*. Chicago: University of Chicago Press.

De Certeau, Michel. 1988. *The Practice of Everyday Life*. Berkeley: University of California Press.

Denis, Eric. 1997. "Urban Planning and Growth in Cairo." *MERIP* (Middle East Report) 27, no. 1:7–12.

Dessouki, Ali E. Hillal, ed. 1982. *Islamic Resurgence in the Arab World*. New York: Praeger.

Diase, Martha. 1996. "Egyptian Television Serials, Audiences, and *The Family House,* a Public Health Enter-Educate Serial." Ph.D. diss., University of Texas at Austin.

Early, Evelyn. 1993. *Baladi Women of Cairo: Playing with an Egg and a Stone*. Boulder, Colo.: Lynne Rienner.

Economist Intelligence Unit. 1996. *Egypt: Country Profile, 1996–1997*. London: EIU.

Eickelman, Dale. 1989. *The Middle East: An Anthropological Approach*. Englewood Cliffs, N.J.: Prentice Hall.

Eickelman, Dale, and James Piscatori. 1996. *Muslim Politics*. Princeton, N.J.: Princeton University Press.

Epstein, David. 1988. "The Gensis and Function of Squatter Settlements in Brasilia." In *Urban Life: Readings in Urban Anthropology,* edited by George Gmelch and Walter P. Zenner. Prospect Heights, Il: Waveland, pp. 412–23.

Featherstone, Mike. 1995. *Undoing Culture: Globalization, Postmodernism, and Identity*. Thousand Oaks, Calif.: Sage.

Fegan, Brian. 1986. "Tenants' Non-Violent Resistance to Landowner Claims in a Central Luzon Village." *Journal of Peasant Studies* 13, no. 2:87–106.

Fernea, Robert. 1993. "Suqs of the Middle East: Commercial Centers Past and Present," In *Everyday Life in the Muslim Middle East,* edited by Donna Lee Bowen and Evelyn A. Early. Bloomington: Indiana University Press, pp. 182-204.

Foucault, Michel. 1979. *Discipline and Punish*. New York: Vintage.

———. 1980a. *The History of Sexuality*. Translated by Robert Hurely. New York: Vintage.

———. 1980b. *Power/Knowledge: Selected Interviews and Other Writings 1972–1977,* edited by Colin Gordon. New York: Pantheon.

———. 1984. *The Foucault Reader,* edited by Paul Rabinow. New York: Pantheon.

Fox, Richard. 1977. *Urban Anthropology: Cities in Their Cultural Settings*. Englewood Cliffs, N.J.: Prentice Hall.

Fraser, Nancy. 1992. "Rethinking the Public Sphere: A Contribution to the Critique of Actually Existing Democracy." In *Habermas and the Public Sphere,* edited by Craig Calhoun. Cambridge, Mass.: MIT Press, pp. 109–42.

Friedland, Roger, and Deirdre Boden, eds. 1994. *NowHere: Space, Time and Modernity*. Berkeley: University of California Press.

Frow, John. 1995. *Cultural Studies and Cultural Value*. Oxford, England: Clarendon Press.

Geertz, Clifford. 1973. *The Interpretation of Cultures*. New York: Basic Books.

———. 1979. "Suq: The Bazaar Economy in Sefrou." In *Meaning and Order in Moroccan Society*, edited by Clifford Geertz, Hildred Geertz, and Lawrence Rosen. Cambridge: Cambridge University Press, pp. 123–313.

———. 1988. *Works and Lives*. Stanford, Calif.: Stanford University Press.

Gerholm, Tomas. 1977. *Market, Mosque and Mafraj: Social Inequality in a Yemeni Town*. Stockholm: University of Stockholm.

Ghosh, Amitav. 1992. *In an Antique Land*. New York: Vintage.

Giddens, Anthony. 1990. *The Consequences of Modernity*. Stanford, Calif.: Stanford University Press.

Gilroy, Paul. 1987. *"There Ain't No Black in the Union Jack": The Cultural Politics of Race and Nation*. London: Hutchinson.

Gilsenan, Michael. 1982. *Recognizing Islam: Religion and Society in the Modern Arab World*. New York: Pantheon.

Gmelch, George, and Walter P. Zenner, eds. 1988. *Urban Life: Readings in Urban Anthropology*. Prospect Heights, Ill.: Waveland.

Goffman, Erving. 1959. *The Presentation of the Self in Everyday Life*. New York: Doubleday Anchor.

Gottdiener, M. 1985. *The Social Production of Urban Space*. Austin: University of Texas Press.

Grunebaum, Gustave. 1955. *The Structure of the Muslim Town*. Memoir no. 81. Ann Arbor, Mich.: American Anthropological Association.

Guggenheim, Scott, and Michael M. Cernea. 1993. "Anthropological Approaches to Involuntary Resettlement: Policy, Practice, and Theory." In *Anthropological Approaches to Resettlement*, edited by Michael M. Cernea and Scott E. Guggenheim. Boulder, Colo.: Westview, pp. 1–12.

Gupta, Akhil. 1992. "The Song of the Nonaligned World: Transitional Identities and the Reinscription of Space in Late Capitalism." *Cultural Anthropology* 7, no. 1:63–79.

Gupta, Akhil, and James Ferguson. 1992. "Beyond 'Culture': Space, Identity, and the Politics of Difference." *Cultural Anthropology* 7, no. 1:6–23.

———, eds. 1997a. *Anthropological Locations: Boundaries and Grounds of a Field Science*. Berkeley: University of California Press.

———. 1997b. "Culture, Power, Place: Ethnography at the End of an Era." In *Anthropological Locations: Boundaries and Grounds of a Field Science*, edited by A. Gupta and J. Ferguson. Berkeley: University of California Press, pp. 1–29.

Habermas, Jurgen. 1983. "Modernity: An Incomplete Project." In *The Anti-Aesthetic: Essays on Postmodern Culture*, edited by Hal Foster. Townsend, Wash: Bay Press, pp. 3–15.

Habitat. 1993. *Metropolitan Planning and Management in the Developing World:*

Spatial Decentralization Policy in Bombay and Cairo. Nairobi: United Nations Centre for Human Settlements.

Hakim, Basim. 1986. *Arabo-Islamic Cities: Building and Planning Principles.* New York: Routledge.

Hall, Edward. 1966. *The Hidden Dimension.* New York: Doubleday.

Hall, Stuart. 1991a. "The Local and the Global: Globalization and Ethnicity." In *Culture, Globalization and the World-System,* edited by Anthony D. King. Binghamton: State University of New York Press, pp. 19–39.

———. 1991b. "Old and New Identities, Old and New Ethnicities." In *Culture, Globalization and the World-System,* edited by Anthony D. King. Binghamton: State University of New York Press, pp. 41–68.

———. 1993. "Culture, Community, Nation." *Cultural Studies* 7:349–63.

El-Hamamsy, Laila. 1975. "The Assertion of Egyptian Identity." In *Ethnic Identity: Cultural Continuities and Change,* edited by George DeVos and Lola Romaucci-Ross. Palo Alto, Calif.: Mayfield, pp. 276–306.

Hamdan, Jamal. 1993. *Al-Qahirah* (in Arabic). Cairo: Dar al-Hilal.

Hanna, Milad. 1978. *I Want a House: A Problem That Can Be Solved* (in Arabic). Cairo: Rose al-Yusuf Foundation.

———. 1993. *Egypt for all Egyptians* (in Arabic). Cairo: Ibn Khaldun Center.

———. 1996. *Housing and Politics* (in Arabic). Cairo: Al-Hai'a al-'Ama lil-Kitab.

———. 1997. *Politicians and Priests behind Bars* (in Arabic). Cairo: Kitab al-Hilal.

Hannerz, Ulf. 1980. *Exploring the City: Inquiries toward an Urban Anthropology.* New York: Columbia University Press.

———. 1996. *Transnational Connections: Culture, People, Places.* New York: Routledge.

Hansen, Art, and Anthony Oliver-Smith, eds. 1982. *Involuntary Migration and Resettlement.* Boulder, Colo.: Westview.

Harvey, David. 1990. *The Condition of Postmodernity.* Cambridge, England: Blackwell.

Hassan, Nawal Mahmoud. 1985. "Social Aspects of Urban Housing in Cairo." *MIMAR* 17 (July-September): 59–61.

———. 1991. "Social Implications of Population Displacement and Resettlement: Cairo's Inner City." Paper presented at the meeting of the Study Group on Social Implications of Population Displacement and Resettlement, July 29–31, Irbid, Jordan.

Hecht, Richard D. 1994. "The Construction and Management of Sacred Time and Space: Sabta Nur in the Church of the Holy Sepulcher." In *NowHere: Space, Time and Modernity,* edited by Roger Friedland and Deirdre Boden. Berkeley: University of California Press, pp. 181–235.

Hegland, Mary Elaine. 1991. "Political Roles of Aliabad Women: The Public-Private Dichotomy Transcended." In *Women in Middle Eastern History: Shifting Boundaries in Sex and Gender,* edited by Nikki R. Keddie and Beth Baron. New Haven, Conn.: Yale University Press, pp. 215–30.

Hessini, Laila. 1994. "Wearing the Hijab in Contemporary Morocco: Choice and Identity." In *Reconstructing Gender in the Middle East,* edited by Fatma

Muge Gocek and Shiva Balaghi. New York: Columbia University Press, pp. 40–56.

Holston, James. 1989. *The Modernist City: An Anthropological Critique of Brasilia*. Chicago: University of Chicago Press.

Honneth, Alex, Kocyba Hermann, and Bernd Schwibs. 1986. "The Struggle for Symbolic Order: An Interview with Pierre Bourdieu." *Theory, Culture and Society* 3, no. 3:35–51.

Hoodfar, Homa. 1997. *Between Marriage and Market: Intimate Politics and Survival in Cairo*. Berkeley: University of California Press.

Hourani, Albert, and S. M. Stern, eds. 1970. *The Islamic City*. Philadelphia: University of Pennsylvania Press.

Huntington, Samuel. 1993. "The Clash of Civilizations?" *Foreign Affairs* 72, no. 3:22–49.

Ibrahim, Barbara Lethem. 1985. "Cairo's Factory Women." In *Women and the Family in the Middle East: New Voices of Change*, edited by Elizabeth Warnock Fernea. Austin: University of Texas Press, pp. 293–99.

Ibrahim, Saad Eddin. 1982. "Islamic Militancy as a Social Movement: The Case of Two Groups in Egypt." In *Islamic Resurgence in the Arab World*, edited by Ali E. Hillal Dessouki. New York: Praeger, pp. 117–37.

———. 1987. "Cairo: A Sociological Profile." In *Urban Crisis and Social Movements*, edited by Salim Nasr and Theodor Hanf. Beirut: Euro-Arab Social Research Group, pp. 87–99.

———. 1992. *The Rehabilitation of President Sadat* (in Arabic). Cairo: Dar al-Shurouq.

Ikram, K. 1980. *Egypt: Economic Management in a Period of Transition*. Baltimore: Johns Hopkins University Press.

Inhorn, Marcia Claire. 1994. *Quest for Conception: Gender, Infertility, and Egyptian Medical Traditions*. Philadelphia: University of Pennsylvania.

Jacobs, Jane. 1961. *The Death and Life of Great American Cities*. New York: Vintage.

Jenkins, Richard. 1992. *Pierre Bourdieu*. New York: Routledge.

Jenks, Chris. 1995. "Watching Your Step: The History and Practice of the Flâneur." In *Visual Culture*, edited by Chris Jenks. New York: Routledge, pp. 142–60.

Joseph, Suad. 1988. "Feminization, Familism, Self, and Politics: Research as a Mughtaribi." In *Arab Women in the Field*, edited by Soraya Altorki and Camillia Fawzi El-Solh. Cairo: American University in Cairo Press, pp. 25–48.

———. 1994. "Brother/Sister Relationships: Connectivity, Love, and Power in the Reproduction of Patriarchy in Lebanon." *American Ethnologist* 21, no. 1:50–71.

Kapchan, Deborah. 1996. *Gender on the Market: Moroccan Women and the Revoicing of Tradition*. Philadelphia: University of Pennsylvania.

Kepel, Gilles. 1993. *Muslim Extremism in Egypt: The Prophet and Pharaoh*. Berkeley: University of California Press.

Khafagy, Fatma. 1983. "Socio-Economic Impact of Emigration from a Giza Village." In *Migration Mechanization and Agricultural Labor Markets in Egypt,* edited by Alan Richards and Philip Martin. Boulder, Colo.: Westview, pp. 135–58.

Khuri, Fuad. 1975. *From Village to Suburb: Order and Change in Greater Beirut.* Chicago: University of Chicago Press.

Krais, Beate. 1993. "Gender and Symbolic Violence: Female Oppression in the Light of Pierre Bourdieu's Theory of Social Practice." In *Bourdieu: Critical Perspectives,* edited by Craig Calhoun, Edward LiPuma, and Moishe Postone. Chicago: University of Chicago Press, pp. 156–77.

Lamaison, Pierre. 1986. "From Rules to Strategies: An Interview with Pierre Bourdieu." *Cultural Anthropology* 1, no. 1:110–20.

Lapidus, Ira M. 1979. "Muslim Cities and Islamic Societies." In *Middle Eastern Cities,* edited by Ira M. Lapidus. Berkeley: University of California Press, pp. 47–79.

Lash, Scott, and John Urry. 1994. *Economics of Signs and Space.* Thousand Oaks, Calif.: Sage.

LaTowsky, Robert J. 1984. "Egyptian Labor Abroad: Mass Participation and Modest Returns," *MERIP* (Middle East Report) 14, no. 4:11–18.

Lefebvre, Henri. 1991. *The Production of Space.* Translated by Donald Nicholson-Smith. Oxford, England: Blackwell.

Leprette, Fernand. 1939. *Egypt: Land of the Nile.* Cairo: R. Schindler.

MacLeod, Arlene Elowe. 1991. *Accommodating Protest: Working Women, the New Veiling, and Change in Cairo.* Cairo: American University in Cairo Press.

Maddox, Richard. 1997. "Bombs, Bikinis, and the Popes of Rock 'n' Roll: Reflections on Resistance, the Play of Subordinations, and Liberalism in Andalusia and Academia, 1983–1995." In *Culture, Power, Place: Explorations in Critical Anthropology,* pp. 275–90.

Mahar, Cheleen, Richard Harker, and Chris Wilkes. 1990. "The Basic Theoretical Position." In *An Introduction to the Work of Pierre Bourdieu,* edited by Richard Harker, Cheleen Mahar, and Chris Wilkes. New York: Macmillan, pp. 1–26.

Malkki, Liisa. 1992. "National Geographic: The Rooting of Peoples and the Territorialization of National Identity among Scholars and Refugees." *Cultural Anthropology* 7, no. 1:24–44.

———. 1997. "News and Culture: Transitory Phenomena and the Field Tradition." In *Anthropological Locations: Boundaries and Grounds of a Field Science,* edited by A. Gupta and J. Ferguson. Berkeley: University of California Press, pp. 86–101.

Marcus, Abraham. 1989. *The Middle East on the Eve of Modernity: Aleppo in the Eighteenth Century.* New York: Columbia University Press.

Massey, Doren. 1994. *Space, Place and Gender.* Minneapolis: University of Minnesota Press.

Mele, Christopher. 2000. *Selling the Lower East Side: Culture, Real Estate, and Resistance in New York City.* Minneapolis: University of Minnesota Press.

Mernissi, Fatima. 1987. *Beyond the Veil: Male-Female Dynamics in Modern Muslim Society.* Bloomington: Indiana University Press.

El-Messiri, Sawsan. 1978. *Ibn al-Balad: A Concept of Egyptian Identity.* Leiden, the Netherlands: E. J. Brill.

Miller, Daniel. 1995. "Introduction: Anthropology, Modernity and Consumption." In *Worlds Apart: Modernity through the Prism of the Local,* edited by Daniel Miller. New York: Routledge, pp. 1–22.

Mitchell, Timothy. 1988. *Colonising Egypt.* Cairo: American University in Cairo Press.

Moore, Barrington. 1984. *Privacy: Studies in Social and Cultural History.* Armonk, N.Y.: M. E. Sharpe.

Muhammad, Prophet. 2000. *Sahih Bukhari.* Vol 1, book 8, no. 441. Translated by M. Muhsin Khan. Retrieved October 31, 2001, from www.usc.edu/dept/MSA/fundamentals/hadithsunnah/bukhari

Muharram, Najwan. 1989. *Hawari . . . with History* (in Arabic). Cairo: Kitab al-Jumhoriyya.

Myntti, Cynthia. 1984. "Yemeni Workers Abroad: The Impact on Women." *MERIP* (Middle East Report) 14, no. 5:11–16.

———. 1999. *Paris along the Nile: Architecture in Cairo from the Belle Epoch.* Cairo: American University in Cairo Press.

Nadim, Asaad, Nawal El-Messiri Nadim, Sohair Mehanna, and John H. Nixon. 1980. *Living without Water.* Cairo Papers in Social Science, vol. 3, no. 3. Cairo: American University in Cairo Press.

Nadim, Nawal al-Messiri. 1985. "Family Relationships in a Harah in Cairo." In *Arab Society: Social Science Perspectives,* edited by Nicholas Hopkins and Saad Eddin Ibrahim. Cairo: American University in Cairo Press, pp. 212–22.

Nagy, Sharon. 1998. "'This Time I Think I'll Try a Filipina': Global and Local Influences on Relationships between Foreign Household Workers and their Employers in Doha, Qatar." *City and Society,* pp. 83–104.

Nelson, Cynthia. 1974. "Public and Private Politics: Women in the Middle Eastern World." *American Ethnologist* 1, no. 3:551–63.

Oldham, Linda, Haguer El Hadidi, and Hussein Amaa. 1987. *Informal Communities in Cairo: The Basis for a Typology.* Cairo Papers in Social Science, vol. 1, no. 4. Cairo: American University in Cairo Press.

Ortner, Sherry. 1995. "Resistance and the Problem of Ethnographic Refusal." *Society for Comparative Study of Society and History* 26:173–93.

———. 1999. "Thick Resistance: Death and the Cultural Construction of Agency in Himalayan Mountaineering." In *The Fate of Culture: Geertz and Beyond,* edited by Sherry Ortner. Berkeley: University of California Press, pp. 136–64.

Ossman, Susan. 1994. *Picturing Casablanca: Portraits of Power in a Modern City.* Berkeley: University of California Press.

Perlman, Janice E. 1982. "Favela Removal: The Eradication of a Lifestyle." In *Involuntary Migration and Resettlement,* edited by Art Hansen and Anthony Oliver-Smith. Boulder: Westview, pp. 225–34.

———. 1989. *French Modern: Norms and Forms of Social Environment.* Cambridge: MIT Press.

Rageh, Abou-Zeid. 1984. "The Changing Pattern of Housing in Cairo." In *The Expanding Metropolis: Coping with the Urban Growth of Cairo,* edited by the Aga Khan Award for Architecture. Singapore: Concept Media, pp. 133–40.

Ray, Larry J. 1993. *Rethinking Critical Theory: Emancipation in the Age of Global Social Movements.* Newbury Park, Calif.: Sage.

Raymond, Andre. 1993. *Le Caire* (in Arabic). Translated by Farag Latif. Cairo: Dar al-Fikr.

Ritzer, G. 1996. *The McDonaldization of Society.* Thousand Oaks, Calif.: Pine Forge.

Robertson, Roland. 1995. "Glocalization: Time-Space and Homogeneity-Heterogeneity," in *Global Modernities,* edited by Mike Featherstone, Scott Lash, and Roland Robertson. Thousand Oaks, Calif.: Sage, pp. 25–44.

Robins, Kevin. 1993. "Prisoners of the City: Whatever Could a Postmodern City Be?" In *Space and Place: Theories of Identity and Location,* edited by Erica Carter, James Donald, and Judith Squires. London: Lawrence & Wishart, pp. 303–30.

Rodenbeck, Max. 1998. *Cairo: The City Victorious.* Cairo: American University in Cairo Press.

Rofel, Lisa. 1992. "Rethinking Modernity: Space and Factory Discipline in China," *Cultural Anthropology* 7, no. 1:93–114.

Rosen, Lawrence. 1979. "Social Identity and Points of Attachment: Approaches to Social Organization." In *Meaning and Order in Moroccan Society,* edited by Clifford Geertz, Hildred Geertz, and Lawrence Rosen. Cambridge: Cambridge University Press, pp. 19–122.

Rugh, Andrea. 1979. *Coping with Poverty in a Cairo Community.* Cairo: American University in Cairo Press.

———. 1984. *Family in Contemporary Egypt.* Cairo: American University in Cairo Press.

Sadat, Anwar el-. 1974. *The October Paper* (in Arabic). Cairo: Hay'at al-Isk'lamat.

———. 1978. *In Search of Identity.* Glasgow: Collins.

———. 1981. *The Basic Relationships of the Human Being: His Relationships with God, Himself, Others, the Universe, and Objects* (in Arabic). Cairo: General Agency for Information.

Al-Safty, Madiha. 1983. "Sociological Perspectives on Urban Housing." In *Urban Research Strategies for Egypt,* edited by Richard Lobban. Cairo Papers in Social Science vol. 6, no. 2. Cairo: American University in Cairo Press, pp. 1–8.

As-Safty, Madiha. [Madiha Al-Safty]. 1987. "Low-Cost Housing: Public versus Private Action in Cairo." In *Urban Crisis and Social Movements,* edited by Salim Nasr and Theodor Hanf. Beirut: Euro-Arab Social Research Group, pp. 117–27.

Sassen, Saskia. 1996. "Whose City Is It? Globalization and the Formation of New Claims." *Public Culture,* no. 8:205–23.

Scott, James. 1986. "Everyday Forms of Peasant Resistance," *Journal of Peasant Studies* 13, no. 2:5–35.

———. 1998. *Seeing Like a State: How Certain Schemes to Improve the Human Condition Failed*. New Haven, Conn.: Yale University Press.

Scudder, Thayer, and Elizabeth Colson. 1982. "From Welfare to Development: A Conceptual Framework for the Analysis of Dislocated People." In *Involuntary Migration and Resettlement*, edited by Art Hansen and Anthony Oliver-Smith. Boulder, Colo.: Westview, pp. 267–88.

Sennett, Richard. 1977. *The Fall of Public Man*. New York: Vintage.

Serjeant, R. B., ed. 1980. *The Islamic City*. Paris: UNESCO.

Seton-Williams, Veronica, and Peter Stocks. 1988. *Blue Guide: Egypt*. London: A & C Black.

Shami, Seteney. 1988. "Studying Your Own: The Complexities of a Shared Culture." In *Arab Women in the Field*, edited by Soraya Altorki and Camillia Fawzi El-Solh. Cairo: American University in Cairo Press, pp. 115–38.

———. 1990. *The Social Implications of Population Displacement and Resettlement: An Overview with a Focus on the Middle East*. Regional Papers, no. 37. Cairo: Population Council.

———, ed. 1994. *Population Displacement and Resettlement: Development and Conflict in the Middle East*. New York: Center for Migration Studies.

———. 1996. "Gender, Domestic Space, and Urban Upgrading: A Case Study from Amman." *Gender and Development* 4, no. 1:17–23.

Sharabi, Hisham. 1988. *Neopatriarchy: A Theory of Distorted Change in Arab Society*. New York: Oxford University Press.

Shorter, Frederic. 1989. *Cairo's Leap Forward: People, Households, and Dwelling Space*. Cairo: American University in Cairo Press.

Singerman, Diane. 1995. *Avenues of Participation: Family, Politics, and Networks in Urban Quarters of Cairo*. Princeton, N.J.: Princeton University Press.

Slater, C. 1996. "Four Moments." In *The World Observed: Reflections on the Fieldwork Process*, edited by B. Jackson and E. D. Ives. Urbana: University of Illinois Press, pp. 18–31.

Springborg, Robert. 1989. *Mubarak's Egypt: Fragmentation of the Political Order*. Boulder, Colo.: Westview.

Stallybrass, Peter, and Allon White. 1986. *The Politics and Poetics of Transgression*. London: Methuen.

Starett, Gregory. 1998. *Putting Islam to Work*. Berkeley: University of California Press.

Steinberg, Florian. 1991. "Architecture and Townscape in Today's Cairo: The Relevance of Tradition." *Ekistics* 58, no. 346:75–86.

Stewart, Desmond. 1968. *Great Cairo: Mother of the World*. Cairo: American University in Cairo Press.

Stewart, Kathleen. 1996. *A Space on the Side of the Road*. Princeton, N.J.: Princeton University Press.

Taher, Nadia Adel. 1986. *Social Identity and Class in a Cairo Neighborhood*. Cairo

Papers in Social Science, vol 9, no. 4. Cairo: American University in Cairo Press.

Taylor, Elizabeth. 1984. "Egyptian Migration and Peasant Wives." *MERIP* (Middle East Report) 14, no. 5:3–10.

Tsing, Anna Lowenhaupt. 1993. *In the Realm of the Diamond Queen: Marginality in an Out-of-the-Way Place.* Princeton, N.J.: Princeton University Press.

Tucker, Judith. 1978. "Economic Decay, Political Ferment in Egypt." *MERIP* (Middle East Report) 65:3–9.

———, ed. 1993. *Arab Women: Old Boundaries, New Frontiers.* Bloomington: Indiana University Press.

Turino, Thomas. 1990. "Structure, Context, and Strategy in Musical Ethnography." *Ethnomusicology* 34:399–412.

Turner, Bryan S., ed. 1990. *Theories of Modernity and Postmodernity.* Newbury Park, Calif.: Sage.

———. 1994. *Orientalism, Postmodernism and Globalism.* New York: Routledge.

Urry, John. 1995. *Consuming Places.* New York: Routledge.

Waterbury, John. 1983. *The Egypt of Nasser and Sadat: The Political Economy of Two Regimes.* Princeton, N.J.: Princeton University Press.

Waters, Malcolm. 1995. *Globalization.* New York: Routledge.

Watts, Michael. 1996. "Islamic Modernities? Citizenship, Civil Society and Islamism in a Nigerian City." *Public Culture,* no. 8:251–89.

Weber, Max. 1978. *Economy and Society,* edited by Guenther Roth and Claus Wittich. Berkeley: University of California Press.

Weir, Shelagh. 1987. "Labour Migration and Key Aspects to Its Economic and Social Impact on a Yemeni Highland Community." In *The Middle Eastern Village,* edited by Richard Lawless, pp. 273–96. London: Croom Helm.

Wilson, Elizabeth. 1992. *The Sphinx in the City: Urban Life, the Control of Disorder, and Women.* Berkeley: University of California Press.

Wright, Gwendolyn. 1983. *Building the Dream: A Social History of Housing in America.* Cambridge, Mass.: MIT Press.

Zenlund, Darrow Gary. 1991. "Post-Colonial Aleppo, Syria: Struggles in Representation and Identity." Ph.D. diss., University of Texas at Austin.

Index

Abdu, Sheikh Muhammad: on Muslim identity, 140

additions (to housing): bribery and, 173, 174; as *hadad* (demolition), 55

Aden, 18

Afghanistan, 138

afrangi, 79; opposed to *baladi,* 77

'afrit (demon), 61; and Muslim-Christian conflict, 125

el-ahali, 103, 124, 152, 162; author's connections with, 8–9, 11; contrasted with *el-masaakin,* 6–7, 81–82, 163–64; and gender, 170; and local identity, 118; markets in, 111; and marriage, 130; mosques in, 23–24, 126, 127, 170; narratives of residents, 163; negative views of relocation, 71–73; use of space in, 63

Ahali Bulaq (people of Bulaq): and rootedness, 76

Ahmed Ibn Talun, 16

'Ain shams, 38, 127; and Bulaq, 76; and relocation, 4, 72

Alexandria: and 1977 riots, 37–38

Algeria, 20, 51; Bourdieu on, 48–49, 95; housing in, 93

Ali, Ismail: and modernization of Cairo, 27

Ali, Muhammad: and building of Cairo, 26–27

Amin Qasim: on Egyptian identity, 140

Andalusia, 18

Animal Feed Factory: mosque for workers of, 120

animals, domestic: and community, 62–65

Appadurai, Arjun 19, 24; on consumption, 179

'ashwua'iyyat ("unplanned" areas), 41

'asl (origin): defined, 84–85; forgetting one's, 85–87; and globalization, 84–87

audio tapes: and migration, 149–51; state control of, 149–50

authority: husband's, 10

al-Azhar, 119

Bab al-Sha'riyah: and relocation, 162; research in, 5

baladi: and *'asl,* 86–87; and Bulaq, 77–80, 82; and class, 77, 79; defined, 77; and *lama,* 80–82; and post-colonialism, 5; and al-Zawiya, 78–83

balcony: and privacy, 98–99

bazaar: studies of, 112

Berman, Marshall, 21, 38, 39, 45, 133, 136; quoted, 37, 51, 84

biyuut ahali (private houses), 5. See also *el-ahali*

body: and the mosque, 130–31; and privacy, 98, 99; and religious identity, 124

Bosnia, 80, 138

Bourdieu, Pierre, 17, 22, 23, 38–39, 44, 48–51, 58, 70; on doors, 93, 95; on the "doxic," 106; quoted, 43, 48, 55, 103, 170 bribery: and housing additions, 173, 174

Bulaq, 127; and *'asl*, 85, 86; as *baladi* area, 77–80, 81, 82; children in, 108–09; and class, 83; community in,94; as less "modern," 133; locals of, 118; location of, 76–77, 79; memories of, 95, 96; relations between Muslims and Christians in, 123–24; relocation from, 4, 6, 134, 163, 164, 169,173; research in, 5; social control in, 65; and al-Zawiya, 7

bus: in Cairo, 116–17; and commute to al-Zawiya, 11; conditions on, 170; and fieldwork, 8; and poverty, 132

Cairo: "city of problems," 167, 169–70; as "the face," 31; founding of, 26; and globalization, 17–21; inclusion in, 158, 167–68, 171–73; infrastructure of, 28; and Islam, 5, 17, 179–80; map of, 3; metro, 169; and migration, 145, 167–68; and modernization of, 2–4, 27–42; and nationalism, 28; new governor of, 160, 169, 173; and 1977 riots, 37–38; "Old," 5; outskirts of, 5–6; population of, 25–26; production of, 16–17, 24, 143–44, 168, 174–78; reform of, 168–70; Sadat's plans for, 135; "strangers in," 12; and technological progress, 168; tourism in, 2, 5, 38; transportation in, 116–17; *Umm al-Dunya* (Mother of the World), 25; and al-Zawiya, 11, 162–64, 166

capital, symbolic: loss of, and relocation, 76–77

censorship: and audio tapes, 149–50

Central Security Forces (*al-Amn al-Markizi*): and Muslim-Christian conflict, 122; and relocation, 70

Chechnya, 138, 180

Christian(s), 14–15; author's relations with, 12–13; church, construction of, 120; clashes with Muslims, 120–26; economic superiority of, 124; and Muslims, 5, 12, 23–24, 181. *See also* Copts

city: and *'asl*, 85; and class, 4–5, 11, 45; and colonialism, 26–27; and fieldwork, 8–17; and gender, 100–03, 114–15; and globalization, 87, 169; governance of, 160, 168; "Islamic," 17, 98; and inequality, 143; and migrants, 167–68; and modernization, 2, 18, 27–28, 133; planning, 30–40, 161, 174–75; population

of, 26; "of problems," 28, 167, 168; production of, 11, 16–17, 18, 22–24, 26–28, 48, 51, 143, 145, 146, 171, 172, 176–77; and poverty, 132; and relocation, 4, 5–6, 18, 51–52, 69–70, 74, 114, 123; and space, 99; transport in (bus), 1, 2, 8, 11, 14, 76, 116, 117, 128, 132, 170, 179, 181

class: and *baladi*, 77, 79; differences, 4–5; and fieldwork, 11–12; and globalization, 84, 143, 178; and housing, 28, 48–49; and information, 14; and *lama*, 80–82; and modernization, 22; and relocation, 18, 30; and rights, 174–75; *sha'bi* and *raaqi*, 82–83; and space, 11–12

coffeehouse (*qahwa*): and gender, 109–11; and *lama*, 109

colonialism: and *baladi*, 77; British, 27; French, 26–27; and production of Cairo, 26–27; resistance to, in Bulaq, 70; and space, 22

Comaroff, Jean: on religion and relocation, 118–19

communication: and migration, 155

communists: and 1977 riots, 37, 38

community: and Bulaq, 75–76, 78–79; and class, 82–83; and domestic animals, 62–65; and everyday norms, 126; and housing alterations, 159; and individualism, 136; and modernity, 134; and the mosque, 126–31; opposed to privacy, 92–93; and religious identity, 117–20, 122; and state control, evasion of, 154; and structure of *el-masaakin*, 46; and *ulfa*, 80–81; and work, 60

computers: and technological renaissance, 169

consumption: and frustration, 179; and status, 51

contraception: perception of, in al-Zawiya, 9–10

control, state: and audio tapes, 149–50

conversion: and marriage, 124

cooperation: neighborhood, against the state, 141–42

Copts: and government policies, 119–20; and Muslims, 110, 117–18, 121–22; protests of, 122; Sadat on, 121. *See also* Christians

cross: tattoo of, 124

dancing: allowance of, 98–99

Dar il-Salam, 80–81

de Certeau, Michel, 16, 23, 50, 168, 171; critique of Bourdieu, 50; quoted, 17, 58, 141, 167; on "spatial practices," 16, 22, 41; on "tactics," 15, 22, 50
desire: and state discourse, 41–42
discourse: on bus, 132; global, 19–21, 68, 70, 143; of modernity, 2–4, 48, 133–40, 179, 180; in mosque, 13, 130–31; negative, and Bulaq, 70–73; religious, and control of women, 102–03; of relocation, 23, 31–34, 35–37, 38–42; state, 16, 22–23, 48, 66, 93, 158, 168, 173–74, 179; state, resistance to, 172–77; of urban planning, 129–30
diversity: in Cairo, 25–26; and housing, 6–7; and *lama*, 80
doors: and isolation, 96; significance of, 93, 94–96
dreams: and global images, 44–45; and modernity, 180
dress: Islamic, 124

education: and mosque, 127, 130–31; religious, 49
Egypt: compared to United States, 83; economic problems of, 28–29; failure of bureaucracy, 39–40; and globalization, 17–21; indigenous population of, 77; and "modern Egyptians," 119; and modernity, 21; and nationalism, 119–20; 1952 revolution, 27; state attitude to Islam, 117; traditions, 125–26
Eickelman: on Morocco, 46
English (language), 86
Europe: travel to, 178

Fallahin, 118; and *el-ahali*, 72; and *'asl*, 85
family, nuclear: and public housing, 93, 94–96
fasting: importance of, 13
Fatimids: and founding of Cairo, 26
Fernea, Robert: and religious identity, 14–15
field work, 7–8, 14; and class, 11–12; and gender, 9–10; and marriage, 9–11; and religious identity, 12–13
"Food Riots," 37–38
Foucault, Michel: on "dividing practices," 33; on power and desire, 41; on space, 22
Fraser, Nancy, 91
French: attacks on Egypt, 28; colonial presence in Cairo, 26–27

fundamentalism, 132–33
fusha (going out), 101

al-Gamaliyya: research in, 5
Garden City, 11; author's apartment in, 54
gaze: of neighbors, 57; and visits, 54
gender: and *baladi*, 87; and coffeehouse, 109–11; and control, 88–90, 99–103, 103–15; and fieldwork, 9–10; and *fusha*, 101; and global discourse, 67–69, 143, 178; and housing, 51; and inequality, 23, 89–90; and information, 106; and market, 111–14; and negative images, 72–73; and production of Cairo, 16–17; and public vs. private, 90–92, 99–103; and relocation, 71; roles, 53, 72, 88–89, 100, 114–15; and rootedness, 74–75; and segregation, 10; and space, 53–54, 59, 60, 61–66, 89–90
Geniza documents, 17–18
Gilsenan, Michael, 57, 91, 96, 112, 114, 119; quoted, 131
globalization: and appropriation of modernity, 180; and *'asl*, 84–87; and class, 18, 178; and Cairo, 17–21; and daily practices, 17; and fast-food chains, 25, 84; and fundamentalism, 132–33; and gender, 67–68, 87, 178; and images, 44, 179; and inequality, 143; and locality, 19, 69–70, 143–44; narratives of, 66–69; and neighborhoods, 166; and religious identity, 131–33; and state discourse, 22–23
government, Egyptian: control, 149–50, 154, 159, 164–65, 166; and anti-government feelings, 12, 180; discourse of, 173–74; incompetence, 132; legislation, 160; and modernity, 24; neglect, 162–63; plans, resistance to, 171–77; presence and absence, 25–26; system of bribery, 174; and unplanned areas, 173
Gulf War, 8

Hanna, Mildad: on relocation, 31, 119, 120, 121, 173
Hall, Stuart, 19; quoted, 118
hara: in Bulaq, 74
Hassan, Nawal: on relocation, 40
Haussman, 168
hijab, 124
Hosni, Abu, 14–15, 17, 18, 67–68, 69, 71, 78, 84, 86, 175, 180; modernity "like a knife," 134; and technology, 135–36, 138

housing: additions to, 48, 50–51, 52–53, 55–58; 174–76; and belonging, 152; and bribery, 173, 174; and class, 28, 48–49; conditions, 31–33; crisis, 31–33; and diversity, 6–7; and domestic animals, 62–65; and gender, 50, 53–54, 59, 60, 61–66; and identity, 151–52; and income, 2–4, 6–7, 178; and marriage, 18, 45, 53, 152–53; and migration, 29, 68, 147; and modernization, 133–34, 154–58, 159–60, 164–66; options, 10–11; problem of, 170; project, stigmatization of, 179; public, and immigrants, 79; and religious identity, 53; and segregation, 73; shortage, 12, 27, 44–45, 141–42; and state control, 2–4, 16–17, 154, 174–77; and status, 153, 157–58, 159; and unplanned areas, 173; value of, 164–65; and visits, 54, 59; and workplace, 57–58, 60

housing, public, 185n11, 186n20, 186nn5, 6, 7, 187n12, 189nn4, 10, 192n7, 193n8; advantages of, 41; cost of, 40; financing of, 30–31; Nasser's plan for, 6, 27–28; and nuclear family, planning of, 34; police presence in, 34; 93, 94–96; and private, 6–7

Houston: as model for Cairo, 28, 135

ibn el-balad: and baladi, 77. See also baladi
identity: and 'asl, 84–87; baladi, 78–79; and Bulaq, 73–76; complexity of, 20–21; cultural, 17, 40; and gender, 9; and housing, 53–54; and place, 45; and relocation, 23, 118; and stigmatization, 70–73; and space, 82–83

identity, Egyptian: and post colonialism, 5; and the West, 140

identity, religious, 9, 15, 117–18, 163; and body, 124; and criticism of government, 180; and difference, 13; and fasting, 13; and fieldwork, 12–13, 14–15; and globalization, 131–32, 132–40; and housing, 53; and "Islamic city," 17; and the "local," 68–69; and migration, 67–68; and modernity, 24, 34, 136–37, 179–80; and mosque, 126–31; and nationalism, 119–20; and pilgrimage, 180; and police, 128; and relocation, 118–19; and space, 120–26; and television, 137–39

images: global, 44, 179; of modernity, 133–40, 154; and relocation, 44, 70–73

Iman: and unity in mosque, 126–27

income, 6–7; and marriage, 7
India, 18, 20, 146, 177, 178
individualism: in the United States, 136
inequality: and gender, 89–90, 106; and information, 106; and public vs. private, 91–92; and symbolic violence, 103–04

infitah: and 1977 riots, 37, 38; "open-door" policy, 22, 29, 37, 38, 84, 94, 144–45
internet: cafés, 169
Iran: squatter settlements in, 175
Iraq: and Egyptian migration, 145
'ishash al-Turguman: demolition of, 36–37; and 1977 riots, 38

Islam: activists, 117, 119–20, 122, 129, 137; and Cairo, 5, 17; and collectivity, 23–24; conversion to, 124; dress, 124; extremism in, 120, 123, 132–33, 137, 179; and "good Muslim," 116–17; and the government, 117, 119; and Islamization, 179–80; and modernization, 136, 137; and television, 137–39; traditions of, and western advances, 125–26, 134, 137

Israel: 1968 war, 28

Jordan, 54; author's connections with, 8, 12, 13; and Egyptian migration, 145; and modernity, 21

Kalam Rigalla: and baladi identity, 78–79
Kihmar, 124
Kulthum, Um, 117
Kuwait, 144, 146, 147, 152, 178; and migration, 18, 20; purchases in, 158; and transnationalism, 8

lama, 109; and diversity, 80–82; and market, 114; negative connotations of, 81–82

Lash, Scott: on "the local," 69
Lebanon, 96, 121
Le Courbusier, 168
Libya, 178; and Egyptian migration, 18, 145; and transnationalism, 8
"local, the": and Bulaq, 73–76; dislocation of, 70–73; and restriction of women, 69; shift of, 69–70

locality: production of, 24, 143–44
London, 178
Los Angeles: as model for Cairo, 28, 135

McDonald's: and globalization, 19
Madinet al-Mohandessin: and class, 28

Madinet Nasr, 11; and class, 28
Madinet al-Salaam, 45, 164
market (*suq*), 101; and *lama*, 109; negative
    image of, 92; and the "public," 91; social
    construction of, 111–14; women's con-
    trol of, 112–14
marriage, 12; and *baladi*, 86–87; between
    Copts and Muslims, 124; and field
    work, 9–11; and housing, 18, 53, 45;
    husband's role, 10; and identity, 9; and
    income, 7; and migration, 67–68, 146,
    152, 157–58; and restricted movement,
    102–03; and stigmatization, 72; and
    ulfa, 80
el-masaakin, 6, 124; and *el-ahali*, 8–9, 71–
    73, 81–82,163–64; and *'asl*, 86–87;
    author's connections with, 9, 11; and
    Bourdieu's study, 49–51; changes
    in, 158–59, 161–62; doors in, 94–96;
    "housing for the people," 6; isolation
    in, 96; and local identity, 118; markets
    in, 111; and marriage, 130; mosques in,
    23–24, 126, 127, 170; and privacy, 47–
    48; problems of, 46–48; relocation to,
    23, 30–34; and *sha'bi*, 83; segregation in,
    73; uniformity of, 161
Masaakin al-Turguman: and Bulaq, 76
Massey: on "the local," 69
Mecca, 124; and pilgrimage, 178
media: state control of, 23
Medina, 124
metro: in Cairo, 169
migration, 50, 93; and al-Zawiya, 7; and
    class, 178; and communication, 147–48;
    and consumer goods, 57, 62; desire for,
    147–48; difficulties of, 147; and gender,
    147–49; and globalization, 18; and hous-
    ing, 147, 148, 151–58; and income, 29, 55,
    146; and locality, 24; and marriage, 67–
    68,146, 152, 157–58; and regulation, 145–
    46; post-Sadat, 144–45; and virginity, 87
El-Missiri: and *baladi*, 77
Misr al-Jididah: and class, 83
modernism: and housing projects, 161–
    62
modernity: appropriation of, 21, 24, 49–
    51, 137–39, 179, 180; critique of, 42, 136;
    discourse of, 48, 49, 133–40; and ex-
    tremism, 137; images of, 21, 38, 39, 41–
    42; and Islam, 181–82; and religious
    identity, 117–18, 136–37; and state plan-
    ning, 2–4; and stigmatization, 70–73;

and *tamaddun*, 133; and technology, 134;
    and television, 137–39; and al-Zawiya,
    79
modernization: adapting to, 49–51; of
    Cairo by Sadat, 27, 28–42; and class, 22;
    cost of, 38–39; discourse of, 29–30, 48;
    failure of, 39; and family, 93, 94–96;
    and housing, 31–33, 154; and privacy,
    32; and religious identity, 179–80; and
    relocation, 18, 30, 35–42
Morocco, 18; and *'asl*, 84–85
Moses, Robert, 168
mosque, 116, 117, 177; and activists, 129;
    authority of, 41; building of, 170; cen-
    trality of, 12, 13, 126–31; and collectivity,
    23–24; discourses in, 13; dress for, 71;
    and education, 127, 130–31, 179; and field
    work, 8; and gender, 69, 92, 101, 102;
    and identity, 115; and modernity, 181–82;
    and 1981 religious clashes, 120–26; and
    the "public," 91; as social space, 126; in
    the United States, 68; and unity, 126–27,
    131; women's feelings for, 127–31
Mubarak, Hosni: and economic reform,
    168–69
Muslim(s), 20; activists, 179; and
    Christians, 5, 12, 23–24, 181; Christians,
    clashes with, 120–26; and Copts, 110,
    117–18, 119–20; dress, 12–13; extremists,
    24; "good," 116–17; and the mosque,
    126; Shi'ites, 26

narratives: of globalization, 66–69
Nasser, Gamal Abdel: and land redistribu-
    tion, 40; and migration, 144; Nasserists,
    119; public housing plan, 6, 16; socialist
    policy of, 27–28
National Democratic Party (NDP), 76,
    181; and Muslim-Christian conflict, 121
nationalism: Asian and African, and Cairo,
    28; and outsiders, 12; and religious iden-
    tity, 119–20; and relocation, 36
al-Nazir: mosque on disputed land, 122
neighbors: cooperation of, 159–60, 164;
    and history, 162–64; and housing addi-
    tions, 165–66
New York, 144, 178
Nile, 25, 31; access to, 74; and Bulaq, 30,
    76, 77; and construction, 29; corniche,
    29, 62, 74
1952 revolution, 35; and *baladi*, 77
1977 riots: and Bulaq, 37–38

1973 war: and Sadat's popularity, 29
niqab, 128

Ottoman empire: and production of
    Cairo, 26–27

Pakistan, 146
Paris, 178; model for Cairo, 27, 28
People's Assembly: and Muslim-Christian
    conflict, 121
Phalangists: and Copts, 121
Philippines, 146
pilgrimage (*hajj*), 177–78, 180
place: and *ulfa,* 80–81
planning, urban: and gaze, 31. *See also*
    Cairo; modernization; relocation; Sadat
police: bribery of, 174; and coffeehouses,
    110–11; and housing projects, 34; and
    Muslim-Christian conflict, 121; and
    Muslims, 117, 128; and planning of Cairo,
    38; presence, in Cairo, 25–26; and relo-
    cation, 35–36, 38, 52; tricking of, 16
postcolonialism: and Egyptian identity, 5
poverty: and government incompetence,
    132; and housing, 2–4
practices, daily: and housing, 58–66; and
    production of Cairo, 16–17; and space,
    22; and state discourse, 41–42
practices, spatial, 24; and production of
    Cairo, 17
prayer: "correct" manner of, 13
pregnancy: and identity, 9–10
privacy, 63; and body, 98, 99; and class,
    79; and dress, 96, 98; foreignness of,
    92–93; and isolation, 96; in *el-masaakin,*
    47–48; and seeing, 96–99, 108; and
    state discourse, 66, 93
private: defined, 91; and doors, 94–96; and
    seeing, 96–99, 108; *vs.* public, 90–115
public: defined, 91; and gender, 99–115; *vs.*
    private, 90–115; and religious identity,
    115; and scarf, 97–98
pyramids: and tourism, 30

Quran, 124, 125, 127, 177, 181, 182; and
    space, 81

raaqi: and class, 79; contrast to *sha'bi,*
    82–83
Ramadan, 140, 146; fasting during, 13; and
    television, 137

religion. *See* Christian(s); Copts; identity,
    religious; Islam; Muslim(s)
relocation, 51; and *'asl,* 85–87; and *baladi,*
    77; and Bulaq, 69–70; and class, 30, 40;
    and community, 75–76, 118–19, 134;
    cost of, 37–39; and diversity, 79, 80–82;
    failure of, 39; feelings about, 7–8; and
    force, 35–36, 38–39, 52; and foreign
    investment, 30–31; and gender, 71; and
    globalization, 169; legitimization of, 77;
    and local identity, 118; and modernity,
    2–4, 18, 30; and Muslim-Christian
    clashes, 123–24; narratives of, 43–45,
    163–64; and price increases, 114; and
    "progress" (*tamaddun*), 133; and protest,
    36–37; and religious identity, 118–19;
    and rootedness, 74–76; and social con-
    trol, 81–82; and space, 22–23, 66; state
    discourse of, 31–34, 35–37, 38–42, 173,
    174; and stigmatization, 70–73; and
    "symbolic capital," 76–79; and al-
    Zawiya, history of, 162–64
resistance: and anti-government feelings,
    12, 171–77; and relocation, 36–37
rights: protection of, and class, 174–75
ritual: and the mosque, 126; and space, 81
rootedness: and *baladi,* 78; and Bulaq, 74–
    76; and gender, 74–75; and *el-masaakin,*
    81–82; and relocation, 74; and *ulfa,* 80–
    81
ruqaq, 62

Sacrifice Feast (*Eid al-Adha*): animals for,
    62, 64–65
el-Sadat, Anwar, 39,138–39; assassination
    of, 123; assumes presidency, 28; as "the
    Believing President," 119; economic
    promises of, 178–79; and globalization,
    18; *In Search of Identity* (1978), 28–29;
    and Islam, 136, 139; and modernization,
    2, 16, 22–23, 30–31, 34, 35–36, 37–40,
    135, 168–69; and 1981 clashes, 122–23;
    and 1977 riots, 37–38; and 1973 war, 29;
    "open-door" policy, 22, 29, 37, 38, 84,
    94, 144–45; and relocation, 30–34
Sa'ides, 118; from Bulaq, 72
Sarajevo, 144
Saudi Arabia, 147; goods from, 57; and
    migration, 8, 18, 20, 145, 149, 152; and
    pilgrimage, 177–78, 180
savings associations: and *ulfa,* 80–81

Schwarzenegger, Arnold, 20, 180
secularization: and modernity, 137
seeing: and privacy, 96–99
segregation: by gender, 10
sexuality: control of, 90–91, 106; female,
    and the mosque, 130–31
al-Sha'b, 36
Sha'bi: and *baladi,* 79; contrast with *raaqi,*
    82–83
Shamm in-nisiim, 125
Shehata, Abdel-Rehim: governor of Cairo,
    167
Shenoudaha, Pope, 124
6th of October: low-income housing, 45
space: appropriation of, 17, 31, 49–51, 52–
    53, 58–66; and *baladi* identity, 78–79;
    and body, 98; centrality of, 21–24; and
    class, 11–12; and colonial power in
    Cairo, 26–27; control of, 171–73, 174–
    77; and cultural identity, 82–83; and
    defilement, 61; and domestic animals,
    62–65; empty, 81; and gender, 53–54,
    66, 90, 92, 99–115; and mosque, 13; and
    privacy, 93–96; private, 124; public,
    116–17, 120–26, 126–31; and resistance,
    171–77; and rootedness, 74; Sadat's poli-
    cies and, 29–30; scarcity of, 45–48, 71;
    and segregation, 73; and socializing, 62–
    63; "spaces of tolerance," 173; and status,
    65–66; and "symbolic violence," 103–
    04; and "tactics," 58–66; transformation
    of, 55–58, 66; use of, and state discourse,
    41–42; women's use of, 106–09; in al-
    Zawiya, 11
state: compensation, 37; criticism of, 110;
    definition of "modern Egyptians," 119;
    discourse, and privacy, 66, 93; dis-
    course, and relocation, 22–23, 31–34,
    35–37, 38–42; discourse, and stigmatiza-
    tion, 70–73; discourse of modernity, 16,
    48; and space, 40–42, 89
stereotypes: in Muslim-Christian conflict,
    125; and relocation, 70–73, 75, 108, 118,
    140
strategies: and gender, 101; and "tactics,"
    50–51; of women, 102–03
Sudan, 77
Suez Canal: nationalization of, 28; open-
    ing of, 27
al-Sunniyin: and mosque, 121, 127; state
    attitude towards, 117

Switzerland, 177, 178
Syria, 77

tactics, 50–51; of appropriation, 42, 58–
    66; and negative images, 72, 73; and
    space, 23. *See also* strategies
al-Tahrir Square, 116
technology: consumer goods, 51; as invest-
    ment, 20; and modernity, 134; "renais-
    sance," 169
restriction of, 102; Sadat's fascination
    with, 135; and status, 54–55, 137–38
telephones: in al-Zawiya, 169
television, 59, 60, 115; and housing, 157,
    158; and modernization, 67; as silence,
    139; struggle over, 86, 102, 137–39
terrorism, 110; and housing projects, 41, 173
tourism: lack of, in al-Zawiya, 5; and mod-
    ernization, 2, 4; and planning of Cairo,
    29, 38
tradition: and *'asl,* 85; Muslim, vs. Egyptian,
    124–25; Muslim, and western advances,
    134
transnationalism, 143; and housing, 29. *See
    also* migration
transportation, public, 1–2, 8, 11, 12, 116–
    17, 177, 181; and fieldwork, 8; and the
    hajj, 180; and preaching, 179
tricking, 50; of powerful, by weak, 15–16;
    and housing, 16–17

ulfa: and place, 80–81
'Umar Ibn al-'Ams, 16
United States, 85, 122; and *'asl,* 86; author's
    education in, 54; critique of, 83, 135–36;
    and globalization, 19–20; links with
    Egypt, 18, 135; and migration, 67–68,
    69; travel to, 178
"Uprising of the Thieves," 37–38
urban: clearance, 6; fabric, and religion,
    119, 132; life, 16–17, 181; life, and mod-
    ernization, 133; localities, production of,
    143, 145, 158–66, 178; planning, 27–28,
    29–30; poor, 2, 132; problems, 16, 27;
    resources, and "fooling," 174–77; space,
    2, 4, 5, 17, 22, 30–31, 39–40, 49, 86, 172,
    175–77; space, and gender, 92; urbaniza-
    tion, 27–28, 132
Urry, John: on "the local," 69

veil: and public vs. private, 90

village: and identity, 118
violence, symbolic, 70; and public space, 103–04
vision: privileging of, 31
visits, 54, 59; and gender, 60

West, the: and *afrangi*, 77; and Cairo, 67–68; Egypt's relation to, 19–21. 27–28; and "the local," 69; Sadat and, 28
women: and "bad manners," 104–05; control of, 88–90, 99–103, 103–09; and globalization, 67–69; and the mosque, 127–31; negative images of, 71; and workplace, 103–09. *See also* gender
work: and gender, 104–09
workplace: and collectivity, 105–06
World Cup, 20

Yemen, 96

Zamalek: and class, 30, 83; location of, 76–77; and space, 11
al-Zawiya al-Hamra, xi; and *'asl*, 85–87; and *baladi*, 79–83; connection with Cairo, 4–6, 11, 162, 166; and globalization, 84; hierarchies in, 77, 79–83; history of, 5–6, 28, 79, 162–64; and local identity, 118; and "modern Egyptians," 119; and modernity, 38, 39; Muslim-Christian clashes in, 5, 120–26; name, 162; population of, 7, 70–73; 79; production of, 24, 164–65, 169–77; religious identity in, 117, 120–26; Sadat visits, 35–36; and space, 11–12; transportation to, 1–2, 116–17. *See also* Bulaq; relocation
Zidane, Zineddine, 20

Compositor:	BookMatters, Berkeley
Text:	10/13 Galliard
Display:	Galliard